EDUCATION IN JAPAN

REFERENCE BOOKS IN
INTERNATIONAL EDUCATION
(General Editor: Edward R. Beauchamp)
VOL. 5

GARLAND REFERENCE LIBRARY
OF SOCIAL SCIENCE
VOL. 329

Reference Books in International Education

Edward R. Beauchamp
General Editor

EDUCATION IN JAPAN
A Source Book

Edward R. Beauchamp
Richard Rubinger

GARLAND PUBLISHING, INC. • NEW YORK & LONDON
1989

Library of Congress Cataloging-in-Publication Data

Beauchamp, Edward R., 1933–
    Education in Japan : a source book / Edward R. Beauchamp, Richard
Rubinger.
      p. cm. — (Reference books in international education ; vol.
5)   (Garland reference library of social science ; vol. 329)
    Includes index.
    ISBN 0–8240–8635–X (alk. paper)
    1. Education—Japan—Bibliography. I. Rubinger, Richard, 1943– .
II. Title. III. Series. IV. Series: Garland reference library
of social science ; v. 329.
Z5815.J3B43   1989
016.37'0952—dc19   88-30049
                                      CIP

STUDIES OF THE EAST ASIAN INSTITUTE, COLUMBIA UNIVERSITY

The East Asian Institute is Columbia University's center for research,
teaching, and publication on modern East Asia. The Studies of the East
Asian Institute were inaugurated in 1962 to bring to a wider public the
results of significant new research on China, Japan, and Korea.

CONTENTS

SERIES EDITOR'S FOREWORD

This series of reference works and monographs in education in selected nations and regions is designed to provide a resource to scholars, students, and a variety of other professionals who need to understand the place of education in a particular society or region. While the format of the volumes is often similar, the authors have had the flexibility to adjust the common outline to reflect the uniqueness of their particular nation or region.

Contributors to this series are scholars who have devoted their professional lives to studying the nation or region about which they write. Without exception they have not only studied the educational system in question, but they have lived and travelled widely in the society in which it is embedded. In short, they are exceptionally knowledgeable about their subject.

In our increasingly interdependent world, it is now widely understood that it is a matter of survival that we understand better what makes other societies tick. As the late George Z.F. Bereday wrote: "First, education is a mirror held against the face of a people. Nations may put on blustering shows of strength to conceal public weakness, erect grand facades to conceal shabby backyards, and profess peace while secretly arming for conquest, but how they take care of their children tells unerringly who they are" (*Comparative Method in Education*, New York: Holt, Rinehart & Winston, 1964, page 5).

Perhaps equally important, however, is the valuable perspective that studying another education system provides us in understanding our own. To step outside of our commonly held assumptions about schools and learning, however briefly, and to look back at our system in contrast to another, places it in a very different light. To learn, for example, how the Soviet Union handles the education of a multilingual society; how the French provide for the funding of public education; or how the Japanese control admissions into their universities enables us to understand that there are alternatives to our familiar way of doing things. Not that we can often "borrow" from other societies; indeed, educational arrangements are inevitably a reflection of deeply rooted political, economic, and cultural factors that are unique to a society. But a conscious recognition that there are other ways of doing things can serve to open our minds and provoke our imaginations in ways that can result in new approaches that we would not have otherwise considered.

Since this series is designed to be a useful research tool, the editors and contributors welcome suggestions for future volumes as well as ways in which this series can be improved.

Edward R. Beauchamp
University of Hawaii

ACKNOWLEDGMENTS

A work of this kind could not be accomplished without the expert assistance of professional librarians. The editors are particularly grateful to the following for guidance and services beyond the call of duty: Ms. Togasaki Tamiyo, Ms. Kurita Junko of the International House of Japan Library, Ms. Fukunaga Matsumiko of the Japan Foundation Library, Ms. Nakamura Yoshiko and Mr. Noguchi Takahiro of the Kyoto University Faculty of Education Library, and Mr. Shiro Saito of the University of Hawaii Library. We would also like to thank Gerard Sullivan, Jan Ibana, Suzanne Culter, Ida Yoshinaga, and Pamela Kido, of the staff of the Center for Japanese Studies, University of Hawaii, for help in preparing the manuscript for publication.

Errors that remain are, of course, the responsibility of the editors.

INTRODUCTION

Over the past several years American interest in Japanese education has grown by leaps and bounds. As a result, there have been numerous accounts, often by "instant experts" who, having spent a week or two in Tokyo, have contributed to shaping American views about Japan and Japanese education. These accounts, although often inaccurate or misleading, have filled the popular media.

The editors believe, therefore, that it is time to update Herbert Passin's *Japanese Education: A Bibliography of Materials in the English Language,* published in 1970 (see item 5 below). Like Professor Passin's earlier work, our book is also included as a "Study of the East Asian Institute of Columbia University." Unlike the earlier work, this one includes brief essays on a number of the most important topics in Japanese education. Since we believe that understanding educational matters requires insight into the historical context, we have tried to place contemporary educational matters in historical perspective.

We have included highly selected bibliographies with each essay. These bibliographies are divided into two categories. The most important citations have been annotated to help readers in their search for further information on the topics of the essays. In addition, we have listed other books and articles which, because they are less directly concerned with education, or were dated, or were less accessible, are not annotated.

The explosion of scholarly interest in Japanese education has multiplied the number of articles and books on the subject far beyond what they were in 1970. To list all the articles on Japanese education since then would require several volumes and has necessitated rather severe limiting of what can be included here. Because the quantity of material has so far outstripped the capabilities of individual researchers to quickly and easily find quality work in specific areas of interest, the effort to be selective and to annotate judiciously was deemed worthwhile.

Selectivity does have drawbacks. The listings here, while comprehensive, are nevertheless incomplete; and, the judgment of the compilers has been used throughout. There has been no attempt to even out coverage; thus the subject matter of the listings and the categories used by the compilers reflects, not only our own interests, but also the content of writings on Japanese education in the West over the past two decades or so. Several criteria have been primary in the selection process: the quality and the usefulness of the material and the ease of access to it. We have generally not included materials published before 1970 and which appear in the Passin bibliography or others (listed below). In several cases, however, either where (as in the case of the historical sections) other materials were not in abundance or where the original piece is of such high quality and has been so often used in subsequent writing that its omission would be glaring, we have included some materials that predate the Passin bibliography.

The purpose of this work is to keep the reader up-to-date with the best scholarship on Japanese education since the late 1960s. Since this is a selective work, the reader should be aware that more comprehensive bibliographies on specific topics and less recent titles are available. For educational issues of the American Occupation of Japan, for example, the reader would be better off with the Eells or Ward and Shulman bibliographies (see items 1 and 7 below). Bibliographies that might be consulted on Japanese education are the following:

1. Eells, Walter Crosby. *The Literature of Japanese Education, 1945-1954*. Hamden, Conn.: The Shoe String Press, 1955.

    Annotates 1,400 publications which appeared between 1945 and 1954. Particularly useful for overlooked articles on the Occupation although many entries are of dubious quality. Over-representation of missionary writings and articles on Christian education.

2. International Christian University Library and International House of Japan Library, comps. *Books on Japan in English: Joint Holdings List of International Christian University Library and International House of Japan Library.* Tokyo: International Christian University Library, 1984.

   An unannotated joint holdings list. For section on "Education and Higher Education" see pp. 318–335.

3. The Japan Foundation, comp. *Catalogue of Books in English on Japan: 1945–1981.* Tokyo: the Japan Foundation, 1986.

4. The Japan Foundation, comp. *An Introductory Bibliography for Japanese Studies.* Tokyo: The Japan Foundation, 1974–. v. 1–. (In progress)

   A continuation of Kokusai Bunka Shinkokai, comp. *K.B.S. Bibliography of Standard Reference Books for Japanese Studies with Descriptive Notes.* Tokyo: Kokusai Bunka Shinkokai, 1959–1973, with emphasis on materials published since 1970. All citations are for Japanese-language materials but the annotations are in English by prominent scholars, and provide insight into the substance and range of Japanese scholarship in a variety of fields. Each volume is published in two parts (part 1, social sciences; part 2, humanities), the parts appearing in alternate years. Education has been included with the social sciences (part 1 of each volume). The latest volume published is vol. v, part 1, in 1986, covering publications of 1979–1980. The annotations on educational material in this volume are by Terasaki Masao, a leading scholar of educational history at Tokyo University and are very informative.

5. Passin, Herbert. *Japanese Education: A Bibliography of Materials in the English Language.* New York: Teachers College Press, 1970.

   Includes 1,500 titles which appeared over the 100-year period from 1870 to 1970. More than half of the entries were published between 1955 and 1967. Particularly good on Occupation materials. Emphasis is on official publications, general descriptions, perspectives of foreign observers. Lists of serial publications by Japanese government and others. Indexed but not annotated.

6. Teichler, Ulrich, and Voss, Friedrich. *Bibliography on Japanese Education*. Munich: Verlag Dokumentation, 1974.

   Supplements the coverage in the Passin bibliography with more entries in European languages and publications in Western languages available in Japan and not generally known in the West. Publications in English and German systematically checked, other European languages according to preferences of compilers. Pre-1945 publications not included. Large number of categories facilitates search for specific topic. Also, index of authors and institutions. Unpublished doctoral dissertations included, but other unpublished material generally not; newspaper articles and pieces from weekly magazines generally not included. Introductory essays in English and German. Not annotated. Emphasis on student unrest and university disputes.

7. Ward, Robert E., and Shulman, Frank J. *The Allied Occupation of Japan, 1945–52: An Annotated Bibliography of Western Language Materials*. Chicago: American Library Association, 1974.

   More than 3,000 annotated entries, including doctoral dissertations, government publications, and serials. Arranged by topics, including education reform. See pp. 638–677 for materials on education.

Our volume is meant as an update and a supplement to the above five works. It is intended primarily for non-specialists who do not have access to the Japanese language. Thus, although Japanese names are written in customary Japanese order, that is, family name first, macrons to indicate long vowel sounds have not been used.

Part I
History of Japanese
Education to 1952

CHAPTER I
GENERAL HISTORIES AND SURVEYS

The Japanese owe much of their early educational tradition to China. Formal education was made possible by the introduction of writing from China in the early fifth century, and in the eighth century T'ang China provided the model for Japan's first school system. As described in the Taiho Codes of 701, a Confucian College (*Daigaku-ryo*) provided training in the Chinese classics to the court nobility in Kyoto and branch schools (*kokugaku*) provided training for the provincial aristocracy. The meritocratic principles of the Chinese examination system were never fully implemented in this early system because they conflicted with a Japanese preference for inherited privilege. During the ninth century aristocratic families set up private schools for their members; and at least one school, that of the Shingon monk Kukai (also known as Kobo Daishi, 774–835) was open to commoners. By the tenth century Confucian scholarship was in decline and court culture centered on a more Japanese form of aesthetic refinement. The development of a phonetic syllabary (*kana*) made possible a vernacular literature and the spread of literacy in the native language.

During the medieval age (twelfth to sixteenth centuries) Zen Buddhism became part of the training of the samurai along with the practical techniques of warfare. Scholarship was sheltered in Buddhist monasteries and priests taught acolytes and other children in their temples, but there were few schools. Not until the prolonged era of stability and peace of the Tokugawa period (1600–1868), did the systematic education of the samurai and extension of popular literacy become possible.

By 1853 when Commodore Perry intruded on Japan's 250 years of isolation from the West, the samurai were not only fully literate but many had been transformed into urban bureaucrats, wielders of the pen rather than the sword. The Neo-Confucian curriculum at official schools trained leaders in the ethical responsibilities of good government through the Chinese classics. The Neo-Confucian insistence on "the investigation of things" stimulated an intellectual flowering. Private academies sprang up by the hundreds to satisfy interests of students in Western science, military technology, foreign language, national studies, and the traditional arts—adding considerably to the complexity and diversity of Tokugawa schooling patterns.

Another important aspect of the Tokugawa legacy was the spread of learning beyond elites to the non-samurai classes. Tens of thousands of local parish schools (*terakoya*) were established without official support by public-spirited citizens to train commoners in the rudiments of reading, writing, and calculation. It is estimated that 40% of the boys and 15% of the girls were receiving formal training outside their homes by the middle of the nineteenth century. This meant that before the modern period Japan had a highly skilled group of leaders, and wide segments of the population were prepared to take advantage of the opportunities that modern education offered.

Following the Meiji Restoration of 1868 education became the foundation for a strong unified state during the Meiji period (1868–1912). Borrowing freely from European and American models, the Meiji leaders planned a national system that would train the population in basic skills and create a citizenry responsive to state goals. In 1872 the Fundamental Code of Education called for a nationally organized system of schools administered by a central Ministry of Education. By 1886 a comprehensive system was implemented by Mori Arinori, the first minister of education, that provided the framework for Japanese education until 1945. Elementary schools were redesigned to inculcate patriotic loyalty, a new Imperial University provided free access to Western higher learning, and middle schools were established to act as elite sorting mechanisms for the narrow channel to higher education. The central mission of the schools to provide service to the state was set forth in the Imperial Rescript on Education of 1890.

Although liberalism and innovation in education gained currency in the 1920s, by the 1930s, with the outbreak of war on the Asian mainland, an extreme form of nationalism and patriotism was inculcated in children through the morals courses (*shushin*) in Japanese schools. The appointment of General Araki Sadao as minister of education in 1938 signalled the complete military takeover of the school system. Elementary schools were reorganized as "people's schools" (*kokumin gakko*); military drill and evacuations to the countryside became ordinary parts of student life.

Following defeat in World War II, Japan was placed under Occupation by the Allied Powers and the educational system was singled out for special attention by Occupation reformers. Under American guidance the goals of postwar education became the development of individual personality and the nurturing of an independent spirit. The School Education Law of 1947 codified an extensive reorganization. The elitist multitrack system of the prewar period was replaced with a single track in a 6-3-3-4 structure. Technical colleges, normal schools, and higher schools were upgraded and absorbed into new four-year colleges on the American model; and a single comprehensive high school replaced the specialized schools of the old system. Compulsory education was extended from six to nine years and the principle of coeducation was established for all schools.

While the expansion of opportunity provided by the Occupation reforms has been welcomed, not all its effects have been positive. Competition for university entrance has, in fact, been exacerbated by greater numbers and the Japanese preference for ranking schools in a hierarchy by prestige. Because the graduate of a highly rated school has a far better chance of securing a desirable job than the graduate of a lesser school, the pressure to enter one of the very few prestigious national universities has become an "examination hell."

Statistics show Japanese education to be among the most successful systems in the world in providing broad access to higher levels of schooling. In 1984 virtually 100% of the age group completed the nine years of compulsory schooling. 93.9% went on to high schools which are non-compulsory (and all but 2.2% graduated); 35.5% of the age group went on to universities or junior colleges (a figure that is second only to the United States but represents a slight falling off from previous years).

Despite these impressive numbers, many Japanese are concerned that the social cost may be too high. Among the many ills blamed on school entrance pressures are a rise in school violence and a profusion of costly "cram" schools (*juku*) which give wealthy families advantages

and undermine the egalitarian thrust of the entire educational system.
Against a backdrop of complaints from business leaders, education
authorities, the media, and the public, a Provisional Council on
Educational Reform was established by Prime Minister Nakasone
Yasuhiro in September 1984 to make recommendations that will guide
Japanese education into the twenty-first century. To what extent the
Japanese will be able to ease pressures and provide greater flexibility in
the school system, without undermining quality, remains to be seen.

A. Histories of Japan

It is generally agreed, among those who teach survey histories of
Japan, that there is no entirely satisfactory single-volume text that
provides balanced treatment of both ancient and modern times and
comprehensive, yet succinct, coverage of major issues in political,
social, economic, cultural, and intellectual history. Nevertheless, while
dissatisfaction remains, there are a number of standard works and an
ever-increasing number of excellent one-volume survey histories that
the student unfamiliar with Japan's educational past may turn to with
profit. Included here are works that cover the entire sweep of Japan's
history, as well as those that survey Japan's modern development from
the mid-nineteenth century to the present. Included also are the best
available reference works to which readers may refer for background
material.

While there are now numerous works of high quality on specific
aspects of Japanese educational history, there is not a single general
survey of the subject. To get some sense of the broad sweep of Japanese
educational history the reader is referred to the general histories listed
below.

8. *Encyclopedia of Asian History.* 4 vols. New York: Charles
   Scribners Sons, 1988.

   Comprehensive coverage of histories of all Asian countries by
   area specialists. Educational topics included.

9. *Encyclopedia of Japan.* 15 vols. Tokyo and New York: Kodansha International, 1983.

The most comprehensive and authoritative source on all aspects of Japanese civilization. An extraordinary feat of collaboration among outstanding scholars in Japan, Europe, and North America. Excellent general interpretive essays as well as shorter, more detailed entries on specific topics. Fine essay on Japanese educational history by Ronald Dore. Informative pieces on a wide range of specific issues and problems in Japanese education.

10. Hall, John Whitney. *Japan: From Pre-History to Modern Times.* New York: Dell, 1971.

Excellent one-volume history that combines good narrative history with a broad interpretive framework. Especially strong on development of political structures; contemporary period given much less stress than earlier periods.

11. Hane, Mikiso. *Modern Japan: A Historical Survey.* Boulder and London: Westview Press, 1986.

A revised edition of a 1972 publication. Intended for the general reader, it provides balance between pre-modern and modern periods, although thin on periods before Tokugawa. It is distinguishable from other one-volume histories in its emphasis on economic, social, and cultural developments and particularly by the space given to the social conditions of the lower classes of society.

12. Keene, Donald. *Anthology of Japanese Literature.* New York: Grove Press, 1955.

A comprehensive and authoritative collection of fine English translations of selections from Japanese literature—from earliest times to the postwar period by a renowned authority.

13. Najita, Tetsuo. *Japan.* Englewood Cliffs, N.J.: Prentice-Hall, 1974.

Short but provocative interpretive essay that traces the development of central themes in Japanese political thought. Suggestive for modern educational studies.

14. Pyle, Kenneth B. *The Making of Modern Japan*. Lexington, Mass., and Toronto: D.C. Heath and Co., 1978.

    Concise survey of main themes in Japan's modern history from reunification in the late sixteenth century through the Occupation. The focus on topics and issues avoids overwhelming the reader with names and dates.

15. Reischauer, Edwin O.; Fairbank, John K.; and Craig, Albert M. *East Asia: Tradition and Transformation*. New York: Houghton Mifflin, 1973.

    A one-volume abridgement of the earlier two-volume classic. Comprehensive treatment of histories of China, Korea, and Japan.

16. Sansom, George B. *Japan: A Short Cultural History*. New York: Appleton-Century-Crofts, 1962.

    Highly literate account of cultural developments set in social, political, and economic settings from early times through the mid-nineteenth century.

17. ———. *The Western World and Japan*. New York: Vintage, 1973.

    Picks up coverage of Japanese cultural history in the mid-nineteenth century and takes it through the 1890s. Focus is on the effects of the intrusion of the West on subsequent development of Japanese history.

18. Tsunoda, Ryusaku; de Bary, Wm. Theodore; Keene, Donald; et al. 2 vols. *Sources of Japanese Tradition*. New York: Columbia University Press, 1964.

    Collection of translated documents and writings of important thinkers from earliest times to the early post-war period. Excellent introductory essays and annotations. Includes excerpts from works that bear on educational matters.

19. Varley, H. Paul. *Japanese Culture*. 3rd ed. Honolulu: University of Hawaii Press, 1984.

Comprehensive cultural history from earliest times to the present. Focus is on the arts and aesthetic traditions.

B. Surveys of Educational History and Collections of Essays

Included here are works that, cover more than one historical period (those dealing with a single period are in later listings) and collections of essays that span periods.

It should be noted that, despite the flood of scholarly work being turned out on Japanese education, survey histories are in short supply. Although there is an enormous bibliography in Japanese, very few survey histories of education are available in English. None has been written since the Keenleyside volume of 1937 (see below). What has been done has focused almost exclusively on the modern period—that is, the Tokugawa period (1600–1868) and afterward. The reader seeking pre-Tokugawa educational history will be disappointed. Listed here are annotations of the best work available in this category. Following that there is appended a secondary list with only minimal comments. The works on the latter are, for the most part, deficient in critical analysis but are listed because of the general lack of adequate resources in this category. Clearly one of the priorities for Western scholarship ought to be an exploration, using modern historical methods, of the pre-Tokugawa tradition of Japanese education.

20. Anderson, Ronald S. *Education in Japan: A Century of Modern Development*. Washington: U.S. Government Printing Office, 1975.

A revised and up-dated version of the same author's earlier *Japan: Three Epochs of Modern Education*. Washington, D. C.: U.S. Office of Education Bulletin No. 11, U.S. Government Printing Office, 1959. A survey of educational policy, administration, curriculum, teaching methods, texts, teacher education, vocational and special education in three periods: prewar, the Occupation, and post-Occupation systems. The emphasis is on policy and official directives. The outlines of systems are useful; there is a wealth of quantitative data heavily favoring the postwar period.

21. Aso Makoto and Amano Ikuo. *Education and Japan's Modernization.* Tokyo: Ministry of Foreign Affairs, 1972.

For a government publication, a remarkably balanced survey of modern educational trends in Japan, by two important scholars of education.

22. Beauchamp, Edward R., ed. *Learning to Be Japanese: Selected Readings on Japanese Society and Education.* Hamden, Conn.: Linnet Books, 1978.

A useful collection of previously published journal articles and book chapters relating both to the roots of modern education and the contemporary scene. The historical section contains: Ronald Dore on the Tokugawa legacy (item 75); Edward Beauchamp on William E. Griffis (item 149); Joseph Pittau on Inoue Kowashi (item 179); Wilbur M. Fridell on ethics textbooks in the late Meiji period (item 153); Richard Smethurst (item 281) and Tsurumi Kazuko (item 318) on different aspects of prewar youth socialization, and Victor Kobayashi on education under the American Occupation. There is a section on the postwar period, one on future directions, and a bibliography. Also contains items 493, 506, 644, 678, 753.

23. Hall, John Whitney. "Education and Modern National Development." In *Twelve Doors to Japan*, pp. 384–426. Edited by John W. Hall and Richard K. Beardsley. New York: McGraw-Hill, 1965.

One of the best general introductions to basic issues in education and social change in Japan. There are brief but useful interpretive essays on the pre-Tokugawa heritage, a survey of the Tokugawa legacy, Meiji policy, the prewar school system, Occupation reforms, and the early postwar system and its problems. A good place to begin.

24. Japanese National Commission for Unesco, ed. *The Role of Education in the Social and Economic Development of Japan.* Tokyo: Ministry of Education, 1966.

    Prominent Japanese scholars of education assess the role of education in Japan's economic development of the 1960s with an abundance of data not often found in English-language publications. The focus on modernization is dated but there are useful sections on industrial and technical education and case studies of educational modernization in Hokkaido, Nagasaki, and Okayama.

25. Kaigo Tokiomi. *Japanese Education: Its Past and Present.* Tokyo: Kokusai Bunka Shinkokai, 1968.

    A single-volume study of Japanese educational history by a leading authority. The chapters on the modern period have largely been superceded by more recent works, but the chapters on earlier periods remain among the best available in English. Charts show changes in the modern system and a brief chronology shows important events in educational history.

26. Keenleyside, Hugh, and Thomas, A.F. *History of Japanese Education and Present Educational System.* Tokyo: Hokuseido, 1937.

    Dated in most respects, but does provide details of administrative machinery and official policy for the prewar educational system.

27. Kikuchi, Baron Dairoku. *Japanese Education.* London: John Murray, 1909.

    Lectures delivered at the University of London in 1907 by the former president of Tokyo Imperial University (1898-1901) and minister of education (1901-1903). Focus is on government policies and structure of the system. There is a brief sketch of Japanese education during the Meiji period focusing on the central position of the Imperial institution. Especially useful are the details of the school system around 1900. There is an interesting section on the teaching of reading in elementary schools. Generally weak in analysis.

28. Kobayashi Tetsuya. *Society, Schools, and Progress in Japan.* Oxford: Pergamon Press, 1976.

    A leading scholar of comparative education at Kyoto University discusses Japanese educational history in comparative context. The book is divided into three sections: historical development, issues of the 1950s and 1960s, and discussion of reforms of the 1970s.

29. Lombard, Frank Alanson. *Pre-Meiji Education in Japan.* Preface by G. Stanley Hall. Tokyo: Kyobunkan, 1913.

    A book that is considerably out of date in most respects, it still provides fascinating discussion of Japan's earliest educational traditions. An analysis of the educational values contained in Japan's early classics—primarily *Kojiki*—suggests what education must have been like before exposure to the Chinese writing system. The author was professor of English at Doshisha University and Kyoto Imperial University.

30. Passin, Herbert. *Society and Education in Japan.* Tokyo and New York: Kodansha International, 1983. Originally published New York: Teachers College Press, 1965.

    After more than twenty years this work remains the single best source for understanding Japanese education from Tokugawa times to the present. It consists of separate essays on Tokugawa education, the Meiji system, the pre-war years, mobility, and education and ideology. These essays provide superb integration of prudent generalizations and interpretive insight based on copious data from Japanese sources. About half of the book is devoted to English translations of important documents in Japanese educational history. The book is thus an invaluable reference source and a useful introduction to Japanese education through the early postwar years.

EDUCATIONAL SURVEYS AND COLLECTIONS OF ESSAYS II

31. Akabori Takashi. *History of Japanese Education.* Tokyo: Kokudosha, 1960.

32. Cross, Edmond. "Japanese Education, 1868–1953." Ph.D. dissertation, Teachers College, 1954. (on microfilm)

33. Hiratsuka Masunori. "Some Important Moments in the History of Japanese Education." *Bulletin of Research Institute of Comparative Education and Culture*. Kyushu University (March 1957) English Edition, No. 1.

    Not as useful as the title suggests.

34. Ishikawa Matsutaro. "Past and Present of the Study of Japanese Educational History." *Present Status of Educational Research in Japan: Supplement to the Proceedings of the International Conference on Educational Research, 1959*. Tokyo: The Organizing Committee, International Conference on Educational Research, 1961.

35. ———. "Tables and Explanatory Notes of the Literature on History of Education." *Japan Science Review: Literature, Philosophy, and History* 7 (1956): 65–68.

    Abstract of a dissertation.

36. Japan, National Institute for Educational Research, "Modernization of Education in Japan." *Research Bulletin of the National Institute for Educational Research* No. 17 (October 1978).

    Concise summary in English of major developments in Japanese educational history from earliest times to the present, with emphasis on post-Meiji.

37. Japanese Department of Education. *History of Japanese Education.* Tokyo: Department of Education, 1910.

    Prepared for the Japan-British Exhibition. Contains brief sections on early educational history.

38. ———. *Outline of Japanese Education.* New York: D. Appleton and Co., 1876. Produced for the Philadelphia Exposition of 1876 by David Murrary.

39. Nakaseko Rokuro. "Highlights in Japan's Educational Development: With Special Reference to the Introduction of Foreign Languages." *Pacific Affairs* 2 (January 1929): 15–19.

40. Yamashita Tokuji. *Education in Japan*. Tokyo: The Foreign Affairs Association of Japan, 1938.

    A 35-page summary of the entire history of Japanese education through the prewar period.

41. Yoshida Kumaji. *A Short History of Education in Japan*. Tokyo: Meguro Book Store, 1922.

    An English summary of work by a major scholar of Japanese educational history.

CHAPTER II
EARLY JAPANESE EDUCATION

A. The Aristocratic Age: Introduction and Assimilation of Chinese Learning

For general developments related to education such as the introduction of Chinese culture, the development of a written language and a native syllabary, and the emergence of a scholarly community during the Aristocratic Age (Nara and Heian periods, the eighth to twelfth centuries), one is directed to the general histories recommended earlier. Here, the focus is on issues that relate to organized education more particularly: the first institution of higher education, the early examination system, the decline of Confucian scholarship in the tenth century and rise of a courtly cult of beauty.

42. Bock, Felicia G. *Classical Learning and Taoist Practices in Early Japan*. Tempe, Arizona: Center for Asian Studies, Arizona State University, 1985. Occasional Papers, No. 17.

   An introduction to and translation of a document published in 927 known as *Engi-shiki*. The introduction discusses the progress of Chinese studies in Japan from the Taika Reform of 645 to the early tenth century. Topics included are the exchange of students and teachers between China and Japan and the establishment of the first institution of higher learning in Japan, the *Daigaku-ryo*.

43. Borgen, Robert. *Sugawara no Michizane and the Early Heian Court.* Cambridge, Mass.: Council on East Asian Studies, Harvard University, 1986.

Contains the best material available in English on the life of a student and scholar at the early Japanese "university" known as *Daigaku-ryo* during the ninth century. See especially Chapter 2, "Student Years," and Chapter 3, "Bureaucrat and Educator."

44. Crump, J.I. *'Borrowed' T'ang Titles and Offices in the Yoro Code.* Ann Arbor: Center for Japanese Studies, University of Michigan, 1952. Occasional Papers, No. 2.

A comparison between early Japanese regulations for an institution of higher learning and the T'ang Chinese regulations upon which they were based. Provides specifics on how foreign educational institutions were transformed to suit Japanese needs as early as the eighth century. See the appendix, pp. 51–56.

45. Hakeda, Yoshito S. *Kukai: Major Works.* New York: Columbia University Press, 1972.

The major English language work on Kukai (774–835), also known as Kobo Daishi, an influential priest and teacher, thought to have systematized the *kana* syllabary, and known as the founder of the Shingon sect of Buddhism. The biographical section includes a discussion of Kukai's private school, *Shugei Shuchi-in*, thought to be the first school in Japan to provide systematic training for the poor, on the model of the T'ang village school.

46. Miller, Richard J. *Japan's First Bureaucracy: A Study of Eighth-Century Government.* Ithaca, N.Y.: Cornell China-Japan Program, 1979.

Contains a brief section on the "Great Learning Bureau" (*Daigaku-ryo*). See pages 105–109.

47. Morris, Ivan. *The World of the Shining Prince: Court Life in Ancient Japan.* New York: Alfred A. Knopf, 1964.

Chapter 7 provides a survey of education and learning in the tenth century. Among important trends described are: the decline of Confucian scholarship and deterioration of the University; the rise of non-academic and non-Chinese inspired forms of culture—particularly the growth of nativist aesthetic refinement in the arts, especially poetry.

48. Murasaki Shikibu. *The Tale of Genji*. Translated by Edward Seidensticker. New York: Alfred A. Knopf, 1978.

    Chapter 21, "The Maiden," provides a view of the sorry state of learning at the University through the eyes of a tenth-century court lady. It also suggests, in a speech by Prince Genji, the continuing importance of systematic Confucian education despite the fact that promotions in the bureaucracy were usually made solely on the basis of birth.

49. Reischauer, Edwin O. *Ennin's Travels in T'ang China*. New York: Ronald Press, 1955.

    Chapter 3, "The Embassy to China" provides a vivid account of a Japanese Buddhist monk's travels in ninth century China— three centuries before Marco Polo wrote his account for the West.

50. Sansom, George B. *A History of Japan to 1334*. Stanford: Stanford University Press, 1958.

    Overview of cultural developments in the Heian period found in the section on "The Rule of Taste," pp. 178–196; brief discussion of the early University in Appendix 3, "A Note on Higher Education, 700-1000," pp. 474–476.

51. Sei Shonagon. *The Pillow of Sei Shonagon*. Translated by Ivan Morris. New York: Columbia University Press, 1967.

    Translation of a tenth-century classic which, like *The Tale of Genji*, describes the "rule of taste" that formed both the style and content of the education of the court nobility.

52. Spaulding, Robert M., Jr. *Imperial Japan's Higher Civil Service Examinations*. Princeton: Princeton University Press, 1967.

    Historical treatment of the examination system in Japan with a focus on the prewar period. Chapter 1, "Trial of the Chinese System," provides an historical context for Japan's decision to adopt a form of the T'ang period Chinese examination system. Details of regulations and administration of exams from the seventh century and discussion of Japanese preference for inherited privilege, which effectively thwarted the institutionalization of meaningful entrance examinations until the modern period.

B. The Medieval Age: The Education of Warriors

Although the medieval age (from the end of the twelfth century through the beginning of the seventeenth century) is usually considered a period of educational decline due to long periods of disruptive warfare, there were, nonetheless, educational developments that had a lasting impact on Japanese culture. Among these were the tradition of military discipline and ethics known as *bushido* (The Way of Warriors), the Buddhist clergy's achievements in preserving Chinese learning and training both acolytes and other children in basic literacy at temples, the patronage by warrior families of cultural centers such as the *Kanazawa Bunko* or the *Ashikaga Gakko*, and, finally, the educational efforts of the early Spanish and Portuguese missionaries who arrived in Japan in the late sixteenth century and established schools for recruiting a native clergy.

As the following list indicates, appropriate English-language materials on education are scarce for this period. Many of the works in English reflect a preponderant interest in the Western presence in Japan by missionaries during the "Christian Century" from the mid-sixteenth to the mid-seventeenth century. English-language works pertaining specifically to education in this period are rare.

53. Boxer, C.R. *The Christian Century in Japan, 1549–1650.* Berkeley, Los Angeles, London: University of California Press, California Library Reprint Series, Edition No. 51, 1974.

    See Chapter V, "Christian Culture and Missionary Life," for interesting discussions of the Jesuit mission press and the founding and running of seminaries to train a native clergy.

54. Cieslik, Herbert. "The Training of a Japanese Clergy in the 17th Century." In *Studies in Japanese Culture*, pp. 41–78. Edited by Joseph Roggendorf. Tokyo: Sophia University Press, 1963.

    Detailed examination of Christian missionary efforts to establish seminaries to train native Japanese clergymen in the late sixteenth and early seventeenth centuries.

55. Elison, George. *Deus Destroyed: The Image of Christianity in Early Modern Japan*. Cambridge, Mass.: Harvard University Press, 1973.

Chapter 3, "The Accommodative Method: The Jesuit Mission Policy and Cultural Contribution," discusses Jesuit educational goals and achievements in Japan and suggests that the latter may have been exaggerated.

56. Steenstrup, Carl. *Hojo Shigetoki*. London and Malmo: Citizen Press, 1979.

See pages 78–82 and 212–223 for discussion of values taught to medieval warriors.

57. ———. "The Imagawa Letter: A Muromachi Warrior's Code of Conduct Which Became a Tokugawa Schoolbook." *Monumenta Nipponica* 28 (Autumn 1973):295–316.

Translation and analysis of a fifteenth-century code of ethics for warriors. Because the document so succinctly summed up the essential values of the samurai class, it became a schoolbook during the Tokugawa period. A useful primary source for samurai values.

58. Suzuki, Daisetz T. *Zen and Japanese Culture*. Princeton: Princeton University Press, 1973.

Chapter 3, "Zen and the Samurai," provides a useful discussion of the moral, philosophical, and religious values of the medieval samurai.

59. Varley, H. Paul. *Samurai*. New York: Dell, 1970.

A brief and highly readable history of the samurai, including discussion of methods of training and codes of conduct.

MEDIEVAL EDUCATION II

60. Cooper, Michael, comp. *They Came to Japan: An Anthology of European Reports on Japan, 1543–1640*. Berkeley, Los Angeles, London: University of California Press, 1965.

Scattered throughout this fascinating collection of European accounts of Japan are observations of child training and intellectual abilities of children.

61. Ebisawa Arimichi. "The Jesuits and Their Cultural Activities in the Far East." *Journal of World History* 5 (1959):344–374.

62. Ishikawa Ken and Ishikawa Matsutaro. "Development of Educational Facilities in the 'Modern Age'—1576–1872." *Education in Japan: Journal for Overseas* 2 (1967):1–16.

*   Japanese Department of Education. *History of Japanese Education.* Cited in item 37, above.

     See pages 38–71, "Middle Ages."

*   Kaigo Tokiomi. *Japanese Education: Its Past and Present.* Cited in item 25 above.

     See Chapter III, "Education of Warriors," pp. 19–30.

*   Kikuchi, Baron Dairoku. *Japanese Education.* Cited in item 27 above.

     See Chapter II, "From the Establishment of the Shogunate to the Restoration," pp. 20–43.

*   Lombard, Frank Alanson. *Pre-Meiji Education in Japan.* Cited in item 29 above.

     See Chapter II, "The Government System of Education (662–1603)," pp. 47–66.

63. Murakami Naojiro. "The Jesuit Seminary of Azuchi." *Monumenta Nipponica* 6 (1943):375–390.

64. Ruch, Barbara. "Medieval Jongleurs and the Making of a National Literature." In *Japan in the Muromachi Age*, pp. 79–309. Edited by John Whitney Hall and Toyoda Takeshi. Berkeley, Los Angeles, London: University of California Press, 1977.

     Focusing on the early rise of a national literature, there are suggestions here of the educational effects of storytelling, simple dramas, and picture books in the commoners' preliterate world.

65. Satow, Ernest. *The Jesuit Mission Press, 1591–1610.* London: Privately printed, 1888.

66. Suzuki, Daisetz T. *The Training of the Zen Buddhist Monk.* Kyoto: Eastern Buddhist Society, 1934.

* Varley, H. Paul. *Japanese Culture*. Cited in item 19 above.
See Chapter 5, "The Canons of Medieval Taste," pp. 84–123.

CHAPTER III
TOKUGAWA EDUCATION:
TRADITION AND CHANGE

No area of life benefitted more from the civilizing effects of two and a half centuries of peace during the Tokugawa period (1600–1868) and the moderate economic growth that accompanied it, than did formal education. Both quantitative and qualitative developments in Tokugawa education conditioned the pace and substance of changes that took place when a modern school system was instituted following the collapse of the Tokugawa shogunate in 1868.

At the beginning of the Tokugawa period there were no schools as such. The samurai leadership class were largely illiterate warriors, and government was carried out without dependence on written decrees. Scholarship and teaching was maintained by Buddhist priests and some Confucian scholars in monasteries established as havens from the endemic warfare of the years preceding Tokugawa Ieyasu's victory at Sekigahara which unified the country in 1600. By the mid-nineteenth century the samurai were fully literate urban bureaucrats, educated systematically in schools organized especially for them by the shogun and domain authorities in all but the smallest of the some 260 feudal domains. Popular education for the non-samurai classes was widespread due to the spontaneous growth of small-scale local schools known as *terakoya*. Some 15,000 of these "little red schoolhouses" are known to have existed, with as many as 4,000 established from 1854 to 1867 alone.[1] Here the rudiments of Japanese reading and writing were taught entirely at local initiative, to townsmen in the cities as well as peasants in farming villages. The best estimate we have suggests that the spread of popular education was comparatively very high, with approximately

40% of the males and 15% of the females receiving some kind of training outside their homes by the end of the Tokugawa period.[2]

But the impact of Tokugawa education was more than quantitative. Some of the functions of modern schooling had already appeared and many of the reform measures that were instituted nationally in the 1870s had already been tried locally, considerably easing the way to a unified national system during the modern period. During the 1860s official schools experimented with graded curricula, hesitatingly opened their doors to some commoners and women, and admitted teachings outside the orthodox Neo-Confucian canon. Innovations were most pronounced, however, in the numerous private academies that sprang up to accommodate unmet educational demand. Entirely free from official control, these academies provided advanced training to students, regardless of class, in practical areas that were largely prohibited in official schools—Western languages, Western military science, navigation, coastal defenses, and natural sciences. With the Western military threat compelling national leaders to recruit competent specialists in technical fields, these schools began to serve as agents of educational change—away from the traditional pattern of hereditary succession to a more modern function of selecting and sorting students into occupational areas by ability and specialized training.[3]

Although growth, innovation, and experimentation marked some sectors of Tokugawa education late in the period, traditional patterns continued to persist, acting as brakes on full-scale reform well into the modern period. Among these were: widespread geographical disparities, severe class and sex distinctions, and lack of systematization in the organization of schooling. The multitude of Tokugawa schools were not evenly distributed throughout the country. There remained wide regional disparities in school availability and educational opportunity throughout the period. The availability, size, and educational content of official schools differed greatly among the domains: some domains required attendance, others had no school at all. The *terakoya* (local parish schools), although widely distributed, were concentrated in urban areas and those provinces with long-standing commitments to education. City schools tended to be larger, more systematized, and more expensive than their rural counterparts; their curricula were directed at the interests of merchants.

Differences in the degree to which the various classes took advantage of learning opportunities in Tokugawa Japan also persisted.

Male members of the samurai class were probably fully literate; they attended schools regularly and for extended periods of time. The curriculum was based on the Confucian classics, but some samurai were exposed to Western learning, the political and cultural nationalism of National Studies, and a variety of heterodox schools of Confucianism. Merchant children in the cities made full use of *terakoya* and became literate and numerate appropriate to their needs. Some took the opportunity for higher learning provided by private academies in the larger cities. The leadership levels of the peasantry were well represented at *terakoya* and academies, and received educations little different from the samurai, but poorer farmers saw little need for formal schooling outside the home and their children attended school irregularly if at all. Women were admitted to a few domain schools in the 1860s, and a few attended academies; they were about equally represented with men in *terakoya* in the merchant sections of larger cities such as Edo (Tokyo).[4]

Despite large numbers of schools in Tokugawa Japan, there remained a notable lack of systematization among them. There were few explicit connections among the diverse types of schools that dotted the landscape and no central or regional authority providing oversight. With the exception of some samurai who were compelled to attend, the great majority of people were free to arrange schooling for their children as they saw fit. The questions of where, when, and how much education should be sought were individual matters. Throughout the Tokugawa period, personal discipleship rather than institutional affiliation remained the basic principle of educational organization.

Thus, the legacy of Tokugawa schooling was multifaceted and complex, providing both advantages and obstacles for the transformation to a modern system. Facilities and personnel were abundant: there were large numbers of experienced teachers, numerous young people had been exposed to at least the basics of reading and writing, and many families had been introduced to a life-style that included school-going for their children. Merit criteria for advancement, comprehensive curricula, and graded programs were known. At the same time, education during the Tokugawa period remained characterized by differences among regions, bias according to class and sex, and lack of systematization in school sequencing.

The goal of formal education in Tokugawa Japan was primarily moral: to gain access to the teaching of the Sages in order to understand proper human relations; and to acquire useful skills, broaden wisdom, and acquire that knowledge appropriate to good government. The means to this moral end was the Confucian canon, beginning with the *Four Books* and the *Five Classics*. These works formed the core of the curriculum for the official schools and the essence of their message was spread via textbooks, itinerant preachers, and scholarly writings for the non-samurai classes as well. The dominant position of Confucian thought in the curriculum of Tokugawa schools has left a mixed legacy. The pedagogical style of Confucian scholars left a tradition of formalism, pedantry, and authoritarian teacher-student relations. And much in Confucian tradition seemed devoted to venerating the past, encouraging the passive absorption of knowledge rather than independent inquiry, and submissive acceptance of the existing social order. Despite this, the central message of Confucian thought—that the way to social prosperity and individual fulfillment lay in learning and education—was heard and acted upon at both official and popular levels. The encouragement of learning and the spread of popular schooling that resulted had consequences unforeseen by feudal authorities, which worked to undermine the basic premises of the existing social order.

The rational element in Confucian thinking and the emphasis on the "investigation of things" created an intellectual life of remarkable diversity and helped make possible an intelligent and critical acceptance of Western ideas. Confucian thought created a set of shared intellectual assumptions and a common professional discourse among the well-educated, which cut across regional and class boundaries. The rise of popular education and the remarkable spread of literacy stimulated personal ambition and extended the horizons of ordinary people beyond the limits imposed by feudal regulations.

Although such things are difficult to trace with precision, one might argue that the Confucian tradition in education has left some legacies to the present. There remains in Japanese educational thinking a strongly held belief that there is a core body of knowledge that all educated citizens need to know and which should be the primary focus of public school curricula. Although the content of this knowledge may change, the commitment to a rather narrowly defined core that should not be set aside for supplemental studies, no matter how immediately practical, may be traced to earlier Confucian practice. Similarly, the idea that a student's success depends not so much on innate ability and "brilliance" as on perseverance, effort and being *majime* (studious) may have its roots in the formalism and discipline of the Confucian educational heritage.

The suggested readings that follow are organized into five groups. Under "Tokugawa Education" is an annotated list of the best English-language writings on Tokugawa education. Although the intellectual developments of the Tokugawa period (and the debates over what constitutes orthodoxy, the contributions of the various heterodox schools, Western studies, National learning, and others) do not relate directly to formal education, the ideas of leading thinkers did form the basis of the readings and curricula at many schools; and a proper understanding of Tokugawa education requires some familiarity with Tokugawa scholarship. Furthermore, the English-language scholarship in this area is of particularly high quality, so under "Intellectual Currents: Neo-Confucianism and National Learning" and "Tokugawa Science and Medicine" unannotated and selected lists are provided for the interested reader. Following this is a section called "Tokugawa Education II" which lists titles thought to be less important or less accessible than the others but still worth attention. Lastly, there is a section, "Tokugawa Education III, Translations from Tokugawa Writings on Education."

NOTES

1. Ishikawa Matsutaro, "Terakoya kara kindai gakko e no mei to an" (From Terakoya to Modern Schools: The Good and Bad), in *Chishiki* (Knowledge), No. 22 (Spring 1981):159; also, Richard Rubinger, *Private Academies of Tokugawa Japan* (Princeton: Princeton Unviersity Press, 1982), p. 5, for a chart of the numbers of schools in different categories in the Tokugawa period.

2. Ronald P. Dore, *Education in Tokugawa Japan* (Berkeley and Los Angeles: University of California Press, 1965), pp. 291–295 and pp. 317–322.

3. The functions of private academies are discussed in detail in Rubinger, *Private Academies of Tokugawa Japan..*

4. Richard Rubinger, "Problems in Research on Literacy in 19th-Century Japan," in *Nihon kyoiku-shi ronso* (Issues in Japanese Educational

History), ed. Motoyama Yukihiko kyoju taikan kinen ronbun shuhen iinkai (Kyoto: Shibunkaku Shuppan, 1988), p. 9.

TOKUGAWA EDUCATION I

67. Aoki, Michiko Y., and Dardess, Margaret B. "The Popularization of Samurai Values: A Sermon by Hosoi Heishu." *Monumenta Nipponica* 31 (Winter 1976):393–413.

Sermons by itinerant preachers were an important means by which the values of the samurai class were transformed into popular terms for peasants, artisans, and merchants. This article discusses and provides a translation of an 1873 sermon by a popular speaker and Confucian scholar in Nagoya.

68. Backus, Robert L. "The Relation of Confucianism to the Tokugawa Bakufu as Revealed in the Kansei Educational Reform." *Harvard Journal of Asiatic Studies* 34 (1974):97–162.

Discussion of the effects of the educational provisions of the Kansei Edicts (1787–1793) on the training of bakufu retainers at the official Confucian school of the Tokugawa.

69. ———. "The Kansei Prohibition of Heterodoxy and its Effect on Education." *Harvard Journal of Asiatic Studies* 39 (1979):55–106.

The effects of the Kansei reforms (1787–1793) on the development of education throughout Tokugawa society—in the domain schools, academies and elsewhere.

70. ———. "The Motivation of Confucian Orthodoxy in Tokugawa Japan." *Harvard Journal of Asiatic Studies* 39 (1979):275–338.

Last of three articles in series on the Kansei edicts; looks at the ideas and personalities of men behind the orthodox reaction in education that led to the Prohibition on Heterodoxy of 1789, the central role played by the bakufu's Shoheiko, and the influence of Chu Hsi Confucianism on the educational world.

71. Bowers, John Z. *Western Medical Pioneers in Feudal Japan*. Baltimore and London: Johns Hopkins University Press, 1970.

Chapters on the contributions of the leading Western physicians in Japan before 1868: Kaempfer, Thunberg, Siebold, and Pompe.

72. Craig, Albert M. "Kido Koin and Okubo Toshimichi: A Psychohistorical Analysis." In *Personality in Japanese History*, pp. 264–308. Edited by Albert M. Craig and Donald H. Shively. Berkeley: University of California Press, 1970.

Includes a comparison of the role of educational background in the development of the personalities of Kido in Choshu and Okubo in Satsuma, with particularly interesting comments on Yoshida Shoin and his school, Shoka Sonjuku.

73. ———. "Science and Confucianism in Tokugawa Japan." In *Changing Japanese Attitudes Toward Modernization*, pp. 133–160. Edited by Marius B. Jansen. Princeton: Princeton University Press, 1965.

Analysis of the impact of Western scientific thought on the Chu Hsi Confucian tradition of Tokugawa Japan through the thought of Yamagata Banto, an Osaka merchant.

74. Dore, R.P. *Education in Tokugawa Japan*. Berkeley and Los Angeles: University of California Press, 1965; reprint ed., London: Athlone Press and Ann Arbor: Center for Japanese Studies, University of Michigan, 1984.

The classic Western study of Tokugawa education now available in reprint form with a new preface by the author. Detailed discussion of the content, goals, and structure of samurai education as well as the content of commoner learning and the significance of its widespread diffusion.

75. ———. "The Legacy of Tokugawa Education." In *Changing Japanese Attitudes Toward Modernization*, pp. 99–131. Edited by Marius B. Jansen. Princeton: Princeton University Press, 1965. Also reprinted in *Learning to Be Japanese* (item 22), pp. 17–41.

Covers essentially the same ground as the final chapter of *Education in Tokugawa Japan* and points out some of the ways that Tokugawa educational tradition and practice were favorable to the initiation of social change. Singled out are positive attitudes toward popular education, training in abstract analysis among elites, the development of a respect for merit rather than status, the stimulation of personal ambition, and the strengthening of a collectivist ideology.

76. ———. "Talent and the Social Order in Tokugawa Japan." *Past and Present*, No. 21 (April 1962): 60–72. Reprinted in *Studies in the Institutional History of Early Modern Japan*, pp. 349–362. Edited by John W. Hall and Marius B. Jansen. Princeton: Princeton University Press, 1968.

A brief but compelling discussion of the ways by which Tokugawa society first achieved a workable compromise between the emphasis on hereditary privilege and the natural tendency of schools and teachers to reward ability; and then how, by the middle of the nineteenth century, the balance had begun to tip in favor of merit criteria in schools and society.

77. ———. "Education: Edo-period Education." *Kodansha Encyclopedia of Japan*. Tokyo and New York: Kodansha Ltd., 1983. Vol. 2, pp. 172–175.

A brief overview based on previous research.

78. Earl, David Magarey. *Emperor and Nation in Japan: Political Thinkers of the Tokugawa Period*. Seattle: University of Washington Press, 1964.

See Chapter 7, "Life of Yoshida Shoin," for a useful summary of the early training, experience, and thought of the headmaster of Shoka Sonjuku, one of the outstanding educational institutions of late Tokugawa Japan.

79. Fukuzawa Yukichi. *The Autobiography of Fukuzawa Yukichi*. Translated by Kiyooka Eiichi. New York: Columbia University Press, 1966.

The life of the outstanding Tokugawa-Meiji period journalist, scholar, and educator including a detailed first person account of student ways at Teki Juku, a Tokugawa-period Dutch studies academy.

80. Hall, Ivan Parker. *Mori Arinori*. Cambridge: Harvard University Press, 1973.

See Chapter 1, "Satsuma Origins," for Mori's early life and training. Particularly useful is the discussion of the Satsuma *goju*, a unique form of young men's association that was instrumental in providing physical training, moral guidance and political awareness to male youngsters in Satsuma prior to the establishment of a modern educational system.

81. Hall, John W. "The Confucian Teacher in Tokugawa Japan." In *Confucianism in Action*, pp. 268–301. Edited by David S. Nivison and Arthur F. Wright. Stanford: Stanford University Press, 1959.

An early piece not to be overlooked on the origins, functions and significance of the *jusha* or Confucian teacher in early modern Japan.

82. Huber, Thomas M. *The Revolutionary Origins of Modern Japan*. Stanford: Stanford University Press, 1981.

See Chapter 2, "The Early Life of Yoshida Shoin," for useful material on the educational background of one of the best known political thinkers and educators of the late Tokugawa period.

83. Jansen, Marius B. "New Materials for the Intellectual History of 19th century Japan." *Harvard Journal of Asiatic Studies* 20 (December 1957):567–597.

Discussion of developments in Western studies in Tokugawa Japan, including institutional changes in the bakufu's center for translation of foreign books.

84. ———. *Sakamoto Ryoma and the Meiji Restoration*. Stanford University Press, 1971.

See "The Education of Sakamoto Ryoma," pp. 77–92, for a discussion of the unorthodox educational paths followed by lower samurai. Also the importance of fencing academies as educational institutions.

85. Jansen, Marius B., and Stone, Lawrence. "Education and Modernization in Japan and England." *Comparative Studies in Society and History* 9 (January 1967):208–232.

A brilliant comparative study of the educational contributions to modernization in Japan and England.

86. Kaibara Ekken (Ekiken). *Onna Daigaku* [Higher Learning, for Women]. In Basil Hall Chamberlain, *Things Japanese*, pp. 502–508. Tokyo and Rutland, Vermont: Charles E. Tuttle, 1971. Also in Passin, *Society and Education in Japan* (item 30), pp. 173–176.

Translation of classic statement of eighteenth-century morality for women.

87. Kornicki, P.F. "The Enmein Affair of 1803: The Spread of Information in the Tokugawa Period." *Harvard Journal of Asiatic Studies* 42 (1982):503–533.

Excellent analysis of pre-modern networks of communication. Discussion of kinds of written materials available in non-printed form and the role of circulating libraries in their dissemination.

88. Marshall, Byron K. "Universal Social Dilemmas and Japanese Educational History: The Writings of R.P. Dore." *History of Education Quarterly* 12 (Spring 1972):97–106.

Interpretive essay on the contributions to Japanese educational history of the social scientist R.P. Dore.

89. Minear, Richard H. "Ogyu Sorai's Instructions for Students: A Translation and Commentary." *Harvard Journal of Asiatic Studies* 36 (1976):5–81.

Concise statement of Neo-Confucian philosophy and pedagogy from a leading student of the Ancient Studies school, with commentary by the translator.

90. Ooms, Herman. *Charismatic Bureaucrat: A Political Biography of Matsudaira Sadanobu, 1758–1829.* Chicago: University of Chicago Press, 1975.

   Good material on the Ban on Heterodoxy of 1789 and its effects on the curriculum of the bakufu college (*Shoheiko*) and the various domain schools. See especially Chapter 6, "The Politics of Ideology."

*   Passin, Herbert. *Society and Education in Japan.* Cited in item 30 above.

   Chapter 2, "Tokugawa Education: A Portrait," analyzes the various pre-modern schools for samurai and commoners, vocational training, school attendance and literacy. Chapter 3, "Portents of Modernity," perceptively discusses the ways in which Tokugawa schooling provided continuities with and helped prepare the way for modern educational reforms during the Meiji period.

91. Rubinger, Richard. *Private Academies of Tokugawa Japan.* Princeton: Princeton University Press, 1982.

   Analyzes the various kinds of private schools which lay entirely outside the purview of official control and thus added significantly to the diversity and complexity of Tokugawa schooling patterns.

92. Shimazaki Toson. *Before the Dawn.* Translated by William E. Naff. Honolulu: University of Hawaii Press, 1987.

   A powerful work of historical fiction which tells how the social and political changes of the late Tokugawa years affected the lives and learning of a village headman and his family along one of the main transportation routes to the capital.

93. Shively, Donald H. "Tokugawa Tsunayoshi, the Genroku Shogun." In *Personality in Japanese History*, pp. 85–127. Edited by Albert M. Craig and Donald H. Shively. Berkeley: University of California Press, 1970.

   Included in this analysis of the fifth Tokugawa shogun's many personal peculiarities is a useful discussion of his support of

Confucian studies and institutions, Buddhism, and his interest in the moral education of the masses.

94. Varner, Richard E. "The Organized Peasant: The *Wakamonogumi* in the Edo Period." *Monumenta Nipponica* 32 (Winter 1977):459–483.

    Analysis of the organization and functions of one of the important non-formal educational institutions of the Tokugawa period, the young men's associations in rural farming villages.

INTELLECTUAL CURRENTS: NEO-CONFUCIANISM AND NATIONAL LEARNING

95. Abe Yoshio. "Characteristics of Japanese Confucianism." *Acta Asiatica* 25 (1973):1–20.

96. Ackroyd, Joyce. *Told Around Brushwood Fire: The Autobiography of Arai Hakuseki.* Princeton: Princeton University Press, 1979.

97. Bellah, Robert N. *Tokugawa Religion: The Values of Pre-Industrial Japan.* Boston: Beacon Press, 1957.

98. ———. "Reflections on the Protestant Ethic Analogy in Asia." In *Beyond Belief*, pp. 53–63. Edited by Robert N. Bellah. New York: Harper and Row, 1970.

99. Craig, Albert M. *Choshu in the Meiji Restoration.* Cambridge: Harvard University Press, 1967.

    See Chapter 5, pp. 126–164.

100. de Bary, Wm. Theodore. *Neo-Confucian Orthodoxy and the Learning of the Mind-and-Heart.* New York: Columbia University Press, 1982.

101. ———. "Some Common Tendencies in Neo-Confucianism." In *Confucianism in Action*, pp. 25–49. Edited by David S. Nivison and Arthur F. Wright. Stanford: Stanford University Press, 1959.

102. de Bary, Wm. Theodore, and Bloom, Irene, eds. *Principle and Practicality: Essays in Neo-Confucianism and Practical Learning.* New York: Columbia University Press, 1979.

* Earl, David Magarey. *Emperor and Nation in Japan: Political Thinkers of the Tokugawa Period.* Cited on item 78 above.
 See Part I, pp. 3–106.

103. Harootunian, Harry D. "Jinsei, jinzai and jitsugaku: Social Values and Leadership in Late Tokugawa Thought." In *Modern Japanese Leadership: Transition and Change*, pp. 83–120. Edited by Bernard Silberman and Harry D. Harootunian. Tucson: University of Arizona Press, 1966.

104. McEwan, J.R. *The Political Writings of Ogyu Sorai.* Cambridge, Mass.: Cambridge University Press, 1969.

105. Maruyama Masao. *Studies in the Intellectual History of Tokugawa Japan.* Translated by Mikiso Hane. Princeton: Princeton University Press, 1974.

106. Matsumoto Shigeru. *Motoori Norinaga.* Cambridge, Mass.: Harvard University Press, 1970.

107. Motoyama Yukihiko. "The Political Thought of the Late Mito School." *Philosophical Studies of Japan* 11 (1975):95–119.

108. Najita, Tetsuo. "Intellectual Change in Early Eighteenth-Century Tokugawa Confucianism." *Journal of Asian Studies* 34 (August 1975):931–944.

* ———. *Japan.* Cited in item 13 above.
 See Chapters 1–3 for Tokugawa thought.

109. ———. *Visions of Virtue in Tokugawa Japan: The Kaitokudo Merchant Academy of Osaka.* Chicago: The University of Chicago Press, 1987.

110. Najita, Tetsuo, and Scheiner, Irwin. *Japanese Thought in the Tokugawa Period, 1600–1868: Methods and Metaphors.* Chicago: The University of Chicago Press, 1978.

111. Nosco, Peter, ed. *Confucianism and Tokugawa Culture.* Princeton: Princeton University Press, 1984.

112. Ooms, Herman. *Tokugawa Ideology: Early Constructs, 1570–1680.* Princeton: Princeton University Press, 1985.

113. Spae, Joseph John. *Ito Jinsai: A Philosopher, Educator and Sinologist of the Tokugawa Period.* Peking: Catholic University of Peking, 1948; reprint ed., New York: Paragon, 1967.

114. Tucker, Mary Evelyn. "Moral and Spiritual Cultivation in Japanese Neo-Confucianism: The Life and Thought of Kaibara Ekken (1630–1714)." Ph.D. dissertation, Columbia University, 1985.

115. Wakabayashi, Bob Tadashi. *Anti-Foreignism and Western Learning in Early Modern Japan.* Cambridge: Council on East Asian Studies, Harvard University, 1986.

116. Yoshikawa Kojiro. *Jinsai, Sorai, Norinaga: Three Classical Philologists in Mid-Tokugawa Japan.* Tokyo: Toho Gakkai, 1983.

TOKUGAWA SCIENCE AND MEDICINE

117. Bartholomew, James. "Why Was There No Scientific Revolution in Tokugawa Japan?" *Japanese Studies in the History of Science* 15 (1976):111–125.

118. Fairbank, John K. "The Influence of Modern Science and Technology on Japan and China." *Explorations in Entrepreneurial History* 7 (1955):189–204.

119. French, Calvin L. *Shiba Kokan: Artist, Innovator, and Pioneer in the Westernization of Japan.* Tokyo and New York: Weatherhill, 1974.

120. Goodman, Grant K. *Japan: The Dutch Experience.* London and Dover, N.H.: The Athlone Press, 1986.

121. Jansen, Marius B. *Japan and Its World: Two Centuries of Change.* Princeton: Princeton University Press, 1980.

122. Kanamaru Yoshio. "The Development of a Scientific Community in Pre-Modern Japan." Ph.D. dissertation, Columbia University, 1980.

123. Keene, Donald L. *The Japanese Discovery of Europe, 1720–1830.* Stanford: Stanford University Press, 1969.

124. Kuwaki Ayao. "Western Sciences in the Later Tokugawa Period." *Cultural Nippon* 9 (July 1941):25–53.

125. MacLean, J. "The Significance of Jan Karel van den Broek (1814–1865) for the Introduction of Western Technology into Japan." *Japanese Studies in the History of Science* 16 (1977):69–90.

126. Nakayama Shigeru. *A History of Japanese Astronomy.* Cambridge, Mass.: Harvard University Press, 1969.

127. ———. "Japanese Scientific Thought." In *Dictionary of Scientific Biography*, vol. 15, pp. 728–758. Edited by C. Gillespie. New York: Scribners, 1978.

128. Ogawa Teizo, ed. *History of Medical Education.* Proceedings of the 6th International Symposium on the Comparative History of Medicine—East and West. Tokyo: Saikon Publishing Co., 1983.

129. Sugimoto Masayoshi and Swain, David L. *Science and Culture in Traditional Japan, AD 600–1854.* Cambridge, Mass.: MIT Press, 1978.

130. Sugita Gempaku. *The Dawn of Western Science in Japan.* Translated by Matsumoto Ryozo and Eiichi Kiyooka. Tokyo: Hokuseido Press, 1969.

131. Tsuge Hideomi. *Historical Development of Science and Technology in Japan.* Tokyo: Kokusai Bunka Shinkokai, 1968.

132. Van der Pas, Peter W. "Japanese Students of Mathematics at the University of Leiden During the Sakoku Period." *Japanese Studies in the History of Science* 14 (1975): 109–116.

TOKUGAWA EDUCATION II

133. Ackroyd, Joyce. "Women in Feudal Japan." *Transactions of the Asiatic Society of Japan* Ser. 3, 7 (November 1959):30–68.

134. Bresler, Lawrence. "The Origins of Popular Travel and Travel Literature in Japan." Ph.D. dissertation, Columbia University, 1975.

135. Fisher, Galen M. "Daigaku Wakumon." *Transactions of the Asiatic Society of Japan* Ser. 2, 16 (May 1938):259–356.

136. ———. "Kumazawa Banzan, His Life and Ideas." *Transactions of the Asiatic Society of Japan* Ser. 2, 16 (May 1938):221–258.

137. ———. "The Life and Teaching of Nakae Toju, the Sage of Omi." *Transactions of the Asiatic Society of Japan* Ser. 1, 36 (1908):25–96.

138. Fukaya Katsumi. "Tokugawa Peasants and the Three Rs." *Japan Interpreter* 13 (Summer 1980):126–128.

139. Inoue Yoshimi. "The Kangien, A Private School for Chinese Classics and Its Disposition Toward Western Learning." *Philosophical Studies of Japan* 11 (1975):121–137.

140. Ishikawa Ken. "On Kaibara Ekken's Thought and Reasoning as Expressed in His Yamato Zokkun." *Cultural Nippon* 7 (1939):23–35.

141. Kaibara Ekken. *Yojokun: Japanese Secret of Good Health.* Translated by Masao Kunihiro. Tokyo: Tokuma Shoten, 1974.

142. Kline, Carol June. "Early Tokugawa Education and Ethics: An Annotated Translation of 'The General Introduction' to *The Five Constants*, by Kaibara Ekken." Masters essay, Columbia University, 1970.

143. Kobayashi Tetsuya. "Tokugawa Education as a Foundation of Modern Education in Japan." *Comparative Education Review* 9 (October 1965):288–302.

144. Langston, Eugene. "The 17th Century Hayashi, a Translation from the Sentetsu Sodan." In *Researches in the Social Sciences on Japan*, pp. 1–32. Edited by John E. Lane. Columbia University East Asian Institute Studies, No. 4 (1957): 1–32.

145. Okuma, Count Shigenobu. *Fifty Years of New Japan.* London: Smith, Elder and Co., 1910; reprint ed., New York: Kraus Reprint Co., 1970. Vol. 2.

146. Shiga Tadashi. "Historical View of the Education of Women Before the Time of Meiji." *Education in Japan: A Journal for Overseas* (Hiroshima University) 6 (1971):1–14.

147. Van Straelen, Henricus. *Yoshida Shoin: Forerunner of the Meiji Restoration.* Leiden: E.J. Brill, 1952.

TOKUGAWA EDUCATION III—TRANSLATIONS FROM TOKUGAWA WRITINGS ON EDUCATION

In addition to translations of Tokugawa period writings on education which have appeared as monographs or as journal articles, and for which separate entries are listed above, extracts from selected Tokugawa educational writings are also available in collected form in:

* Passin, Herbert. *Society and Education in Japan..* Cited in item 30 above.

The section entitled, "Documents on Japanese Education," includes translations of the following Tokugawa period writings arranged by date of publication:

"Laws Governing the Military Households" (1615);
Nakae Toju,"Control of the Mind Is True Learning" (1628);
Yamazaki Ansai, "Principles of Education" (1650);
Ito Jinsai, "On Education" (1666);
Kaibara Ekken, "The Greater Learning for Women" (1672);
Kaibara Ekken, "The Way of Contentment" (1672);
Kumazawa Banzan, "Questions About the Greater Learning";
Dazai Jun, "Essay on Educational Control" (1714);
Ogyu Sorai, "Education" (1721);
Kada Azumamaro, "Petition for the Establishment of a School of National Learning" (1728);
The Kansei Edict (1790);
Hirata Atsutane, "On Japanese Learning" (1811);
Sakuma Shozan, "Reflections on My Errors" (1855);
Yoshida Shoin, "Arms and Learning";
Oshima Takato, "Memorial to the Lord of Nambu Domain" (on educational reform) (1863).

CHAPTER IV
MEIJI EDUCATION: TRANSITION TO MODERN SCHOOLING

The most important institutional development in the history of Japanese education was the creation of a national system of schools by the end of the second decade of the Meiji period (1868–1912). This represented three fundamental shifts that had occurred in the organization of Japanese schooling since Tokugawa times: regional variation in the provision and quality of schooling became more nationally standardized; officially sponsored schools that had exhibited sharp class distinctions became integrated into a system that fostered mobility based on talent; and what had been a loose configuration of mostly private educational arrangements became a compulsory system, having a clearly articulated structure controlled by public authority. Changes in educational policy did not, of course, occur in isolation; the administrative rationalization of the early Meiji years parallels similar developments in many other spheres as the new government consolidated its power and sought to establish a unified, centralized state.

The first three and a half years following the restoration of imperial rule on 3 January 1868 were marked by great confusion and turmoil. Yet, during this time, initial steps were taken and decisions were made that influenced subsequent developments. The government's first priority was establishing a system of higher education that would strengthen the leadership group with the best talents in the country. Initial moves in this direction led, not only to bitter ideological disputes among specialists in Confucian, Shinto, and Western studies over what the contents and goals of higher education ought to be, but to arguments between authorities in Tokyo and Kyoto over where the first university ought to be. During the summer of 1870 the fate of the university was decided: the Confucian domination of higher education in Japan had ended, the Western scholars in Tokyo emerged triumphant in uncontested control over the university.

With the ideological battles over the university settled and the government itself firmly committed to a policy of Westernization, the university became the government's central institution for assimilating advanced and practical knowledge from the West. Accordingly, foreign instructors (called *oyatoi*) were hired in large numbers and students were sent abroad to study to the extent that these two programs accounted for 32% of the government's education budget for 1873.[1]

Plans for a national school system were restrained by political instability and the carryover of attitudes and patterns inherited from the Tokugawa past. Private schools continued to prosper and proliferate, regional disparities continued. But with the establishment of a Ministry of Education (Mombusho) on 2 September 1871, efforts began to focus on creating a nationwide system of public elementary schools.

Based on extensive studies of Western educational systems and on experiments undertaken in local areas in Japan, a comprehensive school system for Japan was drawn up by a committee of twelve and issued by the government on 4 September 1872. On the same day, all schools in the country were ordered closed. They reopened the next day in accordance with detailed provisions of the *Gakusei*, Japan's new school law, usually referred to in English as the Fundamental Code of Education.

The Preamble to the Code indicated that the goals of education under the new system would be quite different from the stress on Confucian morality found in the official schools of the Tokugawa period. The educational thrust was directed toward individual goals, equality among classes, and self-improvement. The country was to be divided into school districts with specified numbers of universities, middle and elementary schools in each. The significance of this first design for education in Japan lies not so much in its specific provisions, for many of them were clearly overambitious and would be replaced by later laws, but in its centralized design and its clear message that henceforth education in Japan was to be a national government enterprise. The new plan established a focal point around which public attitudes would form, and a framework for change as the Japanese struggled with the complicated issues surrounding the creation of a modern school system.

The requirement of four years of compulsory schooling meant that, for most local officials, the essence of the new school law involved establishing public elementary schools and increasing attendance in them. In this, the government's policy was generally successful, although it did not happen over night. After some initial resistance (including school burnings in some cases), the graph of school enrollment shows a gentle upward slope from 1873 until 1905, when school attendance reached nearly universal levels for both boys and girls. Figures for local areas, where rates of school going were particularly low during the Tokugawa period, show dramatic upward swings in the early Meiji period, indicating success for the government's policy of providing uniformity in the availability of schooling and overcoming the regional disparities inherited from the Tokugawa past.[2]

In the content of learning, the legacy of the past remained strong for the first two decades of the Meiji period (1868–1912). Although the government set out detailed guidelines for curriculum and textbooks for elementary schools, it adopted a laissez-faire policy with regard to implementation. Consequently, through the 1880s there continued to be a good deal of mixing of Western, Japanese, and Confucian values in text materials. This changed in 1881 when the Mombusho tightened its control over textbooks and published a list of texts considered appropriate. In 1886 a nationwide system for standardization of texts was implemented, and in 1903 local selection was abolished when Mombusho required all elementary schools to adopt identical, state-approved texts for elementary schools.

Financially, from the point of view of the central government, the school plan of the Fundamental Code was the best of two worlds— government control and local funding. The principle that schools should be supported by the people who use them was basic, and the government's contribution remained comparatively small. During the 1870s Mombusho support for elementary schools never went over 10% of total school income, and in 1882 government support was withdrawn. Although local areas developed a variety of schemes to support schools—from tuition, to interest on endowments, to private donations—the lion's share of income came from taxes assessed on landholders.[3] The financial burden was undoubtedly heavy, and it was one of the chief complaints raised against the schools in the late nineteenth century. It was only in 1900 that tuition in elementary schools was abolished, stimulating a sharp climb in enrollment.[3]

The decade of the 1870s witnessed intensive efforts by the Japanese government at implementing both the higher and lower levels of the school plan set out in 1872. Tokyo University was established in 1877 for the advanced training of future leaders, and more than 20,000 elementary schools were hurriedly put in place throughout the country for lower-level mass education. Although school institutions abounded, during the first decade of the Meiji period the organization of the public system lacked coordination between the levels already formed. According to one Meiji educator, the system resembled lower animals before they developed spinal cords or nervous systems—they were partly controlled by the head, and partly by the tail, with each working independently of the other.

Although the Fundamental Code had mandated a public middle school in each of 256 middle school districts, the prefectures, already strapped financially with expenses for elementary schools, were not able to implement the law. Consequently, throughout the 1870s and early 1880s the university preparatory function of middle schools continued to be carried out by a wide variety of private institutions specializing in Western learning and foreign languages. A series of regulations in the early 1880s began to set regulations for and standardize public middle schools. The very high standards set by these laws kept the number of such schools low, but also helped define them as the best preparation for advanced studies at the university.

The various efforts to reform the school system culminated in 1886 with a series of laws designed by Mori Arinori (1847–1889), the first minister of education in the modern cabinet system. The structure of this system remained essentially unchanged until the Occupation reforms following World War II. Elementary schools were redesigned to inculcate proper character and patriotic loyalty. The newly upgraded Imperial University was to train elites for government service. Between these two, functioning as an elite sorting mechanism, were the middle schools with a dual structure: a five year ordinary middle school followed by a two-year (later three-year) higher middle school. The ordinary middle schools—limited to one in each prefecture—were run by prefectures without assistance from the national government; the higher middle schools (limited to only five in the country at first, then expanded to seven in 1887) were prep schools for the University and were financed out of the national treasury.

If one thinks of the expansion of the elementary schools as progress toward greater numbers, the development of middle schools may be thought of as progress toward greater mobility within the system. Once the middle schools provided articulation between the lower and upper levels of the system, the possibilities for commoners to advance to the higher reaches of schooling increased. This did not happen right away because the constituencies at the top and bottom of the system—samurai at the top, others at the bottom—had been different for so long. But by 1890 the proportion of commoners in the ordinary middle schools went above 50% for the first time; by 1898 the figure was 68% and it continued to rise.[4]

It is well to remember that there were limits to mobility within this system. The ordinary middle schools did not accept girls; and since they were not free, only boys who could afford the fees could attend. But meeting the costs did not require great wealth, so the vertical expansion provided by the middle schools was important for educational mobility.

By 1886 the outlines of a distinctive Japanese organization of schools had appeared. To be sure, the system was not yet fully mature. School attendance did not reach near-universal levels until the first decade of the twentieth century; formalized vocational training was still in its infancy; opportunities for women lagged behind those for men; and there was only one officially recognized university until Kyoto Imperial University was created in 1897. The framework for a modern system was, however, in place. By the twentieth century it could be said that the new school system had succeeded remarkably in raising the general level of educational attainment, and in providing the country with the skills and knowledge required for modern political and economic development. These achievements, however, were not gained without cost.

By the late 1880s educational professionals in the central bureaucracy in the Mombusho were making decisions that had formerly been in the hands of individual teachers. The Mombusho was determining curricula, selecting text material, setting school hours and schedules, preparing examinations, and deciding which teaching methods to be used for the entire nation. Teachers, who had been the focus of educational activities in the Tokugawa period, were now mere parts in a larger, national apparatus.

The shift in the locus of educational authority, from scholars and teachers during the Tokugawa period to the centralized bureaucracy of the late 1880s, inevitably brought with it diminishing possibilities for individual and local influence in the control and practice of education. The process of standardization transformed not only the organization of schools, but their purposes as well. With the establishment of the comprehensive system under Mori Arinori in 1886 and its ideological underpinnings articulated in the Imperial Rescript on Education of 1890, the school system became an effective instrument of national policy. As succeeding decades would make abundantly clear, once the schools became subject to uniform policy decisions their importance for the political goals of the national government increased.

NOTES

1. Nagai Michio, *Higher Education in Japan: Its Take-off and Crash*, trans. by Jerry Dusenberry (Tokyo: University of Tokyo Press, 1971), p. 23.

2. A chart showing changes in school attendance rates in selected local areas is found in Richard Rubinger, "Education: From One Room to One System," in *Japan in Transition: From Bakumatsu to Meiji*, ed. Marius B. Jansen and Gilbert F. Rozman (Princeton: Princeton University Press, 1986) p. 213.

3. Ibid., pp. 216–218.

4. Ibid., pp. 225–226.

MEIJI EDUCATION I

148. Beauchamp, Edward R. *An American Teacher in Early Meiji Japan*. Honolulu: The University Press of Hawaii, Asian Studies at Hawaii No. 17, 1976.

Examination of the career of William E. Griffis as a teacher, first in the Fukui domain school in the late Tokugawa period and then in the predecessor of Tokyo University in the early 1810s.

149. ———. "Griffis in Japan: The Fukui Interlude, 1871." In *Learning to be Japanese*, pp. 42–79. Edited by Edward R. Beauchamp. Hamden, Conn.: Linnet Books, 1978.

Focus on William E. Griffis' experience as an educator in the provincial domain of Fukui prior to the establishment of the modern educational system.

150. Blacker, Carmen. *The Japanese Enlightenment: A Study of the Writings of Fukuzawa Yukichi*. Cambridge: Cambridge University Press, 1964.

See especially Chapter 4, "The New Learning" for Fukuzawa's critique of Neo-Confucian learning and his call for more practical studies based on experience and a critical approach.

151. Dore, R.P. "Education—Japan." In *Political Modernization in Japan and Turkey*, pp. 176–204. Edited by Robert E. Ward and Dankwart A. Rustow. Princeton: Princeton University Press, 1964.

Analyzes the influence of educational factors on political development with respect to: the legacy of Tokugawa schools, the educational of political leaders, the relationship of education to popular political attitudes and to national unity.

152. ———. "Mobility, Equality, and Individuation in Modern Japan." In *Aspects of Social Change in Modern Japan*, pp. 113–150. Edited by R.P. Dore. Princeton: Princeton University Press, 1967.

Discussion of the transformation in methods of selection from systems of patronage and heredity to a merit system and a compulsory system of schools, from Meiji to the postwar period.

153. Fridell, Wilbur M. "Government Ethics Textbooks in Late Meiji Japan." *The Journal of Asian Studies* 29 (August 1970):823–833.

Analysis of content and methods of supervision of textbooks from the turn of the nineteenth century when the government assumed more direct supervision in order to impose stronger national and statist values.

154. Fukuzawa Yukichi. *An Encouragement of Learning.* Translated by David Dilworth and Hirano Umeyo. Tokyo: Sophia University Press, 1969.

The complete translation of the nineteenth-century best-seller by Japan's most influential Meiji reformer and educator.

155. ———. *Fukuzawa Yukichi on Education: Selected Works.* Translated and edited by Eiichi Kiyooka. Tokyo: University of Tokyo Press, 1985.

Extracts from books, editorials from Fukuzawa's newspaper *Jiji shimpo*, speeches, essays, and letters to friends and children on educational matters by the well-known scholar, educator and publicizer of things Western.

156. Gluck, Carol. *Japan's Modern Myths: Ideology in the Late Meiji Period.* Princeton: Princeton University Press, 1985.

See Chapter 5 for the most sophisticated analysis in English of the use of the Imperial Rescript on Education of 1890 to create a new national ethos and the use of national education as the main instrument of its diffusion.

* Hall, Ivan Parker. *Mori Arinori.* Cited in item 80 above.

Detailed examination of the life and education of the first Japanese minister of education. Includes the best examination in English of the unique Satsuma institution of the *goju* or village fraternity which was important in the education of a number of important Satsuma men; fascinating accounts of Mori's experiences abroad as a young man; and careful discussion of the issues surrounding the establishment of the modern school system under Mori as the first minister of education in 1886.

157. Havens, Thomas R.H. *Nishi Amane and Modern Japanese Thought*. Princeton: Princeton University Press, 1970.

Chapters 1–4 provide a useful discussion of the background of Nishi's education in late Tokugawa and early Meiji, the progress of a career that centered around the application of Western knowledge to modernize the Japanese state.

158. Japan, Ministry of Education, Science and Culture. *Japan's Modern Educational System: A History of the First Hundred Years*. Tokyo: Ministry of Education, 1980.

An English language abridgement of *Gakusei Hyakunen-shi*, provides much useful data on institutional history, administrative reforms, chronologies, and lists of statutes relating to education in Japan from the late Tokugawa to the postwar period.

159. Kido Takayoshi. *The Diary of Kido Takayoshi*. 3 vols. Translated by Sidney Devere Brown and Akiko Hirota. Tokyo: University of Tokyo Press, 1983, 1985, 1986. 3 vols.

Scholarly translation of diary of one of the most influential of all Meiji leaders. Volume 2 covers the period of Kido's involvement with the Iwakura Mission, detailing his visits to foreign schools, his awareness of Japan's deficiencies in education, and his involvement in establishment of policies for a modern educational system.

160. Kinmonth, Earl H. "Fukuzawa Reconsidered: *Gakumon no susume* and Its Audience." *The Journal of Asian Studies* 37 (August 1978):677–696.

A revisionist view of the ideas in and influence of Fukuzawa's most popular work. Far from criticizing Tokugawa conventions, for which Fukuzawa is known, Kinmonth sees the purpose of the piece as giving voice and direction to samurai aspirations for personal advancement.

161. ———. *The Self-Made Man in Meiji Japanese Thought: From Samurai to Salary Man*. Berkeley and Los Angeles: Univ. of California Press, 1981.

Beginning with an analysis of *Self-Help* by Samuel Smiles and its popularity among samurai in the 1870s, this book describes the changes that occurred as the ideal of self-advancement through education and employment spread from its samurai origins to the general populace in the next 50 years.

162. Levine, Solomon B., and Kawada, Hisashi. *Human Resources in Japanese Industrial Development*. Princeton: Princeton University Press, 1980.

A study of educational and training institutions that generate the human resources required for modern economic enterprises, focusing on how vocational training institutions emerged and evolved in Japan from the 1870s to the first half of the twentieth century.

163. Marshall, Byron K. "Professors and Politics: The Meiji Academic Elite." *The Journal of Japanese Studies* 3 (Winter 1977):71–97.

The role of the academic elite in shaping the course of political and social change in modern Japan, focusing on the Tomizu incident of 1905 when a professor was fired from his position at Tokyo University for criticizing government foreign policy.

164. Mayo, Marlene. "The Western Education of Kume Kunitake, 1871–1876." *Monumenta Nipponica* 28 (Spring 1973):3–67.

Detailed analysis of the content of the journal of the Iwakura Mission to Europe and America, 1871–1873, and its author. A section entitled, "Education, Religion, and Thought on Progress," describes the Japanese special interest in primary schools in the West. The article uses Kume's journal to discuss what they sought out and how they interpreted what they saw.

165. Nagai Michio. *Higher Education in Japan: Its Take-off and Crash*. Translated by Jerry Dusenberry. Tokyo: University of Tokyo Press, 1971.

A good English translation of an influential book written by a former minister of education. The first half is an analysis of the tasks and problems of higher education in Japan, with a particularly useful essay on the origins and purposes of the university in Japan. The second half provides a series of interpretive essays on the role of the intellectual in Japanese society.

166. ———. "Westernization and Japanization: The Early Meiji Transformation in Education." In *Tradition and Modernization in Japanese Culture*, pp. 35–76. Edited by Donald H. Shively. Princeton: Princeton University Press, 1971.

A discussion with many useful details of the development of Japanese educational structures from 1872 to the 1880s, with some theoretical discussion of the process of adapting Western models to indigenous traditions.

167. Nolte, Sharon H. "National Morality and Universal Ethics: Onishi Hajime and the Imperial Rescript on Education." *Monumenta Nipponica* 38 (Autumn 1983):283–294.

How one Meiji philosopher attempted to harmonize the national morality of the Imperial Rescript on Education of 1890 with universal ethics within a context of widely divergent views of the meaning of the Rescript in the Meiji period. Included is a translation of an essay by Onishi on the meaning of the Rescript.

168. Notehelfer, F.G. *American Samurai: Captain L.L. Janes and Japan*. Princeton: Princeton University Press, 1985.

A scholarly biography of an American misfit of the Civil War period who became an influential educator and spiritual leader of an important group of Christian Japanese in the Meiji period.

169. Passin, Herbert. "Japan." In *Education and Political Development*, pp. 272–312. Edited by James S. Coleman. Princeton: Princeton University Press, 1965.

An overview of themes presented more fully in *Society and Education in Japan* (item 30).

This volume is submitted
FOR REVIEW

Price 42⁰⁰

Date of
Publication 5/89

EDUCATION IN JAPAN
A Source Book
Edward R. Beauchamp and Richard Rubinger

NEW!

This source book of essays and bibliographies covers the complete history of education in Japan. Part One sets the context from Japan's earliest days through 1952, focusing on the Tokugawa, Meiji, and occupation periods and examining foreign influences. Part Two covers major issues, such as higher education, out-of-school learning, international education, teachers and teaching, curriculum, women and minorities, youth problems, preschool, and special education. Part Three contains a selected, annotated bibliography and a list of resources and journals.

c. 300 pages   c. $42
ISBN 0-8240-8635-X   SS329
Spring 1989
Volume 5, Reference Books in International Education

170. ———. "Modernization and the Japanese Intellectual." In *Changing Japanese Attitudes Toward Modernization*, pp. 447–487. Edited by Marius B. Jansen. Princeton: Princeton University Press, 1965.

An essay that attempts to define the role of intellectuals in modern Japanese life also provides, by way of modern antecedents, a good discussion of education and the scholarly life in Tokugawa and Meiji Japan.

171. ———. "Portents of Modernity and the Meiji Emergence." In *Education and Economic Development*, pp. 394–421. Edited by C. Arnold Anderson and Mary Jean Bowman. Chicago: Aldine Publishing Co., 1965.

Concise survey of the educational institutions and practices of the Tokugawa period with thoughtful analysis of continuities and discontinuities with the past during the process of establishing a unified national school system in the Meiji period.

172. ———. "Writer and Journalist in Transitional Society." In *Communication and Political Development*, pp. 82–123. Edited by Lucian Pye. Princeton: Princeton University Press, 1963.

173. Pierson, John D. *Tokutomi Soho, 1863–1957: A Journalist for Modern Japan*. Princeton: Princeton University Press, 1980.

A comprehensive biography of an influential journalist who lived through most of Japan's modern changes, provides, in the first three chapters, fascinating details of Tokutomi's early education in the late Tokugawa and early Meiji periods.

174. Pittau, Joseph. "Inoue Kowashi, 1843–1895, and the Formation of Modern Japan." *Monumenta Nipponica* 20 (1965):253–282. Also reprinted in *Learning to Be Japanese* (item 22), pp. 80–119. The last half of the article, on educational matters, has been reprinted as "Inoue Kowashi (1843–1895) and the Meiji Educational System," in *Modern Japan: An Interpretive Anthology*, pp. 176–189. Edited by Irwin Scheiner. New York: Macmillan Publishing Co., 1974.

Inoue's educational background in Kumamoto in late Tokugawa, his Western training in early Meiji, his important role in the formulation of both the Meiji Constitution of 1889 and the Imperial Rescript on Education of 1890, his career as minister of education, and his views on the nature of the state and education are carefully set out here. The author argues that Inoue was close to Mori Arinori in favoring a national system of education that was essentially utilitarian and designed to serve the purposes of the state. He thus differed from more conservative Confucians such as Motoda Eifu who held morality to be the chief aim of education and politics.

175. Pyle, Kenneth B. *The New Generation in Meiji Japan: Problems of Cultural Identity, 1885–1895*. Stanford: Stanford University Press, 1969.

An examination of the attempts of the first generation of Japanese who attended Western-oriented schools to reconcile the conflicting needs of cultural borrowing and national pride. While not focusing explicitly on specifically educational problems, the book provides a useful discussion of the larger context in which educational controversies of the Meiji period were embedded.

176. Roden, Donald T. "'Monasticism' and the Paradox of the Meiji Higher Schools." *The Journal of Asian Studies* 37 (May 1978):413–425.

Discussion of the effects of a "pedagogy of seclusion" upon the youth culture of the elite university preparatory higher schools of the Meiji period. Exploration of the ways by which the monastic existence at these schools created a pseudo class-consciousness among young men who were being bred for elite leadership.

177. Rubinger, Richard. "Education: From One Room to One System." In *Japan in Transition: From Bakumatsu to Meiji*, pp. 195–203. Edited by Marius B. Jansen and Gilbert F. Rozman. Princeton: Princeton University Press, 1986.

Discussion of major continuities and changes in schools and educational practice from the late Tokugawa period up to the establishment of the modern school system in 1886. Focus on both the quantity and quality of Tokugawa schooling and on major deviations from past practice undertaken by the new Meiji leadership.

178. ———. "Problems in Research on Literacy in Nineteenth-Century Japan." In *Nihon kyoiku-shi ronso*, pp. 1–24. Edited by Motoyama Yukihiko kyoju taikan kinen ronbun shuhen iinkai. Kyoto: Shibunkaku Shuppan, 1988.

A critique, in English, of the available data on literacy in late Tokugawa and early Meiji Japan, with suggestions for future research along lines suggested inWestern literature on literacy in history.

179. Shimazaki Toson. *The Broken Commandment*. Translated by Kenneth Strong. Tokyo: University of Tokyo Press, 1974.

A novel of a young man's self awakening and coming to terms with his outcast origins at a time when, despite rapid advances toward a modern state, traditional attitudes remained predominant. The story is set in a Meiji period primary school and the protagonist's world revolves around his responsibilities as a teacher there.

180. Shively, Donald H. "The Japanization of the Middle Meiji." In *Tradition and Modernization in Japanese Culture*, pp. 77–119. Edited by Donald H. Shively. Princeton: Princeton University Press, 1971.

The resurgence of nativism in the 1880s and 1890s as a reaction to Westernization in education and in other areas of life.

181. ———. "Motoda Eifu: Confucian Lecturer to the Meiji Emperor." In *Confucianism in Action*, pp. 302–333. Edited by David S. Nivison and Arthur F. Wright. Stanford: Stanford University Press, 1959.

Analysis of the role and thought of a professional Confucianist during the period of intense preoccupation with Western ideas. Discussion of Motoda's influence on the emperor as Confucian advisor and in the drafting of the Imperial Rescript on Education of 1890.

182. Soviak, Eugene. "On the Nature of Western Progress—The Journal of the Iwakura Embassy." In *Tradition and Modernization in Japanese Culture*, pp. 7–34. Edited by Donald H. Shively. Princeton: Princeton University Press, 1971.

Useful introduction to the five volumes of journals kept by Kume Kunitake of the trip to Europe and America made by an extraordinary contingent of high Japanese government officials from November 1871 to September 1873 to revise treaties and learn about Western civilization and progress. In the words of the author, the journal "represents a coda to the long first movement of Japan's intercultural learning process."

183. Taira Koji. "Education and Literacy in Meiji Japan: An Interpretation." *Explorations in Economic History* 8 (Summer 1971):371–394.

While generally supporting estimates of substantial growth in the quantity of Japanese literacy in the Meiji period, this article, using comparative data from Europe and America, raises questions concerning the effects of compulsory education on the quality of the population during the Meiji period. There is also a useful discussion of the meaning of the term literacy, background on the interaction between educational and economic development, and inclusion of Japanese data not available elsewhere in English.

184. Tokutomi Kenjiro (Roka). *Footprints in the Snow: A Novel of Meiji Japan*. Translated by Kenneth Strong. Rutland, Vt. and Tokyo: Charles E. Tuttle Co., 1971 (originally published George Allen and Unwin Ltd., New York: 1970).

This novel describes the experience of countless young men who were attracted by Western technology and culture during the Meiji period (1868–1912). Written under the influence of *David Copperfield*, it became one of Japan's most popular novels following its publication in 1901. The story describes the struggle of a penniless boy to rebuild his family's fortunes by succeeding in school and making his way in the world.

185. Tsurumi, E. Patricia. "Meiji Primary School Language and Ethics Textbooks: Old Values for a New Society?" *Modern Asian Studies* 8, Part 2 (July 1974):247–261.

A study of the contents of ethics and language texts used during the 1870s and 1880s that suggests that, in contrast to the view that the content of Japanese education shifted from extreme Westernization to conservative reaction culminating in the Imperial Rescript on Education of 1890, there continued to be a good deal of mixing of Western, Confucian, and Japanese nativist values. At no point, the author suggests, did any one of these areas of thought disappear entirely, and diversity remained.

186. Twine, Nanette. "Toward Simplicity: Script Reform Movements in the Meiji Period." *Monumenta Nipponica* 38 (Summer 1983):115–132.

Overview of early attempts to simplify the cumbersome Japanese language in order to make it more accessible to the masses and thereby more attuned to the needs of a modern state. Proposals to limit the number of Chinese characters, attempts to replace characters with the phonetic *kana* syllabary, and organized efforts to entirely romanize the Japanese language are discussed.

MEIJI EDUCATION II

187. Bowers, John Z. *When the Twain Meet: The Rise of Western Medicine in Japan.* Baltimore: Johns Hopkins University Press, 1980.

188. Kiyooka Eiichi. *A History of Keio Gijuku Through the Writings of Fukuzawa.* Tokyo: Hokuseido Press, 1979.

189. Kuhara Hajime. "Historical Documents of Prefectural Educational Administration in the Meiji Era: A Study Based on the School Documents of Miyagi Prefecture." *Research Bulletin of the National Institute for Educational Research* No. 12 (October 1973):41–43.

190. Lincicome, Mark Elwood. "Educational Discourse and the Dimensions of Reform in Meiji Japan." Ph.D. dissertation, University of Chicago, 1985.

191. Nakayama Shigeru. "The Role Played by Universities in Scientific and Technological Development in Japan." *Journal of World History* 9 (1965):340–362.

192. Tayama Katai. *Country Teacher*. Translated by Kenneth Henshall. Honolulu: University of Hawaii Press, 1984.

193. Watanabe Masao. "American Science Teachers in the Early Meiji Period." *Japanese Studies in the History of Science* No. 15 (1976):127–144.

MEIJI EDUCATION III—TRANSLATIONS OF MEIJI WRITINGS ON EDUCATION

A useful collection of Meiji period documents and writings on education are translated in Herbert Passin, *Society and Education in Japan* (cited as item 30 above), pp. 205–251. Included are the following, arranged by date of publication:

Fukuzawa Yukichi, "Encouragement of Learning" (1872);
Preamble to the Fundamental Code of Education (1872);
Mori Arinori, "Education in Japan" (1872);
Mori Arinori, "Opinion on the Education Law Draft" (about 1879);
Imperial Rescript, "The Great Principles of Education" (1879);
Ito Hirobumi, "Opinion on Education" (September 1879);
"Explanation of School Matters" (17 November 1891);
Uchimura Kanzo, "The Case of Lese Majeste" (1891);
Fukuzawa Yukichi, "Autobiography" (1898);
Nishimura Shigeki, "Memorial to the Minister of Education" (1899);
Okuma Shigenobu, "Education—A Pluralistic View" (1901);
Lafcadio Hearn, "Official Education" (1904).

CHAPTER V
FOREIGN INFLUENCES ON
EDUCATION IN MEIJI JAPAN

Many early Western visitors to Japan have remarked on the Japanese eagerness to entertain foreign ideas, but they have also remarked on how cautious the Japanese are in selecting ideas to be adapted to Japanese conditions. Sir George Sansom, one of the most perceptive students of Japan, concluded: "The power and prestige of a foreign culture seem as if they would overwhelm and transform Japan, but always there is a hard, non-absorbent core of individual character, which resists and in turn works upon the invading influence."[1] His is an excellent description of what happened to educational practices borrowed by Japan from the West.

This tradition of cultural borrowing is deeply embedded in Japanese history. For example, Buddhism from India was introduced into Japan, by way of Korea, around the middle of the sixth century A.D. At about the same time, Chinese and Korean monks, craftsmen, artists, and scholars carried a superior civilization to Japan, and their lessons were quickly accepted and integrated into Japan's national fabric. In the seventh century Prince Shotoku not only played an important role in the promotion of Buddhism, but also was responsible for the importation of a variety of ideas and institutions from China that served to enrich Japanese life. One widely used textbook argues that, "on the whole, the Japanese government of the eighth century presented an amazingly faithful reproduction of the T'ang system."[2] In addition, Japan's writing system is heavily indebted to Chinese ideographs which, although pronounced differently by the Japanese, share the same basic meanings in both the Japanese and Chinese languages.

As early as 1860, several years prior to the Meiji Restoration, the first Japanese diplomatic mission journeyed to the United States. A member of this early mission, Fukuzawa Yukichi (1835–1901), founder of the school that emerged as the prestigious Keio University, took advantage of the opportunity to investigate educational conditions in the young republic. He acquired a solid understanding of modern educational principles during this visit and was instrumental in bringing them back to Japan. He wrote 21 influential volumes, numbering over 14,000 pages, based on his foreign observations and experiences. His *Encouragement of Learning* (1876), for example, is estimated to have sold 420,000 copies in the 1870s and a total of 3.4 million copies in 17 editions during his lifetime.[3] This is an impressive total, even by today's standards, but becomes astounding given the fact that Japan's total population in 1880 was only approximately 37 million people.

With the overthrow of the old regime in 1868 and the restoration of the sixteen year-old Emperor Mutsuhito to the throne, it was clear that the new government was determined to pursue the twin goals of nation building and modernization. Opening itself to the West, after more than two-and-one-half centuries of self-imposed isolation, Japan went on a virtual orgy of borrowing in almost all fields of modern endeavor, not the least of which was education. A modern system of schools was recognized as a prerequisite to carry out this policy. First, such a system could serve as a vehicle of national integration. The existence of over two hundred feudal clans suggested that the loyalty of people was local rather than national, and schools were needed to inculcate loyalty to the national state and the emperor. Secondly, the international environment of the day made it imperative for Japan to modernize quickly if she were to avoid coming under the sway of Western colonial powers. This meant that the nation had to be industrialized and a strong military force brought into being. These changes required the creation of a corps of technically able young men who would modernize the nation, make it an industrial power, and provide it with the strength to survive in an unfriendly world.

The response to this clarion call for reform took two basic forms. The first was the dispatch of hundreds, and then thousands, of Japanese students, usually at government expense, to the United States and Europe to learn the secrets of Western power and prestige. The second was the employment of foreign specialists as teachers, technicians, and experts in a wide variety of fields by the new government. There was even an impressive number of privately sponsored students who joined the ' army' of young Japanese studying abroad.[4]

To their great credit, the Meiji oligarchs quickly recognized the potential of education as a vehicle for modernizing the entire society; and to accomplish this enormous task they began to create a modern educational system. Recognizing their limitations, they set out to examine the educational arrangements existing in the major Western nations—England, France, Germany, and the United States—in an effort to determine not only which elements of those systems were world class, but also, perhaps even more important, which elements were appropriate for Japan in her present state. They thus began a practice that still exists today. They sent out intelligent and well-prepared officials, often possessing keen powers of observation, to study foreign education, to collect materials bearing on the subject, and to serve as experts on education in foreign countries upon their return.

In 1872, the so-called Iwakura Mission was sent to the United States and Western Europe in order to lobby for revision of the so-called "unequal treaties" (trade agreements signed under duress with Western powers in the 1850s and 1860s) but also to learn about the current state of American education. This was reflected in the letters of credentials, from the Meiji Emperor to President Ulysses S. Grant, which stated that "It is our purpose to select from the various institutions prevailing among the enlightened nations such as are best suited to our present condition, and adopt them, in gradual reforms and improvements of our policy and custom, so as to be on an equality with them."[5] Tanaka Fujimaro (1845–1909), senior secretary of the newly established Department of Education, along with several assistants served as the Iwakura Mission's educational specialists. Upon his return, Tanaka wrote 15 volumes describing Western education as he had observed it. Tanaka and his assistants were received by the U.S. Commissioner of Education, John Eaton, who provided them with a great deal of information and assisted them in making contacts with prominent American educators.[6]

Determined to borrow selectively, that is to take the best features of what the West could offer, the Japanese imported experts from many countries. They looked to France for principles of criminal law and French scholars were brought to Japan to create a criminal code. French military officers were engaged to teach strategy and tactics to the Japanese army and, when the French were defeated in the Franco-

Prussian War, the Japanese promptly replaced them with Prussian military advisors.

Although the Japanese decided to model the administrative structure of public education on the highly centralized French pattern, creating a Ministry of Education at the center for both policy implementation and day-to-day administration, a strong American influence was reflected in the popularity of American books on education, and the training of a number of influential future Japanese educators in the United States. During the period following the American Civil War, the educational thought of Johann Heinrich Pestalozzi (1746–1827) was influential in the United States. A number of Japanese educators, including Takamine Hideo (1854–1910) travelled to the United States to study at the Oswego (New York) Normal School, a hotbed of Pestalozzian pedagogy. There the young Japanese came under the influence of Edward A. Sheldon, one of the major American disciples of the great Swiss reformer. Upon returning to Japan, Takamine and his compatriots were influential in spreading the American version of Pestalozzi's thought throughout Japan. In addition, Izawa Shuji (1851–1917) studied at Bridgewater Normal School and Kozu Senzaburo at Albany Normal School. Upon returning home, all three made extensive contributions to the modernization of Japanese education. Izawa and Takamine introduced new pedagogical methods, based on the educational theory of Pestalozzi, with Izawa publishing the first Japanese book on pedagogy, based on his college lecture notes. In addition, Kozu and Izawa introduced new theories and practices for music education. Takamine, a prominent biochemist, successfully pursued a scientific career that kept him in close contact with both nations.

Mori Arinori, serving as Japan's first diplomatic representative to the United States, and later minister of education, carefully identified the most prestigious figures in the American educational establishment; and on 3 February 1872, he sent them identical letters requesting their advice for the future development of Japanese education. Among the matters on which he invited comment were:

The effects of education
1. upon the material prosperity of the country;
2. upon its commerce;
3. upon its agricultural and industrial interests;
4. upon the social, moral, and physical condition of the people; and
5. its influences upon the laws and government.

Among the American educators responding to Mori's request was a Rutgers Professor of Mathematics, Dr. David Murray, who, at least in part because of the excellence of his response, was invited to Japan to serve as the first national superintendent of schools and colleges and advisor to the Department of Education. One of the elements of Murray's reply which undoubtedly appealed to the Japanese was his insistence that an educational system must reflect its national culture. "There are," he wrote, "traditional customs with which it would be unwise to undertake to subvert. There are institutions already founded which are revered for their local and national associations, which without material changes may be made the best elements of a new system."[7]

Murray remained in Japan from August 1873 to December 1879 and made important contributions to the development of Japanese education. His activities included inspecting schools, planning curricula and courses of study, and establishing an educational museum in Tokyo in addition to advising on school construction. Murray also accompanied Japanese officials to set up a Japanese educational exhibit at the Philadelphia Exposition of 1876. Particularly significant in Murray's approach to Japanese education was his role as a brake on the ideas of the more extreme advocates of Western learning. A strong cultural relativist, Murray argued strenuously against Mori Arinori's unsuccessful attempt to replace the Japanese language with English, and in favor of replacing the ubiquitous foreign textbooks of the 1870s with Japanese versions.

Teacher education in Japan was centered at the Tokyo Normal School where, in 1872 Marion M. Scott, a former San Francisco grammar school principal, served as a teacher and model. Scott's teaching reflected the elementary school methods used in the United States, and he organized new courses of study as well as introducing blackboards to Japanese schools. The early graduates of this institution soon staffed the new prefectural normal schools, further spreading the influence of American educational thought.

At the university level, however, the German model was thought most appropriate for Japanese conditions and shaped development of Japanese higher education for many years. Foreign influences were somewhat tempered, however, by a conservative resurgence that began to take hold around 1880.

Another brief period of Western influence occurred during the so-called Taisho democracy of the 1920s, when the Japanese evinced a significant interest in progressive education in general and in John Dewey's educational thought in particular. But the subsequent rise of the military to national power cut short many promising experiments and plunged the nation into the educational morass that would be the target of the next major period of Western influence, the 1945–1952 Occupation of Japan by the allied powers.

In several important ways the American Occupation of Japan was the single greatest experiment in social engineering that the world has seen. In this sense the entire Occupation was an educational enterprise, but the attempts to engender radical social change by reforming the institutions of formal education were, in themselves, virtually unparalleled. The underlying tone was set during the postsurrender planning which began while the outcome of the war was still in doubt. American planners decided that the U.S. government was committed to the postwar demilitarization, democratization, and decentralization of Japan and her people.

The report of the first United States Education Mission to Japan, in the spring of 1946, advised the Occupation authorities how to implement those principles in the education sector. The mission's recommendations ranged from a proposal for greater individualization of instruction to one for a 6-3-3 school ladder and nine years of compulsory education. That the Japanese were willing to embrace these and other recommendations of the mission is as much a tribute to their continuing openness to foreign ideas as to their inferior role after being defeated on the field of battle. One of the most important legacies of Occupation was the creation, in 1946, of the Education Reform Committee as an advisory body to the prime minister. In 1952 this panel evolved into the influential Central Council for Education, which in its early years was independent of the Ministry of Education, reporting directly to the prime minister. Although today its members are appointed by the education minister, the Central Council for Education has been a major arena for debate over educational reforms.

As the Occupation drew to a close, the "hard, non-absorbent core" of the Japanese character that Sansom described, exerted itself and the excesses of the period were corrected in a "reverse course." Even while this was occurring, however, the Japanese tradition of reform continued. Recognizing the need to remain abreast of world trends in education, the

Ministry of Education established a National Institute for Educational Research (NIER) to, among other things, "exchange educational information with education and educational institutions in other countries."[8] Today NIER is comprised of seven research departments, one of which is charged with collecting information about educational trends throughout the world. In addition, many Japanese schools of education have distinguished researchers studying educational conditions in other countries. The result is that government policy makers have continuous access to an impressive pool of education specialists knowledgeable about worldwide trends in education. By the mid-1970s there was increasing talk in the Japanese media and in political and educational circles about the need for "a third major reform" of Japanese education. This ferment has continued to the present and, in 1984, Prime Minister Nakasone appointed an Ad Hoc Committee on Educational Reform (*Rinkyoshin*) to make appropriate recommendations. Once again, Japanese observers fanned out throughout the world to seek ideas and practices that might be relevant and adaptable to the Japanese situation.

NOTES

1. Sir George B. Sansom, *Japan: A Short Cultural History* (New York: Appleton, Century and Crofts, 1962), p. 15.

2. Edwin O. Reischauer and John K. Fairbank, *A History of East Asian Civilization: East Asia: The Great Tradition*, Vol. 1 (Boston: Houghton Mifflin Company, 1960), pp. 484–486.

3. Fukuzawa Yukichi, *An Encouragement of Learning*. trans. with an Introduction by David A. Dilworth and Umeyo Hirano (Tokyo: Sophia University Press, 1969), p. xi.

4. Hazel J. Jones, *Live Machines: Hired Foreigners and Meiji Japan* (Vancouver: University of British Columbia, 1980), pp. xv–xvi, 59.

5. Kenji Hamada, *Prince Ito* (Tokyo: San-seido, 1936), pp. 65–66.

6. Ronald S. Anderson, *Education in Japan: A Century of Modern Development* (Washington, D.C.: United States Government Printing Office, 1975), p.5.

7. Robert Schwantes, *Japanese and Americans: A Century of Cultural Relations* (New York: Harper & Brothers, 1955), p. 130.

8. NIER, *National Institute for Educational Research: A Brief Outline* (Tokyo: NIER, March 1983), p. 2.

FOREIGN INFLUENCES ON JAPANESE EDUCATION I

194. Allen, George C. *Appointment in Japan: Memories of Sixty Years.* London: The Athlone Press, 1983.

G.C. Allen first went to Japan in 1922 as a teacher at the Nagoya Commercial College and died sixty years later, widely acknowledged as an outstanding economic historian of modern Japan. Allen's comments on Japanese education and students over six decades provide a rich lode of information.

195. Anthony, David F. "The Administration of Hokkaido Under Kuroda Kiyotaka, 1870–1882: An Early Example of Japanese-American Cooperation." Ph.D. dissertation, Yale University, 1951.

Focuses on Kuroda Kiyotaka's role in the origins and work of the Kaitakushi (Hokkaido Colonization Commission), including its educational activities.

196. Ashmead, John, Jr. "The Idea of Japan, 1853–1895: Japan as Described by Americans and Other Travelers from the West." 2 vols. Ph.D. dissertation, Harvard University, 1951.

Analysis of the writings of about 200 American and English travellers in Japan and their influence on Japanese culture.

197. Baelz, Erwin O.E. *Awakening Japan: The Diary of a German Doctor; Erwin Baelz.* Edited by his son, Toku Baelz. Bloomington: Indiana University Press, 1974.

An analysis of the medical contributions and experiences of Baelz, who lived and worked in Japan from 1876 to 1905.

198. Barr, Pat. *The Coming of the Barbarians: The Opening of Japan to the West, 1853–1870*. New York: E.P. Dutton, 1967.

A useful, popularized account of the coming of Westerners to Japan. Includes material directly and indirectly related to both schooling and the broader introduction of ideas and technology.

199. ———. *The Deer Cry Pavilion: A Story of Westerners in Japan, 1868–1905*. New York: Harcourt, Brace & World, 1968.

A continuation of her earlier book, named after the so-called *Rokumeikan*, ("Deer Cry Pavilion"), opened in 1883 as a social center.

200. Beck, Clark L., and Burks, Ardath W., eds. *Aspects of Meiji Modernization: The Japan Helpers and the Helped*. New Brunswick: Transaction Books, 1983.

Four papers and a commentary on the foreign employee phenomenon in Meiji Japan. Contributing to this slim volume are Ardath Burks, Marius Jansen, John Maki, Fujita Fumiko and Donald Roden.

201. Black, John R. *Young Japan: Yokohama and Yedo; A Narrative of the Settlement and the City from the Signing of the Treaties in 1858, to the Closing of the Year 1879*. 2 Vols. Yokohama: Kelly and Company, 1883; reprint ed., New York: Oxford University Press, 1968.

One of the earliest records of life in the port settlements. Useful for its reflection of the attitudes of foreigners in late-Tokugawa and early-Meiji Japan toward many things, including education.

202. Blum, Paul C. *Yokohama in 1872, A Rambling Account of the Community in which the Asiatic Society of Japan Was Founded*. Tokyo: The Asiatic Society of Japan, 1963.

Blum, a long time resident of Yokohama, provides a valuable description of the development of Yokohama from an oceanside village to a modern metropolis.

203.   Boxer, C. R. *Jan Campagnie in Japan, 1600–1850.* 2nd ed. The Hague: Martinus Nijhoff, 1959.

Continuation of many of the basic arguments contained in his *Christian Century in Japan* (item 53).

204.   Burks, Ardath, ed. *The Modernizers: Overseas Students, Foreign Employees and Meiji Japan.* Boulder, Colorado: Westview Press, 1985.

An expanded coverage of the topics treated by participants to the 1967 bicentennial anniversary conference of Rutgers University. Contributors include internationally known specialists of the *yatoi* phenomenon from both Japan and the United States. Contains items 222, 224, 227, 230, 235, 239, 240, 268.

205.   Capron, Horace. "Agriculture in Japan." In *Report of the Commissioner of Agriculture for the Year 1873*, pp. 364–374. Washington, D.C.: U.S. Government Printing Office, 1874.

A landmark report of American contributions to Japanese agricultural education.

206.   ———. *Reports and Official Letters to the Kaitakushi.* Tokei: Kaitakushi, 1875.

Valuable primary source material on the educational (and other) activities of the Hokkaido Colonization Commission.

207.   Carey, Otis. *A History of Christianity in Japan.* 2 vols. New York: Fleming H. Revell, 1909.

An indispensable guide to the educational activities of nineteenth century missionaries to Japan.

208.   Clark, Edward W. *Life and Adventures in Japan.* New York: American Tract Society, 1878.

Everyday experiences of an American teacher in early Meiji Japan. Provides flavor of problems of living and teaching in the Japan of the time.

209. Cortazzi, Sir Hugh. *Dr. Willis in Japan: British Medical Pioneer, 1862–1877.* London: The Athlone Press, 1985.

Former British Ambassador to Japan provides a fascinating account of the fifteen years spent in Japan by Dr. William Willis. Willis worked with the British Legation from May 1862 to December 1869, after which he moved to the southern port city of Kagoshima to run a hospital for five years. Willis was responsible for introducing many Western medical techniques to Japan.

210. ———. *Victorians in Japan: In and Around the Treaty Ports.* London: The Athlone Press, 1987.

An anthology of impressions and observations of what it was like to be a foreigner in early Meiji Japan. This useful volume sheds much light on the life of Westerners in late-nineteenth century Japan.

211. ———. "Yokohama, Frontier Town, 1859–1866." *Asian Affairs* 17, Part 1 (February 1986): 3–17.

212. ———. *Mitford's Japan: The Memoirs and Recollections, 1866–1906, of Algernon Bertram Mitford, The First Lord Redesdale.* London: The Athlone Press, 1985.

Although not dealing directly with educational questions, this is an important book for students of late-nineteenth-century Japanese education. It provides the valuable context within which education took place and helps to explain the nature of its development.

213. Curti, Merle, and Birr, Kendall. *Prelude to Point Four: American Technical Missions Overseas, 1838–1938.* Madison: University of Wisconsin Press, 1954.

Contains helpful material on the contributions of Americans to nineteenth century Japanese development.

214. Dulles, Foster Rhea. *Yankees and Samurai: America's Role in the Emergence of Modern Japan, 1791–1900.* New York: Harper & Row, 1965.

215. Fox, Grace. *Britain and Japan, 1858–1883.* New York: Oxford University Press, 1968.

Best study of British activities in Japan during early Meiji, and an important source of information of Britain's educational role in Japan of the time.

216. Fujita Fumiko. "'Boys, Be Ambitious': American Pioneers on the Japanese Frontier, 1871–1882." Ph.D. dissertation, City University of New York, 1988.

An excellent account of Horace Capron and his American colleagues who worked hard to modernize the Japanese frontier of Hokkaido during the Meiji period. Includes a great deal of material relevant to education.

217. Hara Yoshio. "From Westernization to Japanization: The Replacement of Foreign Teachers by Japanese Who Studied Abroad." *The Developing Economies* 15 (December 1977):440–461.

One of the reasons for Japan's successful modernization while fending off undue Western influence was her commitment to replace foreigners with trained Japanese as quickly as possible. This study provides insights into how this task was accomplished.

218. Helbig, Frances Y. "William Elliot Griffis: Entrepreneur of Ideas." M.A. thesis, University of Rochester, 1966.

Sketchy but useful study of one of the first teachers to bring Western style education to the interior (Fukui) of Japan in the early Meiji period.

219. Holtham, Edmund Gregory. *Eight Years in Japan, 1873–1881.* London: Kegan Paul and Trench, 1883.

Firsthand account of life in Japan during early Meiji.

220. Hopper, Helen M. "The Conflict between Japanese Tradition and Western Learning in the Meiji Intellectual Mori Ogai (1862–1922)." Ph.D. dissertation, Washington University, 1976.

    An interesting account of the effects of Western thought and practice, and an important Meiji intellectual's attempt to resolve the conflicts between tradition and modernity.

221. Iglehart, Charles W. *A Century of Protestant Christianity in Japan.* Tokyo: Charles Tuttle, 1960.

    An important account of Protestant educational activities in Japan, before and during the Meiji period.

222. Ishizuki Minoru. "Overseas Study by Japanese in the Early Meiji Period." In *The Modernizers: Overseas Students, Foreign Employees, and Meiji Japan* (item 204), pp. 161–186.

    Interesting analysis of the three stages of Japanese students abroad: the Elementary Stage (1862–1867), the Expansion Stage (1868–1874), and the Consolidation Stage (1875–1881).

223. Jones, Hazel J. "The Formulation of Meiji Policy Toward the Employment of Foreigners." *Monumenta Nipponica* 23 (1968):9–30.

    Analysis of how the Meiji authorities maneuvered to acquire the foreign expertise needed to propel Japan into the modern world and, at the same time, to maintain her control over the foreigners in Japan.

224. ———. "The Griffis Thesis and Meiji Policy Toward Hired Foreigners." In *The Modernizers: Overseas Students, Foreign Employees, and Meiji Japan* (item 204), pp. 219–253.

    Advances the view of William Elliot Griffis that Japanese used foreigners as nothing more than "helpers" in the modernization process, and were very careful not to give them any real authority. This was in direct opposition to the view of Basil Hall Chamberlain that the foreigners were "the makers of the new Japan."

225. ———. *Live Machines: Hired Foreigners and Meiji Japan.* Vancouver: University of British Columbia Press, 1980.

Revised version of her doctoral dissertation, "The Meiji Government and Foreign Employees, 1868–1890" (University of Michigan, 1967). This is the first full scale scholarly study of the *yatoi* phenomenon in English.

226. ———. "The Meiji Government and Foreign Employees, 1868–1900." Ph.D dissertation, University of Michigan, 1967.

Helpful summary of the relationship between foreign employees and the Meiji government.

227. Kaneko Tadashi. "Contributions of David Murray to the Modernization of School Administration in Japan." In *The Modernizers: Students, Foreign Employees, and Meiji Japan* (item 204), pp. 301–321.

One of the few studies of Murray, the first national superintendent of education in Japan (1873–1879), who played a major role in Meiji educational reforms.

228. Maclay, Arthur Collins. *A Budget of Letters from Japan: Reminiscences of Work and Travel in Japan.* New York: A.C. Armstrong & Son, 1886.

One of the more interesting personal experiences of teaching in Meiji Japan. Maclay's time was spent in northern Honshu, well outside the relative comforts of Tokyo or the treaty ports.

229. Morse, Edward S. *Japan Day by Day 1877, 1878–1879, 1882–1883.* 2 vols. Boston: Houghton Mifflin, 1917.

Morse was one of the most important foreigners in Meiji Japan; a man whose educational and intellectual contributions were great. These volumes provide us with a detailed account of his activities in Japan.

230. Motoyama Yukihiko. "The Educational Policy of Fukui and William Elliot Griffis." In *The Modernizers: Overseas Students, Foreign Employees and Meiji Japan* (item 204), pp. 265–300.

One of Japan's outstanding historians, Professor Motoyama applies historical methods to the study of educational policy in Fukui domain in late-Tokugawa and early Meiji Japan. The role of William Elliot Griffis receives full treatment. This is must reading for all students of the topic.

231. Nakamura, Hiroshi. "The Contribution of Foreigners." *Journal of World History* 9 (1965):294–319.

A very useful survey of the contributions of foreigners to the development of Japan.

232. Nishihira Isao. "Western Influences on the Modernization of Japanese Education, 1868–1912." Ph.D. dissertation, The Ohio State University, 1972.

A case study of how Western educational thought influenced the development of Meiji education.

233. Pressesian, Ernest L. *Before Aggression: Europeans Prepare the Japanese Army.* Tucson: University of Arizona Press, 1965.

A useful but often overlooked study of how Europeans taught Japanese modern military organization, strategy, tactics, etc.

234. Roden, Donald. "In Search of the Real Horace Capron: A Historiographical Perspective on Japanese-American Relations." *Pacific Historical Review* 55 (November 1986): 549–575.

A contemporary analysis of the role played by Americans in general, and former American commissioner of agriculture, Horace Capron, in particular.

* Sansom, Sir George B. *The Western World and Japan: A Study in the Interaction of European and Asiatic Cultures* (cited in item 17 above).

An early but, perhaps, still the best study of Western influence on Meiji Japan. This book deals with education in the broadest sense.

235. Schwantes, Robert S. "Foreign Employees in the Development of Japan." In *The Modernizers: Overseas Students, Foreign Employees, and Meiji Japan* (item 204), pp. 207–217.

Argues that the Japanese anticipated the modern practice of foreign specialists to accelerate the development process. In addition, the Japanese were wise to bear the entire cost of employing foreigners (thereby retaining control), and to simultaneously train replacements for these foreign specialists.

236. ———. *Japanese and Americans: A Century of Cultural Relations*. New York: Harper & Brothers, 1955.

The section on Meiji Japan is a dated, but still indispensable, treatment of the subject. This book is a treasure trove of information on individuals and their contributions.

237. Storry, Dorothie. *Second Country: The Story of Richard Storry and Japan, 1913–1982*. Woodchurch: Paul Norbury Publications, 1986.

Storry, one of Britain's greatest historians of Japan, is memorialized by his wife in this volume. Several chapters provide valuable materials on Storry's rich experience.

238. Umetani, Noboru. *The Role of Foreign Employees in the Meiji Era in Japan*. Tokyo: Institute of Developing Economies, 1971.

Contains much important and often hard-to-find material on a number of foreigners in Japan.

239. ———. "William Elliot Griffis' Studies in Japanese History: Their Significance." In *The Modernizers: Overseas Students, Foreign Employees, and Meiji Japan* (item 204), pp. 393-407.

After briefly detailing the major events in Griffis' work in Japan, the author analyzes his major contributions before turning to Griffis in his role as historian. Umetani's evaluation of Griffis the historian is a positive one.

240. Watanabe Masao. "Science Across the Pacific: American-Japanese Scientific and Cultural Contacts in the Late Nineteenth Century." In *The Modernizers: Students, Foreign Employees, and Meiji Japan* (item 204), pp. 254–293.

Watanabe systematically describes America's nineteenth century scientific contributions to Japan in mathematics, physical science, chemistry, seismology, biology (including Darwinism), archaeology, anthropology, etc. He concludes that science was introduced "independently of the humanities and the religious aspect of Western culture," which resulted in a chasm separating science and the humanities in Japanese thought from the very beginning of the modern period.

241. Watanabe Minoru. "Japanese Students Abroad and the Acquisition of Scientific and Technical Knowledge." *Journal of World History* 9 (1965):254–293.

Provides some important detail on Japanese students as "bridges" between Western science and Japanese development.

242. Whitney, Clara A.N. *Clara's Diary: An American Girl in Meiji Japan.* Edited by M. William Steele and Tamiko Ichimata. Tokyo: Kodansha, 1979.

The diary of Clara Whitney provides a fascinating glimpse into the life of an American family in Japan between 1875 and 1884, a period of consolidation for the Meiji government. Originally brought to Japan as the result of an invitation from Mori Arinori to set up a national business college, Clara's father saw this plan fall through when the Tokyo authorities refused to agree to Mori's plan.

243. Yokoyama Toshio. *Japan in the Victorian Mind: A Study of Stereotyped Images of a Nation, 1850–1880.* London: Macmillan, 1987.

Not only traces the ways in which British writings about Japan changed during the Victorian era, but also analyzes the process by which these writings shaped popular British attitudes about Japan.

FOREIGN INFLUENCES ON JAPANESE EDUCATION II

244. Amioka, Shiro. "Changes in Educational Ideals and Objectives (From Selected Documents, Tokugawa Era to the Meiji Period)." In *The Modernizers: Overseas Students, Foreign Employees and Meiji Japan* (item 204), pp. 323–357.

245. Arima Seiho. "The Western Influence on Japanese Military Science, Shipbuilding and Navigation." *Monumenta Nipponica* 14 (1964):352–379.

246. Brooks, Van Wyck. *Fenollosa and His Circle*. New York: E.P. Dutton, 1962.

247. Burks, Ardath. "William Elliot Griffis: Class of 1869." *The Journal of the Rutgers University Library* 19 (1966):91–100.

248. Bush, Lewis. *77 Samurai: Japan's First Embassy to America*. Tokyo: Kodansha, 1968.

249. Chisolm, Lawrence W. *Fenollosa: The Far East and American Culture*. New Haven: Yale University Press, 1963.

250. Church, Deborah C. "The Role of American Diplomatic Advisors to the Japanese Foreign Ministry, 1872–1887." Ph.D. dissertation, University of Hawaii, 1978.

251. Fraser, Mary Crawford. *A Diplomat's Wife in Japan: Sketches at the Turn of the Century*. Edited by Hugh Cortazzi. Tokyo: John Weatherhill, 1982.

252. Gowen, Herbert H. *Five Foreigners in Japan*. New York: Books for Libraries Press, 1967.

253. Griffis, William E. *The Mikado's Empire*. 2 vols. New York: Harper and Brothers, 1877. Reprint ed., Tokyo: Jiji Press, 1977.

254. Harris, Neil. "All the World a Melting Pot? Japan at American Fairs, 1876–1904." In *Mutual Images: Essays in American-Japanese Relations*, pp. 24–54. Edited by Akira Iriye. Cambridge, Mass.: Harvard University Press, 1975.

255. Henry, Joseph. *The Papers of Joseph Henry.* Vol 1. Edited by Nathan Reingold. Washington, D.C.: Smithsonian Institution Press, 1972.

256. Hokkaido Prefectural Government (Archives Section, General Affairs Department). *Foreign Pioneers: A Short History of the Contributions of Foreigners to the Development of Hokkaido.* Sapporo: Hokkaido Prefectural Government, 1968.

257. Huffman, James L. "Edward Howard House: In the Service of Meiji Japan." *Pacific Historical Review* 56 (May 1987):231–258.

258. Iriye, Akira. *Across the Pacific: An Inner History of American-East Asian Relations.* New York: Harcourt, Brace and World, 1967.

259. Iwao, Seiichi. "A Dutch Doctor in Old Japan." *Japan Quarterly* 8 (April–June 1961):170–178.

260. Jones, Hazel J. "Bakumatsu Foreign Employees." *Monumenta Nipponica* 29 (1974):305–327.

261. Lehmann, Jean-Pierre. *The Image of Japan: From Feudal Isolation to World Power, 1850–1905.* London: George Allen and Unwin, 1978.

262. Mayo, Marlene J. "The Iwakura Mission to the United States and Europe, 1871-1873." Columbia University East Asian Institute Studies No. 5. New York, 1959.

263. Medzini, Meron. *French Policy in Japan During the Closing Years of the Tokugawa Regime.* Cambridge: Harvard University Press, 1971.

264. ———. "Leon Roches in Japan (1864–1868)." In *Papers on Japan.* Vol. 2. Cambridge: Harvard East Asian Institute Studies, 1963.

265. Metraux, Daniel A. "Lay Proselytization of Christianity in Japan in the Meiji Period: The Career of Edward Warren Clark." *New England Social Studies Bulletin* 44 (June 1986):40–50.

266. Netherlands Association for Japanese Studies. *Philipp Franz von Siebold: A Contribution to the Study of Historical Relations between Japan and the Netherlands.* Leiden: Leiden University, Center for Japanese Studies, 1978.

267. Rohan, Kieran M. "Lighthouses and the *Yatoi* Experiences of R.H. Brunton." *Monumenta Nipponica* 20 (1965):65–80.

268. Rosenberg, Emily S. *Spreading the American Dream: American Economic and Cultural Expansion, 1890–1945.* New York: Hill and Wang, 1982.

269. Rosenstone, Robert A. "Learning from Those 'Imitative' Japanese: Another Side of the American Experience in the Mikado's Empire." *The American Historical Review* 85 (June 1980):572–595.

270. Saito Masaru. "Introduction of Foreign Technology in the Industrialization Process—Japanese Experience Since the Meiji Restoration (1868)." *The Developing Economies* 13 (June 1975):168–186.

271. Schwantes, Robert S. "American Relations with Japan, 1853–1895: Survey and Prospect." In *American-East Asian Relations: A Survey,* pp. 87–128. Edited by Ernest R. May and James C. Thomson, Jr. Cambridge, Mass.: Harvard University Press, 1972.

272. Taylor, Sandra C. *Advocate of Understanding: Sidney Gulick and the Search for Peace with Japan*. Kent: Kent State University Press, 1984.

273. Thompson, James C., Jr., Stanley, Peter W. and Perry, John C. *Sentimental Imperialists: The American Experience in East Asia*. New York: Harper & Row, 1981.

274. Umetani, Noboru. "Foreign Nationals Employed in Japan During the Years of Modernization." *East Asian Cultural Studies* (1971).

275. Yamamoto, Masaya. "Image-Makers of Japan: A Case Study in the Impact of the American Protestant Foreign Missionary Movement, 1859–1905." Ph.D. dissertation, Ohio State University, 1967.

CHAPTER VI
PREWAR AND WARTIME EDUCATION:
DEMOCRATIC EXPERIMENTS AND INDOCTRINATION

The administrative system established through a series of education laws in 1886 by minister of education, Mori Arinori, and the ideological underpinning of the new system provided in the Imperial Rescript on Education of 1890 remained in place until 1945. The system was, however, forced to meet increasing demands for education at all levels. Because the Japanese had opted for an elitist system that kept the entranceway to the more prestigious academic tracks very narrow, there were bound to be pressures at the point of entry to the middle schools, higher schools, and universities. Because the system was centrally controlled and designed to serve the interests of the state, it eventually fell prey to the rise of militarism in the 1930s.

The system, as set out in the late nineteenth century, was essentially an elaborate sorting mechanism that streamed students into separate, and virtually non-transferable, tracks at critical points. Following six years of compulsory elementary education (it had been increased to six years in 1907) the first streaming occurred: between boys and girls. Although elementary schools were coeducational, middle schools were not. Girls went on to a number of specialized girls schools, primarily vocational and normal schools. For boys, there were two tracks that could be followed: one that led to higher education, and the other that terminated with middle school. For the latter, there was a wide variety of vocational, technical, and normal schools. For the former, there was the five-year academic middle school. The sorting out following middle school was the most radical of all. Because of the small number of higher schools preparatory to the even smaller number of universities, the number of successful entrants was low. Only one out of thirteen middle school graduates could expect to enter higher school, and only one out of twenty-five was admitted to the prestigious higher schools that opened the way to the imperial universities. Normally, there were seven times more applicants than openings. Because this stage was decisive for a child's future, the university being the main channel to better positions in business or government, the pressure for success became known as *shiken jigoku*, or "examination hell." The critical test was for entrance to the three-year higher school. From there, students passed almost automatically into the imperial universities. Those who failed the higher school exams had several choices: terminating their education, going into normal school, attending military school, or attending "technical school" (*semmongakko*). The last provided a wide range of professional training, and through them one could become a doctor, lawyer, dentist, engineer, architect, or pharmacist—but at a lower level than those trained at universities. The women's universities, at the highest level within the track for women, were ranked at the *semmongakko* level.[1]

The hierarchical organization of Japanese schools intensified the competition. Among the 45 prewar universities, the imperial universities ranked highest; and, among these, Tokyo Imperial stood first. Next came the remaining government schools and a small number of prestigious private schools, such as Keio and Waseda. Far below these came the remaining private schools. The result of this elitism was not only the severe competition for entrance to the good schools, but a concentration of the best students in a small number of elite government schools.

Once in the university, the pressure relaxed. The successful entrant was virtually assured a diploma, the passport to the better positions in Japanese society. Thus, the pressures in the Japanese school system were, and still are, the reverse of the American. Where American schools are relatively relaxed and noncompetitive at the beginning levels and gradually more demanding as the level rises, in Japan the system is competitive at the early stages and more easygoing after that.

The rate of attrition in the prewar system was extremely high. Of every 1,000 elementary school entrants, about 5 would enter university.[2] Today, the figure is something like 36 in every 100. The reasons were not only the competitiveness of the system, but the economic hardship of supporting a student beyond the compulsory elementary level.

The educational system was subjected to a number of additional pressures as the temper of the times changed. Following the Sino-Japanese War (1894–95) there were demands for vocational training, so vocational middle schools and *semmongakko* for higher technical training were introduced. Beginning in 1918, significant expansion of higher education was undertaken, as the status of "university" was extended beyond the imperial universities for the first time to some of the *semmongakko* such as Keio and Waseda. Thus, while in 1918 there had been just 5 imperial universities with about 9,000 students, in 1930 there were 46 universities with almost 70,000 students.

The late 1920s saw a resurgence of interest in reformist ideas in education derived from the West. The New Education Movement promoted a child-centered pedagogy, teachers unions were organized, and student movements opposed to the nationalist education of the Ministry of Education arose. The government responded with repression, and promoted, as an alternative to leftist ideology, a return to the "Japanese spirit" through an increasing emphasis on morals courses (*shushin*) in schools.

Following the Manchurian "incident" of 1931, educational policy became increasingly nationalistic; and after the Sino-Japanese War broke out in 1937, educational content was dominated by militarism. With the outbreak of war in the Pacific, elementary schools were reformed as *kokumin gakko* (people's schools) entirely dedicated to inculcation of militaristic ideology. During the worst periods of destruction, in 1944 and 1945, the schools ceased to function in any significant way, and many rural schools had to evacuate students to sanctuaries in the mountains, away from Allied bombing targets.

NOTES

1. Based on discussion in Herbert Passin, *Society and Education in Japan* (New York: Teachers College Press, 1965), pp. 103–108.

2. Ibid., p. 108.

PREWAR AND WARTIME EDUCATION I

276. Bartholomew, James R. "Japanese Modernization and the Imperial Universities, 1876–1920." *The Journal of Asian Studies* 37 (February 1978):251–271.

Rejecting the prevailing view, the argument is made that German influence on Japanese universities has been exaggerated, that universities were an essential element in Japan's modern development, and that they were well equipped to support the rise of modern science.

277. Dower, John W. *War Without Mercy: Race and Power in the Pacific War*. New York: Pantheon Books, 1986.

Although not a book ostensibly about education in the formal sense, it is a study of racial prejudices—how they are formed and are transmitted through language with devastating effects. Drawing on songs, slogans, cartoons, propaganda films, secret reports, official documents, and learned treatises, the author shows how "war words" from the savage epithets of the battlefield to the sophisticated labels of scholars contributed to the savagery of the war in the Pacific.

278. Kobayashi, Victor N. *John Dewey in Japanese Educational Thought*. University of Michigan Comparative Education Dissertation Series, No. 2 (1964).

Discussion of the history and influence of the ideas of John Dewey in Japan particularly during the "progressive" 1920s which saw a resurgence of independent schools and innovative thinking in education.

*   Marshall, Byron K. "Academic Factionalism in Japan: The Case of the Todai Economics Department, 1919–1939." *Modern Asian Studies* 12 (October 1978):529–551. Annotated in item 527 below.

279. ———. "Growth and Conflict in Japanese Higher Education, 1905–1930." In *Conflict in Modern Japanese History: The Neglected Tradition*, pp. 276–294. Edited by Tetsuo Najita

and J. Victor Koschmann. Princeton: Princeton University Press, 1982.

Analysis of erosion of what once had been cohesion between the bureaucratic elite in government and the intellectual elite in universities stemming from enormous expansion in higher education in the early twentieth century, increasing bureaucratization and professionalization at the Ministry of Education, and decentralization of control over universities. Whereas in the late-nineteenth century Tokyo and Kyoto Universities had been an integral part of government educational policy, by the 1920s they, and other universities had become the sources of challenges to governmental authority.

*   ————. "The Tradition of Conflict in the Governance of Japan's Imperial Universities." *History of Education Quarterly* 17 (Winter 1977):385–406. Annotated in item 528 below.

280.   Roden, Donald T. *Schooldays in Imperial Japan: A Study in the Culture of a Student Elite.* Berkeley, Los Angeles, and London: University of California Press, 1980.

A powerful and well-written account of student culture of the very few who made it through the selection process to become students at the prewar higher schools. Analysis, based on primary materials written for and by students, of the functions and some of the excesses of elitist ideology and practice in the prewar period.

281.   Smethurst, Richard J. *A Social Basis for Prewar Japanese Militarism: The Army and the Rural Community.* New York: Columbia University Press, 1974.

How, between 1910 and 1945, the Japanese Army attempted to spread nationalistic ideology, tried to ensure popularity for the military, and built a solid basis of popular support for the army in rural areas of the country. Chapter 2 looks at Army efforts to educate rural youth through a variety of non-formal educational institutions such as youth associations, training centers, youth schools, and women's associations outside of the national school system. This chapter, "The Army, Youth, and Women" is reprinted in *Learning to Be Japanese* (item 22), pp. 137–166.

282. Smith, Henry D., II. *Japan's First Student Radicals.* Cambridge, Mass.: Harvard University Press, 1972.

A study of the *Shinjinkai* (New Man Society), the leading prewar left-wing student movement in Japan from its creation in 1918 to its suppression in the 1930s. Following a very useful introductory chapter on the prewar university system, the book looks at the roots of modern student unrest in Japan, makes comparisons between pre- and postwar student movements, and then concentrates on the nature and importance of the *Shinjinkai*.

* Spaulding, Robert M. *Imperial Japan's Higher Civil Service Examinations.* Cited in item 52 above.

A study of the way Japan came to reject the traditional criterion of heredity and accepted the examination system and the merit principle as the key to regulating access to position in the civil bureaucracy. Included are impressive details on the administration and content of the prewar civil service examinations, a useful comparative history of Japanese higher education, and a brief discussion of the Chinese origins of the early Japanese examination system.

283. Takane, Masaaki. *The Political Elite in Japan: Continuity and Change in Modernization.* Berkeley, Calif.: Center for Japanese Studies, Institute of East Asian Studies, University of California, 1981.

Influences on education of feudal status and social mobility. For the pre-war period, see Chapter 7, "The Emergence of an Education-Oriented Society."

284. Tsurumi, E. Patricia. *Japanese Colonial Education in Taiwan, 1895–1945.* Cambridge, Mass., and London: Harvard University Press, 1977.

Detailed examination of Japanese educational policy during its period of colonial administration of Taiwan. Focusses on comparisons between Japanese educational policies in its colony and educational policies at home, as well as the effects of colonial policy on the people colonized.

*   Wray, Harold J. "A Study in Contrasts: Japanese School Textbooks of 1903 and 1941–1945." *Monumenta Nipponica* 28 (1973):69–86. Annotated in item 884 below.

PREWAR AND WARTIME EDUCATION II

285. Daniels, Gordon. "The Evacuation of School-Children in Wartime Japan." *Proceedings of the British Association for Japanese Studies.* 2, Part 1 (1977):100–116.

*   Hall, Robert K., and Gauntlett, J.C. *Kokutai no Hongi: Cardinal Principles of the National Entity of Japan.* Annotated in item 314 below.

286. Ponsomby, Richard. "Japanese Education Viewed by an Englishman." *Cultural Nippon* 3 (March 1935):303–318.

287. Suh Doo Soo. "The Struggle for Academic Freedom in Japanese Universities Before 1945." Ph.D. dissertation, Columbia University, 1953.

288. Wray, Harold J. "Militarism in Japanese Textbooks, 1903–1945: A Content Analysis." *Malaysian Journal of Education* 13 (December 1976):51–72.

PREWAR AND WARTIME EDUCATION III— TRANSLATIONS OF PREWAR AND WARTIME WRITINGS ON EDUCATION

A useful collection of prewar and wartime documents and writings on education are translated in Herbert Passin, *Society and Education in Japan* (cited in item 30 above), pp. 252–269. Included are the following, arranged by date of publication:

Amur Society, "An Anniversary Statement" (1930);
Educational Study Group Proposed Reform Plan (December 1936);
"Principles of the National Polity" (1937);
Extracts from Morals Textbooks, 1930s and 1940s;
Educational Reform of 1941;
Ministry of Education, "Policy on Instruction" (1943).

CHAPTER VII
EDUCATION UNDER THE
OCCUPATION (1945–1952)

World War II came to a close on 14 August 1945 when Japan accepted the Allied terms of surrender laid down by the Potsdam Declaration of 26 July 1945. The first American forces arrived at Yokosuka on August 28, and the formal surrender took place aboard the battleship Missouri, in Tokyo Bay, on 2 September 1945. This was quickly followed by the creation of the Supreme Command for the Allied Powers (SCAP), under the command of General Douglas MacArthur, and a specific staff section called the Civil Information and Education (CI&E) Section. The ensuing occupation ended six years and eight months later, with the Treaty of San Francisco, on 28 April 1952. During this long interval the Allied, primarily American forces, worked to transform formerly militaristic Japan into a democratic society.

When the Emperor's representatives formally signed the instrument of surrender, Japan lay numb and prostrate before a conquering army. Almost 2 million Japanese were dead and millions more were wounded. Suffering was extensive, but no single group suffered more than the young. Japan's educational system was in shambles. An American estimate of conditions on the day of surrender found 18 million students idle, over 4 thousand schools destroyed and thousands more heavily damaged. In addition, available teachers were screened for militaristic leanings, and most textbooks were deemed unsuitable because they were filled with militaristic propaganda considered unsuitable for pedagogical purposes. Finally, more than one of every three institutions of higher education lay in ruins, thousands of teachers were homeless, hungry, and dispirited, and many of their pupils had been moved to safer areas. In short, there was no functioning educational system.

The Occupation's initial objectives were most authoritatively set forth in the "United States Initial Post-Surrender Policy for Japan." This document stated that "[the] ultimate objective" of American policy was "to foster conditions which will give the greatest possible assurance that Japan will not again become a menace to the peace and security of the world and will permit her eventual admission as a responsible and peaceful member of the family of nations." Among the measures deemed essential for fulfilling this objective was "the abolition of militarism and ultra-nationalism in all their forms; . . . the strengthening of democratic tendencies and processes in governmental, economic and social institutions; and the other encouragement and support of liberal political tendencies in Japan."[1] Thus, the major early goals of the Occupation of Japan were the demilitarization, democratization and decentralization of Japanese society.

The authority possessed by General MacArthur was absolute, as evidenced by the instructions he received from President Truman:

> 1. The authority of the Emperor and the Japanese government to rule the State is subordinate to you as Supreme Commander for the Allied Powers. You will exercise your authority as you deem proper to carry out your mission. Our relations with Japan do not rest on a contractual basis, but on an unconditional surrender. Since your authority is supreme, you will not entertain any question on the part of the Japanese as to its scope.
>
> 2. Control of Japan shall be exercised through the Japanese Government to the extent that such an arrangement produces satisfactory results. This does not prejudice your right to act directly if required. You may enforce the orders issued by you by the employment of such measures as you deem necessary, including the use of power.[2]

In retrospect it is clear that MacArthur's use of this enormous power was circumspect and wise, but in the hands of a lesser man, this great experiment in social engineering could easily have been a disaster for both nations.

The Occupation authorities recognized from the outset that schools had played a major role in the inculcation of nationalism and militarism in pre-war youth, and that these same schools could now be used in the same fashion to build a new, democratic society. Thus, educational reform was a crucial element in the United States determination to transform Japan from an aggressive, military dictatorship into a peace-loving democracy. When Japan surrendered in the late summer of 1945, those Americans charged with planning the eventual occupation of Japan shared an essentially common view of prewar and wartime Japanese education and the role it had played in Japan's military expansion into much of Asia and Oceania.

Before and during World War II, American policymakers saw Japanese education as a vehicle for carrying out the intent of the 1890 Imperial Rescript on Education. The Imperial Rescript on Education, promulgated by the Emperor Meiji on 30 October 1890, remained the official statement of the principles underlying Japanese education until it was scrapped by the Occupation authorities. The Rescript gave both legal form and, perhaps more significantly, moral force to an educational system which supported the rise of militarism and ultranationalism during the late-1920s and 1930s. William Sebald, a career State Department officer who served as an advisor to General MacArthur during the Occupation, has written that prewar Japanese education,

> had been used by the country's leaders as part of a policy of developing an obedient and subservient population. Schools had been transformed, primarily into agencies of indoctrination in militarism and ultranationalism. For many years teachers and students had drawn their inspiration from the Imperial Rescript on Education . . . , with the result that the importance and integrity of the individual were dwarfed by the growing power of the state.[3]

The 1890 Imperial Rescript on Education is, therefore, a key document from several points of view. On the one hand, it defines that particular combination of Shinto beliefs, Confucian virtues, and Western statism to which all loyal Japanese were expected to adhere; and in so doing, it sets down the principles from which much of the militaristic and ultranationalistic emphasis in education developed. It clearly subordinates the individual to the good of the state, and promotes unthinking acceptance of, and blind obedience to, instructions from above. An Office of Strategic Services (OSS) document on Japanese education, prepared during World War II, concludes that "[t]he attitude that education should be for the purposes of the State rather than for the liberation of the individual has permeated the entire system. Elementary school instruction has been dedicated to the development of unquestioning loyalty. The Department of Education's exclusive copyright over textbooks, held since 1903, has made it possible to intensify this process of indoctrination." The minister of education, in a speech in 1941, called for "the eradication of thoughts based on individualism and liberalism, and the firm establishment of a national moral standard with emphasis on service to the state."[4]

Having surrendered her sovereignty to the Allies, Japan entered into a period in which the policymaking function was no longer in her hands. As an occupied nation, all Japan could hope for was that through persuasion and political skill she could at least have an influence on the educational policy that the Americans formulated and sought to implement. On the part of the vanquished Japanese, the terrible scars of war led them to acquire a strong aversion toward the military and a distaste for war. At the same time, the victorious Occupation authorities systematically set about to dismantle the prewar institutions and structures which they saw as having caused Japan's slide into the abyss of militarism and nationalism. The Japanese generally supported these actions of the Occupation authorities and demonstrated their commitment to non-violence and peace by embracing Article 9 of the 1946 Constitution, which forever renounced war as an instrument of the national policy.

The initial phase of the Occupation educational reform efforts was often authoritarian and almost completely negative. The Civil Information and Education (CI&E) Section, created by the SCAP, worked closely with the highly centralized Ministry of Education. This new organization, reinforced by surviving remnants of the prewar Japanese willingness to accept and obey instructions from above, enabled the American authorities to use the existing instruments of government to implement educational reforms. (Questions of the extent of Japanese cooperation with and/or manipulation of the American authorities are beyond the scope of this chapter.) The Occupation proceeded to censor textbooks, magazines, films, etc., as well as to purge teachers whose pre-Occupation activities were deemed to be either undemocratic or actively supporting the military's policies.[5] Thus, one of the great ironies of this period was that in encouraging the democratization of Japanese education, the actions of the all-powerful Occupation forces were often not very democratic.

This phase of the Occupation was marked by a stream of highly specific American directives designed to tear down the existing anti-democratic educational structures. This initial frenzy of activity should not be surprising as American pre-surrender planning for the Occupation had begun as early as the summer of 1942. The training of personnel for the eventual Occupation of Japan also began at that time and by the following year many of America's most prestigious institutions began training Occupation personnel not only in the intricacies of military government, but also in the language, culture and history of Japan. During this preparatory period, American planners were able to draw upon the experience and expertise of hundreds of missionaries, businessmen and scholars who had lived and worked in prewar Japan. Thus, long before the end of the World War II, American policymakers had thought through the purposes of the forthcoming occupation and had a reasonable sense of what they wanted to accomplish. This is not to suggest that the Occupation enjoyed smooth sailing, but merely that the Americans were probably as well prepared for their difficult task as could be expected under the circumstances.

Anticipating the thrust of American reforms, the Japanese began making changes even before the Occupation authorities made any demands upon them. Even before American troops landed, and the Occupation had begun, the Ministry of Education abolished the old Wartime Education Law and, on 15 September 1945, promulgated a new "Educational Policy Towards Construction of a New Japan." Although "democracy" was not specifically mentioned, the general thrust of this document was clearly toward the elimination of militarism and its replacement with a democratic educational system. It is significant that the Japanese not only anticipated the overall direction of American educational policy, but also made an early effort to accommodate themselves to it. While it is true that this action demonstrated political realism, it also suggests that some remnants of earlier democratic tendencies still existed.

This behavior on the part of the Japanese is significant in that it suggests that they entered the Occupation period with only a single, potentially contentious issue. The sole official stand taken by the government was in defense of the imperial system, and enough assurance appears to have been given so that this did not become a problem for most leaders. There is no evidence to suggest that the Japanese used the nineteen days between surrender, on August 14, and the Occupation on September 2, to devise ways in which to thwart the Occupation by way of an anti-Occupation conspiracy in high places. The Japanese government remained intact and was predisposed, however

much it was unhappy with the war's conclusion, to accept the
Occupation and to implement its orders.

American actions taken in the early days of the Occupation
reinforced this climate with the issuance of four sweeping educational
directives in the autumn and early winter of 1945, essentially clearing
away much of the foundation of prewar Japanese education. These
directives reoriented Japanese education from militaristic to democratic
ends, provided a framework for purging teachers with "militaristic and
nationalistic" tendencies, abolished State Shinto, and suspended all
courses in moral education, history, and geography that had served as
primary instruments of nationalistic indoctrination. On 1 January 1946
the Emperor issued an Imperial Rescript denying his divinity and
endorsing the principles of the 1868 Charter Oath which had served as
the basis for educational modernization in the early Meiji period. These
actions essentially completed the negative phase of educational reform,
and forced the American authorities to think seriously about what the
new structure they were committed to building would look like.
Fortunately, American pre-surrender planning for the occupation was
based on several assumptions which were particularly relevant for the
reform of Japanese education. The United States, for example, did not
envision the destruction of Japan's cultural heritage and the imposition
of American values and institutions. American planners, in fact,
believed that rather than destroying Japanese culture, they could use it
as far as possible, in establishing new attitudes of mind and assumed
that a peaceful postwar Japan "presupposed the existence of those in the
country who would be predisposed to accept the [liberal American]
vision and carry out the task of reconstruction along liberal lines."[6]

What appeared to be wrong with Japanese schools, in the eyes of
most American policymakers, was that they were unlike American
schools. American-initiated educational reforms were, therefore,
designed to help foster the conditions that would inevitably lead to a
functioning democratic system based on the American model. This
meant that the Occupation would have to transform the prewar
orientation of the Japanese (with its emphasis on filial piety, the
perfection of moral powers, group cohesion and harmony, loyalty and
obedience to the Emperor and nation) into one harmonious with the
often contradictory goals of the United States in Japan.

One of the first steps taken by the relatively inexperienced
Americans, in charge of reforming Japanese education was to request

that a high-level educational mission be sent to Japan to provide advice and, perhaps more importantly, a legitimation of their plans for reform. A 27-member mission under the chairmanship of Dr. George D. Stoddard (former New York State Commissioner of Education and President-Elect of the University of Illinois), arrived in Japan in March 1946. Consisting primarily of school administrators and education professors, the First United States Education Mission to Japan (USEMJ) can be fairly described as representing the mainstream of American progressive educational thought and virtually innocent of any knowledge of either Japan or Japanese education.[7]

In order to provide a legitimate counterpart group with which the USEMJ could work, the Japanese government was directed to form a committee of leading Japanese educators "to facilitate the work of the Educational [sic] Mission." The directive to create this committee also decreed that it would be a standing committee whose charge would be "to advise the Ministry of Education on the reform of Japanese education."[8]

Although General MacArthur told the Japanese that the Mission's Report, issued under his imprimatur, should be viewed as "suggestions" for reform and not as a SCAP master plan, it is not surprising that this message was taken with a grain of salt by the Japanese. Both the tone and recommendations of the Report so faithfully articulated the fundamental tenets of American notions of democratic education that both the Japanese and many CI&E personnel interpreted it as containing the *real* wishes of the "American Shogun."

True to its American heritage, the Mission rejected most of the elements of prewar Japanese education, and insisted on the democratization and decentralization of that nation's highly centralized enterprise into a system in which the centralized power of the Ministry of Education would be broken, and local communities would control their own educational destiny. The American mission also urged the dismantling of the highly differentiated multi-track system of prewar days to be replaced by an American-style 6-3-3 educational ladder with the first nine years compulsory and free, the substitution of social studies for moral education, a greater emphasis on physical and vocational education at all levels, the encouragement of adult education and modern methods of guidance, and the transformation of teacher education by integrating it into four year universities.

With a single exception the Mission's recommendations merely echoed the principles advanced by the pre-surrender planners. This exception, however, dealt with the sensitive area of language reform. The Mission wanted to "overcome the linguistic supports of the spirit of national isolation and exclusiveness," inherent in the Japanese language. This was to be accomplished by not only substituting Roman script for Chinese characters, but also abandoning *hiragana* and *katakana* (Japanese phonetic syllabaries). Not surprisingly this was the only major recommendation that was not embraced by the Japanese.

Decentralization was viewed by the Mission, as well as by CI&E, as the key to reforming Japanese education along democratic lines. The centralized power of the Ministry of Education was, in the Mission's words, "the seat of power for those who controlled the minds of Japan." After all, local control of American schools had kept them "close to the people" and out of the hands of the machinations of national government, and this system would confer the same benefit on Japan. The Americans, however, failed to consider that their decentralized system was an organic outgrowth of an enormous geographical expanse and the "rugged individualism" which flourished on the frontier. Japan, on the other hand, was a small, heavily populated island nation which placed great emphasis on cooperation and harmony. Throughout its modern history, Japan had a centralized educational system and education functioned to serve the needs of the state, not to fulfill the potential of the individual.

With the latter point in mind, the USEMJ strongly urged that the powers of the Ministry of Education be curtailed from a control organ to that of an *advisory* organ providing only advice and assistance to local educational entities. Although abolishing the Ministry of Education had been seriously considered, the combination of the Ministry's political influence, and the need of the Occupation authorities to use the Ministry's administrative skills to implement Occupation policy made this option a dead letter.

Given the assumptions inherent in the decentralization argument, the next logical step was to enhance local decision-making by advocating locally-elected school boards. In 1948, the required legislation was put in place. The following year, further legislation was passed that stripped the Ministry of Education of most of its power and confined its activities to advising, gathering data, and conducting research studies. The system of school inspection was scrapped, and the practice of tight, centralized control over school textbooks was modified but not abandoned. This was a very controversial experiment from the outset. The system never worked as it was intended to, and it was replaced in 1956 by the Local Education Administration Act, which eliminated the popular election of school board members and their power over the educational budget.

Among the Mission's other major recommendations were urgings that the curriculum and methods of education be expanded beyond the old pattern of a single textbook and teacher's manual. Moreover, it proposed that: individualization according to student needs and abilities be instituted; the content and approach of moral education be overhauled and no longer treated as a separate subject in the curriculum; a 6-3-3 system be installed and compulsory schooling be extended to nine years; normal schools be transformed into four-year institutions to better prepare teachers in content and democratic pedagogy; the educational opportunities of women be expanded; and guidance be stressed in the schools. For good or ill, all of these recommendations spoke to a dominant faith in American educational theory and practice.

As a number of scholars, Japanese and American, have pointed out, many of these reforms—such as coeducation, comprehensive schools and local control—were deeply rooted in the American democratic model, but were dysfunctional when transported to the Japanese context. The Japanese educational authorities, however, had little choice but to officially accept the recommendations of the Mission's report and, indeed, these recommendations became the basis for a series of important educational laws implemented between 1947 and 1949.

While reforms were being pondered by the men and women of CI&E, the legal foundation of postwar education was being constructed. After much discussion a new constitution was passed by the Diet on 7 October 1946, to come into effect on 3 May 1947. Unlike the American Constitution which fails to mention education, the Japanese document specifically states that "All people shall have the right to receive an equal education correspondent to their ability, as provided by law. All people shall be obliged to have all boys and girls under their protection receive ordinary education as provided by law. Such compulsory education shall be free."[9]

In March 1947 two signal pieces of legislation guaranteeing the basic educational provisions of the Constitution were put into place, the Law of Fundamental Education and the School Education Law. The former replaced the 1890 Imperial Rescript on Education as the basic document governing Japanese education and boldly set forth as a policy statement many of the democratic principles advocated by the Occupation: "Having established the Constitution of Japan, we have shown our resolution to contribute to the peace of the world and welfare of humanity by building a democratic and cultural state. The realization of this ideal shall depend fundamentally on the power of education."[10] This law established the principle that all major educational regulations would be made by parliamentary procedure. The several provisions of this law called for the full development of personality, respect for academic freedom, equality of educational opportunity for all without discrimination of any kind, coeducation at all levels, education for citizenship.

The School Education Law, on the other hand, set down the administrative nuts and bolts of the new school organization from kindergarten through university education and included creating a 6-3-3-school ladder and raising the school-learning age to 15. These statutes were accompanied by a series of related laws (Social Education Law, Board of Education Law, etc.) that, taken collectively, constitute the heart of the Occupation's reform of Japanese education.

By 1949 the major accomplishments of the Occupation were completed. The political and strategic imperatives of the emerging "Cold War" caused American policymakers to reassess their plans for the future of Japan and to ally themselves more closely with conservative Japanese interests.[11] The reforming zeal of America had, thus, abated, and the environment in Japan underwent an important change. By the time American control was withdrawn in the spring of 1952, American reformers had succeeded in clearing away most of the old undemocratic structures, replacing them with ones more to their liking; they had also replaced those individuals identified as hostile to democracy with Japanese who seemed committed to democratic values; they had provided Japanese educators with new curricula, textbooks and methodologies. In short, they had given their best effort, and as they withdrew to the sidelines, they could only hope that their best effort was good enough.

Hovering in the background of these events was the growing threat of Communism as perceived by American policymakers. Supported by skillful organizers and timely exploitation of economic and political grievances, the Japan Communist Party (JCP), with its 100 thousand members and 3 million non-party supporters, was seen as a threat to stability. Political leaders in Washington, had concluded that Japan could be a reliable frontline ally against Soviet power in East Asia. In order to accomplish this, it would be necessary to rebuild Japan's industrial potential and to find a way to skirt the constitutional prohibition of a Japanese military force. The Occupation began to undergo a subtle redirection, designed to buttress the nation's economy and suppress the increasing strength of the JCP.

Helping to consolidate this change was the outbreak of the Korean War in June 1950, which accelerated the Occupation's so-called "red purge" and virtually crippled the JCP as a serious threat to Japanese political stability. Ultimately, the Japanese came to perceive the Occupation as "inconsistent." When challenged by opposing political ideas, the Occupation authorities acted in conflict with their political rhetoric. While preaching democratic virtues and condemning prewar "thought control," the Americans moved to suppress communist political activities. While advocating the freedom of individuals to pursue political action, the American authorities moved to effectively prosecute what it considered to be "dangerous thoughts." These apparently undemocratic actions by the advocates of democratization inevitably contributed to a fundamentally anti-American student movement in the 1960s.

Although Japan's military defeat and the subsequent American actions to dismantle the prewar system resulted in fundamental changes in the nation's educational orientation, and even though most Japanese supported the changes which had occurred, several of the American reforms seemed, in the eyes of many, to throw the baby out with the bath water. With the return of sovereignty in April, 1952, the Japanese began a careful reexamination, and then systematically modified or changed those things which they believed were not in harmony with the nation's political and cultural traditions. Among major educational revisions were the scrapping of the American-imposed school board system and the reinstitution of the Ministry of Education's centralized control over the educational system, particularly in the areas of administration, curriculum and textbook selection. This process is usually referred to as the "reverse course," but did not signal a rejection of democracy as a concept and a return to "the bad old days." It was not a question of returning to a *status quo ante bellum*, but merely reflected a belief that if the Japanese were to have democracy, they were determined to have a variant that was consistent with their traditions and culture. Although centralization reasserted itself, this was not necessarily anti-democratic. Local control over education, as the study of American education amply demonstrates, does not necessarily result in a greater degree of equality or fairness, and can result in racial discrimination, religious bigotry, textbook censorship, and other undemocratic acts. One can also make the argument, and many Japanese did, that a centralized system ensured that every child from Okinawa to Hokkaido enjoyed "equality of educational opportunity" because of the relatively equal physical facilities throughout the country, a uniform curriculum administered by the Ministry of Education, equal access to the same textbooks, teachers of relatively equal competence, and a uniform set of national standards.

Although not without its defects, the American role in reshaping postwar Japanese education was generally a positive one. The Occupation purged the worst of the militaristic teachers and administrators and created a check of the power of the Ministry of Education for the first time in Japanese history. In addition, it provided a model of one type of democratic education that remains the basic framework for education in Japan. The Occupation also opened Japan to fresh educational thought, including Marxist and antidemocratic ideas, that it had not known since the 1920s. One of the Occupation's most notable achievements was the opening of educational opportunities to the single largest "minority" group in Japan—its women. The Occupation laid down the legal principles for the emancipation of Japanese women, and the American imposed Constitution of 1947 provided a legal guarantee of gender equality that is still not found in the U.S. Constitution.

NOTES

1. U.S., JCS 1380/15 (November 3, 1945). Modern Military Section.

2. U.S., Joint Civil Affairs Committee 48. 30 August 1945. "Basic Initial Post-Surrender Directive to the Supreme Commander for the Allied Powers for the Occupation and Control of Japan." Record Group 319, Records of the Army Staff. ABC 387 Japan (15 February 1944), Sec. 19.

3. Quoted in Thomas P. Rohlen, *Japan's High Schools* (Berkeley: University of California Press, 1983), pp. 63–64.

4. U.S., Office of Strategic Services, n.d. Modern Military Branch.

5. For details see Hans Baerwald, *The Purge of Japanese Leaders Under the Occupation* (Berkeley: University of California Press, 1959).

6. Edward R. Beauchamp, "Educational and Social Reform in Japan: The First United States Educational Mission to Japan, 1946," in *The Occupation of Japan: Educational and Social Reform*, ed. Thomas W. Burkman (Norfolk: The MacArthur Memorial, 1982), p. 178. A summary of the *Report of the [First] United States Education in Japan* (New York: Teachers College Press, Columbia University, 1965), pp. 278–284.

7. Ibid., p. 188.

8. Japan, Imperial Ordinance No. 373, "Organization of Japanese Education Reform Committee" (9 August 1945). In *Education in the New Japan*, Vol. II (Tokyo: GHQ, CIES, May 1948), pp. 89–90.

9. Herbert Passin, *Society and Education in Japan* (New York: Teachers College Press, 1965), p. 287.

10. Ibid., pp. 293–294.

11. John Dower, *Empire and Aftermath: Yoshida Shigeru and the Japanese Experience, 1878-1954* (Cambridge: Harvard University Press, 1979), pp. 369–470.

THE OCCUPATION I

289. Abe Yoshishige. "An Address to the U.S. Education Mission." *School and Society* 64 (August 3, 1946):73–75.

Remarks of the then Minister of Education urging members of the U.S. Education Mission to resist the temptation to impose an American brand of education on defeated Japan, but rather to respect his nation's cultural traditions and assist the Japanese to develop an educational system that is both democratic and Japanese.

290. Allen, Lafe F. "Educational Reform in Japan." *Yale Review* 36 (Summer 1947):705–716.

An optimistic summary of educational reform undertaken in the first months of the Occupation. Allen does, however, point out that low teacher salaries, the shortage of physical facilities, and the handful of Americans assigned to the reform of education are serious problems that must be faced.

*   Anderson, Ronald S. *Education in Japan: A Century of Modern Development.* Cited in item 20 above.

Out-of-date on some details, but perhaps still the single best general treatment of the broad outlines of modern Japanese education. Contains both historical and topical chapters. Anderson was an education officer in southern Japan and his section on the Occupation is informed by this experience.

291. Baerwald, Hans H. *The Purge of Japanese Leaders Under the Occupation.* Publications in Political Science, vol. 8. Berkeley: University of California Press, 1959.

The author, a veteran of the Occupation, provides a scholarly analysis of the purge program, including its evolution, problems and an evaluation of its effectiveness.

292. Bakke, E. Wight. *Revolutionary Democracy: Challenge and Testing in Japan.* Hamden, Conn.: Archon Books, 1968.

Skeptical view of the Occupation's attempts to reform Japan. Bakke argues that it is unlikely that, given the nature of Japanese society, the Japanese can assimilate ideas and practices radically different from those they have lived with for centuries.

293. Ballantine, Joseph W. "The New Japan: An American View." *Far Eastern Survey* 17 (December 22, 1948):286–288.

Treats SCAP educational policies as representing the core values of the philosophical underpinnings of the Occupation.

294. Battistini, Lawrence H. *Postwar Student Struggle in Japan.* Tokyo: Charles Tuttle Company, 1956.

Although the author deals with the Japanese student problem over a broader time span than merely the Occupation period, approximately half of this work focuses on the former. Battistini also looks at the communist influence on the student movement.

295. Beauchamp, Edward R. "Educational and Social Reform in Japan: The First United States Education Mission to Japan, 1946." In *The Occupation of Japan: Educational and Social Reform* (item 300), pp. 175–193.

Description and analysis of the role of the First U.S. Education Mission to Japan. The author describes the political character of the Mission and suggests that a lack of knowledge about Japanese education accounts for the ethnocentric nature of the Mission's Report.

296. Blumhagen, Herman H. "Nationalistic Policies and Japanese Public Education from 1928 to March 31, 1947." Ed.D. dissertation, Rutgers State University, 1957.

Critical of the first year-and-a-half of educational reform, which he believes was characterized by undue haste. Blumhagen questions the wisdom of abolishing such things as state Shinto, *shushin*, etc., which could have been used to improve public and private morality.

297. Borton, Hugh. "Occupation Policies in Japan and Korea." *Annals of the American Academy of Political and Social Science* 255 (January 1948):146–155.

A general analysis of the Occupation up to 1948 with some attention to the educational reforms instituted by SCAP. Useful for providing a contextual framework within which one can evaluate the role played by educational reform.

298. Brickman, William W. "Education in the Occupied Countries." *School and Society* 22 (January 26, 1952):52–61.

Primary value of this piece is the comparative framework it provides in discussing educational reform in Germany and Italy as well as in Japan.

299. Brines, Russell. *MacArthur's Japan*. New York: Lippincott, 1948.

Useful journalistic account of the first three years of the Occupation by a newspaperman who served in prewar Japan. Although not primarily dealing with education, Brines provides useful data from prewar Japan that helps his readers better understand overall Occupation policies. Finally, he provides some perceptive comments on individual American policymakers in Japan and Japanese reactions to them. See pages 233–249.

300. Burkman, Thomas W., ed. *The Occupation of Japan: Educational and Social Reform*. Norfolk, Virginia: MacArthur Memorial, 1982.

Proceedings of a 1980 conference sponsored by the MacArthur Memorial; contains twenty papers on a wide variety of topics dealing with the educational and social dimensions of the Occupation. A good place to begin reading about America's educational activities in early postwar Japan. Contains items 295, 303, 320, 345, 348, 349, 353, 356, 358, 381, 383.

301. Busch, Noel F. *Fallen Sun: A Report on Japan*. New York: Appleton Century, 1948.

This journalistic account of the Occupation's early years is useful only because it evokes some of the atmosphere of the period allowing one to have a sense of the victor-vanquished relations between Americans and Japanese. See pages 66–82.

302. Cassidy, Velma H. "The Program for Reeducation in Japan: A Survey of Policy." In *Documents and State Papers*. Washington, D.C.: U.S. Government Printing Office, 1948.

Based on official American documentation, this publication provides an optimistic view of the course of educational reform in Japan. See pages 3–31.

303. Daniels, Gordon. "Perspectives on Education and Land Reform." In *The Occupation of Japan: Educational and Social Reform* (item 300), pp. 457–469.

Suggests that British perspectives on the Occupation of Japan contained numerous contrasts between liberals who sympathized with SCAP's energetic policies and diplomats who were exceedingly cool towards social experiments.

304. Dempsey, David. "Occupation Policy: German and Japan." *Antioch Review* 6 (March 1946): 143–154.

Education policies in Germany and Japan are considered separately. Dempsey cites recommendations made by various authorities and describes actual steps taken up to early 1946.

305. Dore, Ronald P. "The Ethics of the New Japan." *Pacific Affairs* 25 (June 1952):147–159.

Dore's article consists of a translation and analysis of the 1951 teacher's guide to moral education; one of the early salvos in the conservative's quest to promote a substitute for the 1890 Imperial Rescript on Education. The appearance of this document caused such an uproar when it was announced that the government was forced to withdraw it. Dore concludes that the fact that public opinion forced the government to back down is a good sign that democracy in Japan is possible.

306. Duke, Benjamin C. "American Education Reforms in Japan Twelve Years Later." *Harvard Educational Review* 34 (Fall 1964):525–536.

An analysis of both the Occupation's educational reforms and the so-called "reverse course" following the end of the Occupation. Critical of the conservative politicians' role in scrapping a number of progressive educational reforms.

307. ———. "The Irony of Japanese Postwar Education." *Comparative Education Review* 3 (February 1963):212–217.

Duke suggests that the conservative political forces in Japan, abetted by the United States, are undermining the Occupation's hard won democratic education reforms. He points to the return of moral education, the re-centralization of education under the control of the Ministry of Education, the return of appointed boards of education and the increasingly active role taken by the Ministry in opposing the Japan Teachers Union.

308.   ———. *Japan's Militant Teachers: A History of the Left-Wing Teachers' Movement*. Honolulu: University Press of Hawaii, 1973.

Includes a good description of the role of the Japan Teachers Union during the period of the American Occupation.

309.   Fearey, Robert A. *The Occupation of Japan, Second Phase: 1948–1950*. New York: Macmillan Company, 1950.

Analysis of reforms on Japanese population, their accomplishments, failures and future prospects. See pages 33–46.

310.   Gayn, Mark. *Japan Diary*. New York: William Sloane Associates, 1948.

Disenchanted view of the Occupation from December 1945 to October 1946 in which he sees democratization as a failure, sabotaged by old guard Japanese.

311.   Hall, Robert K. "The Battle of the Mind: American Educational Policy in Germany and Japan." *Columbia Journal of International Affairs* 2 (Winter 1948):59–70.

An interesting and provocative assessment of American education policy in Japan by a controversial participant in the early Occupation efforts to bring about reform. Hall is critical of American efforts because policy statements are often confused with the actual implementation done at the local level by poorly trained, and often indifferent, American personnel. He concludes that poorly trained, unprofessional participants virtually ensure a program's failure.

312.   ———. *Education for a New Japan*. New Haven: Yale University Press, 1949.

After outlining the state of Japanese education immediately following surrender in late 1945 and early 1946, Hall argues that the two most important things to be done to ensure a democratic education system are to devise a decentralized administrative structure, and to replace the Chinese character-based language system with a phonetically based one. Hall's arguments, especially on language, give the reader a sense of the controversy which dogged him in Japan.

313. ———. "Education in the Development of Postwar Japan." In *The Occupation of Japan: The Proceedings of a Seminar on the Occupation of Japan and Its Legacy to the Postwar World*, pp. 117–148. Edited by L.H. Redford. Norfolk, Virginia: MacArthur Memorial, 1976.

An insider's view of the political and policy dynamics of educational reform during the early years of the Occupation.

314. ———. *Kokutai no Hongi [Cardinal Principles of the National Entity of Japan]*. Translated by John O. Gauntlett. Cambridge, Mass.: Harvard University Press, 1949.

One of the most significant educational documents of pre-Occupation Japan, it was used as a manual or guidebook for teachers of ethics. This translation and analysis provides an important understanding of the educational system which the American reformers sought to change.

315. ———. *Shushin: The Ethics of a Defeated Nation*. New York: Columbia University, Teachers College, 1949.

A selection of translated materials taken from prewar Japanese textbooks along with the historical context within which the teaching of ethics evolved. Hall argues that change in Japanese ethical principles is essential for creation of a democratic educational system. Perhaps most valuable for the non-Japanese reader, however, are the translated and annotated selections taken from official prewar Japanese elementary textbooks.

316. Hartford, Ellis F. "Problems of Education in Occupied Japan." *Journal of Educational Sociology* 23 (April 1950):471–488.

Hartford surveyed 69 Japanese professors in teacher-training institutions and found that the three most significant problems facing Japanese education were (1) fear of communist infiltration into the education system, (2) fears over the shortage of teachers and the ability of the system to attract young people into teaching, and (3) lack of adequate financial support for education.

317. Kawai Kazuo. *Japan's American Interlude*. Chicago: University of Chicago Press, 1960.

Although published only eight years after the Occupation ended, this book is perhaps still the best, most balanced treatment. Contains two excellent chapters on lower education and higher education. See pages 183–224.

318. Kobayashi, Victor N. "Japan: Under American Occupation." In *Strategies for Curriculum Change: Cases from 18 Nations*, pp. 181–207. Edited by R. Murray Thomas et al. Scranton, Pa.: International Textbook Co., 1968. Also in *Learning to Be Japanese* (item 22), pp. 181–207.

A reliable discussion of curriculum reform during the Occupation that suggests the reformers greatest contribution may have been implanting the idea of democratic education into Japanese thinking, rather than anything more concrete.

319. Maeda Tamon. "The Direction of Postwar Education in Japan." *Japan Quarterly* 3, 4 (October–December 1956):414–425.

Maeda, who briefly served as Minister of Education at the Occupation's outset, depicts the Occupation reforms as a mixed bag. Although he gives high marks to the establishment of social science courses, improvements made in middle schools, etc., he is highly critical of many of the higher education reforms, especially the transformation of specialized schools into universities.

320. Mayo, Marlene J. "Psychological Disarmament: American Wartime Planning for the Education and Re-Education of Defeated Japan, 1943–1945." In *The Occupation of Japan: Educational and Social Reform* (item 300), pp. 21–127.

Exhaustive study of American pre-surrender planning for educational reform which was focused on placing a future Japan "firmly within its global economic and security systems."

321. Morito Tatsuo. "Educational Reform and Its Problems in Postwar Japan." *Teachers College Record* 60 (April 1959):385–391. Also in *International Review of Education* 1 (1955):338–351, and *Prospect and Retrospect of Japanese Education* (see item 322 below).

Morito, president of Hiroshima University, the first minister of education to preside over the new school system, argues that while an authentic revolution took place in Meiji Japan, the Occupation merely reformed an existing system. Morito is critical of the postwar system of education on several grounds including lack of moral principles, fragmentation, lack of financial resources, and above all, the re-politicization of education by leftist teachers.

322. ———. *Prospect and Retrospect of Japanese Education*. Tokyo: Institute for Democratic Education, 1961.

Pamphlet published by the influential Institute for Democratic Education that contains two of Morito's essays: "Prospect and Retrospect in Japanese Education" and "The Core of the Peace Problem," an early essay in favor of peace education.

323. Murakami Shunsuke and Iwahashi Bunkichi. "Post-war Reconstruction of Japanese Education and Its Social Aspects." *Journal of Educational Sociology* 29 (March 1956):309–316.

Discussion of Occupation's education reforms including administrative reorganization, expansion of opportunities for working youth, new teaching materials, etc.

324. Nishi Toshio. *Unconditional Democracy: Education and Politics in Occupied Japan, 1945–1952*. Stanford, California: Hoover Institution, 1982.

There is a valuable book lurking inside this loosely organized and often simplistic description of American educational reform efforts during the Occupation. Despite this caveat, it is must reading for students of the Occupation because of the wealth of data it contains.

325. Nishimoto Mitoji. "Educational Changes in Japan after the War." *Journal of Educational Sociology* 26 (September 1952):17–26.

Nishimoto focuses on the introduction of the 6-3-3 school ladder into Japanese education and discusses its impact. To a lesser extent, Nishimoto also treats problems relating to textbooks, teaching methods, etc.

326. Orr, Mark T. "Military Occupation of Japan (1945–1952)." In *Year Book of Education 1954*, pp. 413–424. London: Evans, 1954.

A wide ranging overview of the attempts of the Occupation to democratize Japanese education by a former Chief of the Education Division of CI&E.

327. Passin, Herbert. *The Legacy of the Occupation—Japan*. New York: East Asian Institute, Columbia University, 1968.

A judicious retrospective view by a participant in the Occupation. One of America's leading experts on Japanese education, Passin gives high marks to those education reforms which produced a more democratic classroom atmosphere.

328. Quigley, Harold S. "The Great Purge in Japan." *Pacific Affairs* 20 (September 1947):299–308. Reprinted in *The New Japan: Government and Politics*. Edited by Harold S. Quigley and J.E. Turner. Minneapolis: University of Minnesota Press, 1956.

Thousands of teachers accused of militarism and ultranationalism were among many more Japanese purged from public life following the war. Quigley provides a valuable overview with statistical data and analysis of this part of the Occupation.

329. Roden, Donald. "From 'Old Miss' to New Professional: A Portrait of Women Educators Under the American Occupation of Japan, 1945–1952." *History of Education Quarterly* 23 (Winter 1983):469–489.

 Roden describes the role of an American woman, Helen Hosp Seamans, who served as advisor on women's higher education and was responsible for introducing the idea of deans of women in Japanese higher education. Roden describes the ten-week training course Seamans organized for this purpose and evaluates her role in advancing higher education for women.

330. Sansom, Sir George B. "Education in Japan." *Pacific Affairs* 19 (December 1946):413–415.

 In this brief letter, Sansom, perhaps the finest western scholar of Japanese history, takes issue with the Report of the First U.S. Education Mission that most Japanese were virtually illiterate.

331. Shimbori Michiya. "The Fate of Postwar Educational Reform in Japan." *School Review* 68 (Summer 1960):228–241.

 A generally favorable evaluation of American-imposed educational reforms by a well known Japanese sociologist. Shimbori points out, however, that a number of these reforms were imposed without understanding the Japanese context and have resulted in new problems. He argues, for example, that the shift from a dual- to a single-educational ladder seriously damaged vocational education, and the extension of compulsory education to nine years seriously strained the nation's resources.

332. Smethurst, Richard J. "The Origins and Politics of the Japan Teachers' Union, 1945–1956." In *Studies in Japanese History and Politics*, pp. 115–160. Edited by Richard K. Beardsley. Ann Arbor: University of Michigan, 1967.

 This pioneering postwar study of the Japan Teachers Union (*Nikkyoso*) shows that SCAP feared its emergence and often disruptive tactics, while in the immediate postwar years, it displayed a permissive attitude toward the union.

333. Smith, Thomas V. "Ethics in the Japanese Educational
      Curriculum. *Ethics* 56 (July 1956):297–302.

      In this article Smith argues for his view of what "ought" to
      constitute the moral philosophy of a democratic society. He
      concludes with several recommendations for the teaching of
      ethics in Japan.

334. ———. "Personal Impressions of Current Education in Italy,
      Germany and Japan." *Educational Record* 28 (January
      1947):21–32.

      Thomas Smith was probably the only American official to
      play a significant role in the Occupations of Germany, Italy, and
      Japan, so his analysis carries an interesting, built-in comparative
      perspective.

335. Spinks, Charles N. "Indoctrination and Re-Education of Japan's
      Youth." *Pacific Affairs* 3 (March 1944):56–70.

      The author is highly skeptical that democratic education can
      be instituted in Japan very quickly. Although defeat rocked belief
      in the old ideology, he argues that only a gradual introduction of
      democratic ideals should be undertaken by the Occupation
      authorities.

336. Taylor, George E. "The Japanese State of Mind." *Virginia
      Quarterly Review* 29 (Spring 1953):175–186.

      George Taylor, a conservative China specialist, details the
      support of Japanese intellectuals in clearing away the vestiges of
      Japanese militarism, but suggests that a close "intellectual
      intimacy" has not resulted from this common cause. Taylor
      attributes this to the signing of a peace treaty, the security pact,
      and the subsequent American encouragement for Japanese
      rearmament. He urges the vital need for the United States to
      regain the understanding and support of Japanese intellectuals for
      both the health of Japanese democracy and American interests in
      the world.

337. Textor, Robert B. *Failure in Japan: With Keystones for a
      Positive Policy.* New York: John Day, 1951.

Textor's thesis is that the Occupation started successfully, but lost its direction in the latter years of Occupation. He argues that if we are to retrieve our initial successes, the United States must free the Japanese economy from excessive concentrations of power (including that of American business), encourage the practice of civil liberties, remove restrictions from organized labor, encourage a greater proliferation of information and cultural exchange opportunities, move toward a greater civilian domination of Occupation activities, and, finally, internationalization of the Occupation. An important book that caused a sensation when it first appeared.

338. Trainor, Joseph C. *Educational Reform in Occupied Japan: Trainor's Memoir.* Tokyo: Meisei University Press, 1983.

The importance of this book is that it was written by Joseph Trainor, Chief of CI&E's Education Division from July 1949 to January 1952. A controversial figure, Trainor tells his side of the many battles he engaged in during his lengthy service in the Occupation.

339. U.S. Department of State. "Policy for the Revision of the Japanese Educational System." *Department of State Bulletin* 16 (April 17, 1947):746–747. Also in *Current Notes on International Affairs* 19 (November-December 1948):740–742.

Directive of the Far Eastern Commission deals with democratic ideology, teacher recruitment and training (including purging ultranationalist teachers), curricula, textbooks, and teaching methods.

340. ———. *Report of the [First] United States Education Mission to Japan.* Tokyo: SCAP, 1946. Also published as Department of State Publication 2579, Far Eastern Series 11. Washington, D.C.: U.S. Government Printing Office, 1946.

Undoubtedly the single most important document relating to education during the Occupation, this Report contains recommendations that became the blueprint for SCAP reforms. It ranges from a discussion of philosophy of education to specific reform proposals in virtually all categories of the educational enterprise.

341.   ————. *Report of the Second United States Education Mission to Japan*. Washington, D.C.: U.S. Government Printing Office, 1950.

Favorable assessment of the implementation of the earlier U.S. Mission's recommendations, but does identify those areas which were lagging behind.

342.   Van Staaveren, Jacob. "The Educational Revolution in Japan." *Educational Forum* 16 (January 1952):229–240.

An optimistic recounting of educational reforms including the spread of student government, textbook reform, a new social studies curriculum, teacher unions, the founding of the International Christian University, and others.

343.   Vining, Elizabeth G. *Windows for the Crown Prince*. Philadelphia: Lippincott, 1952.

Ms. Vining was brought to Japan to serve as English tutor to Crown Prince Akihito, from 1946–1952 and this book describes that experience.

*   Ward, Robert E., and Shulman, Frank J., comps. *The Allied Occupation of Japan, 1945-1952: An Annotated Bibliography of Western-Language Materials*. Chicago: American Library Association, 1974 (item 7).

By far the best bibliography on the Occupation of Japan, with extensive annotations. Especially useful for identification, description and location of an enormous amount of materials produced by General MacArthur's forces between 1945 and 1952. Simply indispensable. See especially pp. 638–677 for materials on education.

344.   Wildes, Harry E. "The War for the Mind in Japan." *Annals of the American Academy of Political and Social Science* 294 (July 1954):1–7.

Generally critical of SCAP, charging that it took education reform too lightly.

345. Wray, Harry J. "Decentralization of Education in the Allied Occupation of Japan, 1945–1952." In *The Occupation of Japan: Educational and Social Reform* (item 300), pp. 143-174.

Wray views American insistence on educational decentralization as a serious mistake. This wouldn't have happened, he suggests, if MacArthur had listened to those Americans who understood Japanese customs and culture.

346. Zook, George F. "The Educational Missions to Japan and Germany." *International Conciliation* No. 427 (January 1947):3–19.

A comparative analysis of the American Education Missions to Japan and Germany, focusing on the process of choosing the members for each mission, the knowledge of the country possessed by each mission's members as well as the topics studied by both.

THE OCCUPATION II

347. Adams, Donald, and Oshiba Mamoru. "Japanese Education After the Americans Left." *Peabody Journal of Education* 39 (July 1961):9–12.

348. Allinson, Gary D. "Japan's Second Bureaucracy: Civil Service Reforms and the Allied Occupation." In *The Occupation of Japan: Educational and Social Reform* (item 300), pp. 471–497.

349. ———. "A Methodological Epilogue [on Studies of the Occupation]." In *The Occupation of Japan: Educational and Social Reform* (item 300), pp. 509–514.

350. Anderson, Paul S. "The Reorientation Activities of the Civil Education Section of the Osaka Civil Affairs Team: A Case

Study in Educational Change." Ph.D. dissertation, University of Wisconsin, 1954.

351. Baltz, William M. "The Role of American Educators in the Decentralization and Reorganization of Education in Postwar Japan (1945–1952)." Ed.D. dissertation, State University of New York, Buffalo, 1965.

352. Benoit, Edward G. "A Study of Japanese Education as Influenced by the Occupation." Ed.D. dissertation, Michigan State University, 1958.

353. Bowles, Gordon. "Comments on Papers Presented at the Fourth Symposium on the Occupation of Japan: Educational and Social Reform. In *The Occupation of Japan: Educational and Social Reform* (item 300), pp. 515–522.

354. Doi, James I. "Educational Reform in Occupied Japan, 1945–1950: A Study of Acceptance of and Resistance to Institutional Change." Ph.D. dissertation, University of Chicago, 1952.

355. Duke, Benjamin C. "Educational Developments in Asia: Japan's New Role." *School and Society* 91 (November 30, 1963):369–371.

356. Graebner, Norman A. "Occupation Policy and the Schools of Yokohama." In *The Occupation of Japan: Educational and Social Reform* (item 300), pp. 219–230.

357. Griffith, Harry E. "Japanese Normal School Education." Ed.D. dissertation, Stanford University, 1950.

358. Hopper, Helen M. "Kato Shizue, Socialist Party MP and Occupation Reforms Affecting Women, 1945–1948: A Case Study of the Formal vs. Informal Political Influence of Japanese Women." In *The Occupation of Japan: Educational and Social Reform* (item 300), pp. 375–399.

359. Kerlinger, Frederick N. "The Development of Democratic Control in Japanese Education: A Study of Attitude Change in Shikoku, 1948–1949." Ph.D. dissertation, University of Michigan, 1953.

360. Kishimoto Kojiro and Takemura Shigekazu. "Education in Japan After 1945." *Education in Japan Journal for Overseas* (Hiroshima University) 1 (1966):25–37.

361. Kitamura Fusako. "A Study of the Japan Teachers Union and Recommendations for Improvement." Ed.D. dissertation, Teachers College, Columbia University, 1962.

362. Kodama Mitsuo, ed. *Education in Japan: Educational Documents of Occupied Japan.* Vol. 1. Tokyo: Meisei University Press, 1983.

363. Loomis, Arthur K. "Compulsory Education in Japan." *Educational Forum* 27 (November 1962):15–24.

364. Makino Tatsumi. "Post-war Democratization in Japan: Japanese Education." *International Social Science Journal* 13 (1961):44–56.

365. Miwa Keiko. "Analysis of the Effect of Major American Ideas upon the Organization of Japanese Higher Education from 1946 to 1967." Ed.D. dissertation, Washington State University, 1969.

366. Mochida Eiichi. "The Reform of Boards of Education and Its Aftermath." *Journal of Social and Political Ideas in Japan* 1 (December 1963):43–47.

367. Murata Suzuko. "A Study of the Impact of the American Educational System on Higher Education in Japan." Ph.D. dissertation, Indiana University, 1969.

368. Naoi, John Y. "The Educational Reformation in Japan After World War II." Ph.D. dissertation, Catholic University of America, 1955.

369. Nelson, John M. "The Adult-Education Program in Occupied Japan, 1945–1950." Ed.D. dissertation, University of Kansas, 1954.

370. Nishimoto Yoichi. "Improving Moral Education in the Upper Elementary Grades in Japan." Ed.D. dissertation, Teachers College, Columbia University, 1962.

371. Ogawa Taro. "Reflections on Postwar Education." *Journal of Social and Political Ideas in Japan* 1 (December 1963):24–30.

372. Orr, Mark T. "Education Reform Policy in Occupied Japan." Ph.D. dissertation, University of North Carolina, 1954.

373. Oshima Yasumasa. "Education in Japan, 1945–1963." *Journal of Social and Political Ideas in Japan* 1 (1963):2–10.

374. Ota Takashi. "A Study of Educational Practices in the Postwar Period." *Journal of Social and Political Ideas in Japan* 1 (December 1963):116–121.

* "Report of the [First] United States Education Commission Mission to Japan, submitted to the Supreme Commander for Allied Powers, March 30, 1946." Washington, D.C.: U.S. Government Printing Office, 1946 (item 340).

* *Report of the Second United States Education Mission to Japan.* Washington, D.C.: U.S. Government Printing Office, 1950 (item 341).

375. Scalapino, Robert. "American Occupation of Japan Perspectives After Three Decades." *Annals of the American Academy of Political and Social Sciences* 428 (November 1976):104–113.

376. Schwantes, Robert S. "Educational Influence of the United States of America." *Contemporary Japan* 26 (May 1960):442–458.

377. Sugimoto Yoshio. "Equalization and Turbulence: The Case of the American Occupation of Japan." Ph.D. dissertation, University of Pittsburgh, 1973.

378. Tanaka Kotaro. "The Theory of the Fundamental Law of Education." *Journal of Social and Political Ideas in Japan* 1 (1963):33–37.

379. Tatara Toshio. "The Allied Occupation and Japanese Public Welfare: An Overview of SCAP Activities During the Early Phase." In *The Occupation of Japan: Educational and Social Reform* (item 300), pp. 309–332.

380. Todd, Vivian Edmiston. "Education and Social Reforms Through the Enlightened Curriculum Development." In *The Occupation of Japan: Educational and Social Reforms* (item 300), pp. 243–251.

381. Vining, Elizabeth G. "The View From the Other Side." In *The Occupation of Japan: Educational and Social Reform* (item 300), pp. 201–207.

382. Williams, Justin. "Completing Japan's Political Reorientation, 1947–1952: Critical Phase of the Allied Occupation." *American Historical Review* 73 (June 1968):1454–1469.

383. Wilson, Donald V. "Social Welfare Personnel and Social Work Education During the Occupation of Japan, 1945–1948." In *The Occupation of Japan: Educational and Social Reform* (item 300), pp. 333–347.

Part II
Contemporary Japanese Education: Problems and Issues

CHAPTER VIII
ORGANIZATION AND STRUCTURE
OF JAPANESE EDUCATION

Legal Bases of Education

One of the major contributions of the United States to Japanese education was the legal framework enacted during the Allied Occupation of Japan (1945–1952). The first of three basic legal underpinnings was the American-imposed, liberal Constitution which, promulgated on 3 November 1946, and taking force on 3 May 1947, established a democratic system of government on the ruins of a failed militarism. Unlike the American Constitution, there are specific references to education in the Japanese document. For example, all forms of discrimination—including gender discrimination—are outlawed and academic freedom is guaranteed.

The second piece of legislation governing postwar education is the School Education Law of 29 March 1947, which laid down the so-called 6-3-3-4 school ladder, i.e., six years of elementary schooling followed by three years at lower secondary, three years at upper secondary school, topped off by a four-year university curriculum. This single track replaced the specialized multiple tracks of prewar days, and the age of compulsory attendance was raised from 12 to 15 years, which ensured that all youth completed at least the lower secondary school.

The third key document undergirding contemporary education in Japan is the Fundamental Law of Education, passed by the Diet on 31 March 1947. It replaced the 1890 Imperial Rescript on Education as the basic educational policy and blueprint for democratic education. It provides that "Education shall aim at the full development of personality, striving for the rearing of the people, sound in mind and body, who shall love truth and justice, esteem individual value, respect labour and have a deep sense of responsibility, and be imbued with the independent spirit, as builders of a peaceful state and society."

More concrete provisions provide for nine years of free compulsory schooling, respect for academic freedom, equal educational opportunity for all, and the promotion of a broad social education "by the establishment of such institutions as libraries, museums, citizens' public halls," etc. In addition, partisan political activity and the teaching of religion in publicly supported schools is prohibited.

There has been a great deal of educational legislation in the postwar years, but none of it has had the fundamental character of the three documents described above. These enactments have shaped the basic course of Japanese education in the postwar period.

The Ministry of Education (Mombusho)

The Ministry of Education, Science and Culture is the competent authority over educational matters of a formal nature in Japan, with responsibilities ranging from the drafting of bills, preparation of budgetary requests, setting curriculum standards and textbook authorization to the operation of a variety of national schools, museums, children's centers, citizen's halls, etc. Administratively, the Ministry consists of five bureaus: elementary and secondary education, higher education, social education, physical education, and administration. The minister of education is the chief executive officer, a cabinet-level post to which he is appointed by, and serves at the pleasure of, the prime minister. Since Japan's resumption of sovereignty in 1952, with the exception of the prominent scholar Nagai Michio's tenure in the mid-1970s, all ministers of education have been Liberal Democratic Party (LDP) politicians and sitting members of the Diet.

Perhaps the single most important characteristic of modern Japanese education is its centralized nature. Very little that occurs in Japanese education takes place without the knowledge and approval of the educational bureaucrats in the Mombusho. This, its supporters argue, ensures high, uniform standards in every school from Okinawa to Hokkaido, while critics contend that such control inhibits innovation and discourages creativity.

More than a dozen advisory councils work under the aegis of the Mombusho. The most important of these is undoubtedly the Central Council for Education (*Chukyoshin*), established in 1952; its origins can be traced to the Japanese Educational Reform Council, which was originally created as a counterpart to the U.S. Education Mission of 1946. The members of this influential organization are primarily conservative academicians, are appointed by the minister of education and charged with advising him on policy questions dealing with education, science and culture.

More influential in the formation of educational policy, however, are the Liberal Democratic Party Education Committee (*Bunkyo bukai*) and the Education Committee of the Japan Federation of Employers' Association (*Nikkeiren kyoiku iinkai*). The former is composed of all former ministers of education as well as those senior Diet members with a serious interest in educational questions (often referred to as the LDP "education tribe," or *bunkyozoku*). The latter, through its close ties with the LDP, forcefully represents the views of economic leaders on educational questions. The Ministry of Education tends to be deferential toward the advice proffered by these powerful political and economic groups.

Compulsory Education and School Finance

All children are required to attend school, from age six through age fifteen. Virtually all children complete the nine years of compulsory education. In each of the 47 prefectures and each of the more than 3,000 municipalities there is an appointed board of education, which serves as the local educational authority. Prefectural boards of education, consist of five members appointed by the governor, with the consent of the prefectural assembly, and hold office for four years. Municipal boards of education consist of three to five members appointed by the mayor, with the consent of the municipal assembly, and hold office for four years.

Compulsory education in both Japan and the United States is legally free. Unlike the system in the United States, however, the Japanese system of financing education does not earmark local taxes for educational purposes. The responsibility for support of public education is shared by the national, prefectural and municipal governments, with each providing for its own educational activities with funds raised from its taxes and other sources of income. In addition, there exists a rather complicated formula by which the national government equalizes the financial resources available to schools within each of the 47 prefectures. National schools and institutions of higher education are completely funded by the national government, and locally-controlled public schools receive a significant portion of their operating expenses from the Ministry of Education and, in some cases, the Ministry of Home Affairs.

School Year

Unlike many Western countries, in Japan the school year corresponds to the fiscal year and, thus, begins on April 1 and ends on March 31 of the following year. At both the elementary and lower secondary level the school year is divided into three terms: April to July; September to December; and January to March. Upper secondary schools adopt either a two- or three-term school year, and universities generally follow a two-semester pattern. Holidays occur in summer, winter (before and after the New Year), and spring. Although there has been much discussion about the desirability of changing the academic year along the lines of the Western pattern, such a change has not yet been made.

School Ladder

Kindergartens (*yochien*): Imported from Germany during the early Meiji Period, the kindergarten today caters to children ranging in age from three to six. Although non-compulsory, kindergarten enrollments have dramatically increased in recent years as parents have come to view them as a necessary prequisite for their children's success in Japan's highly competitive educational system. Approximately 60% of kindergartens are privately operated. In publicly-operated schools, fees are charged according to parents' ability to pay.

In addition to kindergartens, there is also a system of day care centers (*hoikuen*) operated by the Ministry of Health and Welfare. Created around the turn of the century to serve children of the poor, the *hoikuen* now serve a more comprehensive clientele. Although most children attending these institutions are between the ages of three and five, many *hoikuen* accept younger children. Here, too, fees are adjusted to family income.

Elementary Schools (*shogakko*): Children who have reached age six are required to attend the six-year elementary school which seeks to provide a general education adapted to the child's stage of mental and physical development. All children, except those with marked physical or mental disabilities, are grouped heterogeneously and are promoted automatically each year. A majority of elementary classrooms are self-contained and in the early grades teachers usually remain with the same pupils for more than a year. Pupils, however, receive specialized instruction in music, fine arts and physical education.

Lower Secondary Schools (*chugakko*): Virtually all children complete the six-year elementary school together and attend the required three-year lower secondary school until the end of the school year in which they have reached age 15. Almost all youth complete this level of schooling, and the vast majority go to some form of non-compulsory secondary education which tends to be more highly differentiated. The required curriculum at this level includes Japanese language, social studies, moral education, mathematics, science, music, fine arts, industrial arts (boys), homemaking (girls), and physical education. Foreign languages are required, with a substantial majority choosing English, followed by Chinese, French and German.

Upper Secondary Schools (*kotogakko*): The Japanese version of the American senior high school, the upper secondary school attracts upwards of 96% of students who complete the compulsory, lower secondary school. At this point schooling is more highly differentiated and no longer free, with tuition being charged by both public and private schools. Students can choose between full-time (three years) and part-time and correspondence schools which last for four years. Approximately two-thirds of upper-secondary school students attend general education, academic high schools designed to prepare them for university entrance examinations. The rest tend to cluster in more specialized vocational programs (technical education, agriculture, commerce, domestic arts, etc.). The common upper-secondary school curriculum includes Japanese language, social studies, mathematics, science, music, fine arts, domestic arts, foreign languages and physical education.

Junior Colleges (*tanki daigaku*): Imported from the United States during the Occupation, junior colleges provide upper secondary school graduates with two- or three-year programs in a variety of fields. These institutions primarily attract female students.

Technical Colleges (*koto semmon gakko*): Unlike junior college or universities, students move to the technical colleges directly from the lower secondary school and take a five-year program designed to produce the middle-level technicians whose training is so essential to a strong Japanese economy. They offer courses in mechanical, electrical and chemical engineering and related fields.

Universities (*daigaku*): The approximately 450 public and private four-year universities in Japan vary in quality at least as much as in other countries. The most prestigious Japanese universities are the former (prewar) Imperial Universities (now national universities), with Tokyo and Kyoto at the apex of the pyramid. The academic quality of private universities varies greatly, but there is general agreement that Keio, Waseda, Doshisha, International Christian (I.C.U.), and Sophia are among the best. Admission to most of the best universities is dependent upon one's success in the institution's competitive entrance examination, although some effort is being made to reform the system to place more emphasis on grades, recommendations, extracurricular activities, etc. Some of the best institutions, however, include a feeder system of elementary and secondary schools. Once students become part of this system, they face a comparatively smooth path to the university as long as they perform satisfactorily.

Special Schools (*tokushu kyoiku gakko*): School facilities for the physically and mentally handicapped were mandated by the School Education Law of 1947. Special schools include schools for the blind, deaf, and other handicapped individuals. Each has an elementary and lower secondary department, and many have a kindergarten and/or upper secondary department.

Miscellaneous Schools (*kakushu gakko*): A wide variety of schools, differing in size, curriculum and quality, exist outside the regular system; they offer study in auto repair, bookkeeping, cooking, computer technology, cosmetology, midwifery, photography, typing, etc. Depending on the particular school to which one applies, graduation from either lower or upper secondary school is a prerequisite. Although most provide vocational and practical training, some offer courses in the humanities and foreign languages. The length of course varies from one to three years.

ORGANIZATION AND STRUCTURE OF JAPANESE EDUCATION I

There is a fair amount of material published in English, primarily by the Ministry of Education, on the basic organizational and structural elements of Japanese education. Should one wish to go beyond this basic data, however, the materials are skimpy. Western scholarship has focused mainly on controversies. As soon as the controversy recedes, so does the amount of material available to study.

384. Adachi Kenji. "An Interpretation of Article X of the Fundamental Law of Education." *Journal of Social and Political Ideas in Japan* 1 (December 1963):58–62.

Adachi rejects Japan Teacher Union's interpretation of Article X of the Fundamental Law of Education and supports the Ministry of Education's legal right to control school curriculum (compare item 401 below).

385. Aquilla, Frank D. "Japanese Management Practices: The Educational Hula Hoop of the 80's." *National Association of Secondary School Principals Bulletin* 66 (November 1982):91–96. Reprinted as "Japanese Management in Schools: Boon or Boondoggle?" *Clearing House* 57 (December 1983):180–186.

Describes a number of popular Japanese management concepts, including quality circles, situational management, lifetime employment, worker involvement, etc. Although urging caution, Aquilla suggests ten possible applications to educational administration.

386. Beauchamp, Edward R. "The Development of Japanese Education Policy, 1945–1985." *History of Education Quarterly* 27 (Fall 1987):299–324.

Analysis of the development of Japanese educational policy since the end of World War II in the context of current reform activities.

387. Bonner, James S. "Japanese Quality Circles—Can They Work in Education." *Phi Delta Kappan* 63 (June 1982):681.

Describes the concept of quality circles successfully used in Japanese industry and how it was applied in the Muskegon, Michigan schools to improve communication among employees and management.

388. Cummings, William K. *Education and Equality in Japan.* Princeton: Princeton University Press, 1980.

Although not directly dealing with the organization and structure of Japanese education, Cummings provides important insights into the day-to-day operation of primary schools in Kyoto. The best single source in English for primary education in Japan. A very positive perspective.

389. Duke, Benjamin C. "Educational Administration and Supervision in Japan." *International Review of Education* 2 2 (1976):479–490.

An analysis by a longtime resident scholar describing how Japanese educational administration and supervision has contributed to the success of Japanese education.

390. ———. "The Japanese Supreme Court and the Governance of Education." *Pacific Affairs* 53 (Spring 1980):69–88.

An excellent, if brief, description of the ways in which Japanese education has been shaped by the decisions of Japan's high court in the postwar period.

391. "Education in Asia and Oceania: Japan." *Bulletin of the UNESCO Regional Office in Asia and Oceania.* 20 Bangkok: UNESCO, June 1979, pp. 94–103.

General survey of education in Japan in late 1970s.

392. Friedman, Neil K. "Education as a Political Issue in Japan." Ph.D. dissertation, Stanford University, 1977.

Contains important materials on such political issues as control of public schools, the issue of educational opportunity in Japan, etc.

393. George, Paul S. *Theory Z School: Beyond Effectiveness.* Columbus, Ohio: National Middle School Association, 1983.

   Argues that the performance of American schools might be enhanced by emulating certain successful American businesses having much in common with Japanese corporations.

394. "Japan—Educational Reform." *Education in Asia and the Pacific: Reviews, Reports* and Notes 22 (December 1985):1–14.

   Translation of the 22 March 1984 Report of the Conference on Culture and Education, set up by Prime Minister Nakasone to advise him on educational reform.

395. Japan, Ministry of Education, Science and Culture. *Educational Standards in Japan: The 1970 "White Paper on Education."* Tokyo: Ministry of Education, March 1971.

   English-language translation of an official document prepared to inform Japanese public about educational standards in Japan compared to those in the U.S., England, France, West Germany, and the Soviet Union.

396. ———. *Statistical Abstracts of Education, Science and Culture.* Tokyo: Research and Statistics Division, Minister's Secretariat, Ministry of Education, 1979 and 1981.

   Chapter 1 introduces the organizational pattern of Japanese education, followed by chapters of statistics on school education, social education, physical education, science, culture, international exchanges, educational administration and finance.

397. Kerlinger, Frederick N. "Educational Affairs Board: Precursors of Modern Japanese Boards of Education." *History of Education Quarterly* 5 (1954):91–96.

   A dated but still useful summary of a topic which raised a great deal of controversy during the early postwar period. Kerlinger was one of the few Americans to study this subject.

398. Kishimoto Kojiro. "Controversies Concerning the Head Teacher System." *Education in Japan: A Journal for Overseas* (Hiroshima) 9 (1979):43–51.

    A survey of the heated controversy between the Ministry of Education and the Japan Teachers Union over the appointment of teachers to the quasi-administrative position of head teacher during the mid-1970s.

399. Kogut, Leonard S. "Quality Circles: A Japanese Management Technique for the Classroom." *Improving College and University Teaching* 32 (Summer 1983):123–127.

    Describes the use of quality circles in three undergraduate chemistry courses at Penn State.

400. Mori Takao. "On the Duties of the Vice-Principal." *Research Bulletin of the National Institute for Educational Research* 7 (1966):29–36.

    One of the few studies in English which provides information on the roles and duties of a Japanese school administrator.

401. Munataka Seiya. "The Fundamental Law of Education." *Journal of Social and Political Ideas in Japan* 1 (December 1963):54–58.

    Munataka supports the position of Japan Teachers Union which argues that under Article X of the Fundamental Law of Education, the Ministry of Education and local boards of education are "organs of educational administration." On this basis the JTU argued that Ministry and local school boards have no legal right to control curriculum development.

402. Nishida Kikuo. "Educational Administration in Japan." *Bulletin of the Unesco Regional Office for Education in Asia* 15. Bangkok: UNESCO, 1974, pp. 70–84.

    Primarily valuable for useful, hard to obtain, statistical data about Japanese education in the mid-1970s.

403. Okihara Yutaka. "Pupil Participation in School Cleaning: A Comparative Survey." *East West Education* 1 (Spring 1980):29–38.

This routine task is handled in different ways in different countries, and the Japanese model offers insight into how this seemingly unimportant school function has real pedagogical value.

404. Organization for Economic Cooperation and Development. *Educational Policy and Planning in Japan.* Paris: OECD, 1973.

Contains the major background documents used by an OECD team in 1970 to examine the Japanese educational enterprise. Includes a detailed account of pedagogical, administrative, financial and quantitative aspects of Japanese education, including a wealth of statistical data.

405. ———. *Review of National Policies for Education: Japan.* Paris: OECD, 1971.

An external evaluation of Japanese education by a team of distinguished scholars which include E.O. Reischauer and R.P. Dore. This report has been very influential in the shaping of Japanese education since 1973.

406. Pahg Seong Woo. "Conceptual Schema and Approaches of Studies on Educational Administration in Japan." *East West Education* 2 (Fall 1981):47–52.

Discusses the somewhat different meaning of educational administration within the Japanese context.

407. Park Yung H. "Big Business and Education Policy in Japan." *Asian Survey* 22 (1982):315–336.

An updated version of item 408.

408. ———. "Central Council for Education, Organized Business, and Politics of Educational Policy-Making in Japan." *Comparative Education Review* 19 (1975):296–311.

A successful attempt to explain the complexities of educational policymaking in postwar Japan, and especially the role played by the business community in shaping education as a vehicle for economic development.

409. Pascale, Richard T. "Communication and Decision Making Across Cultures: Japanese and American Comparisons." *Administrative Science Quarterly* 23 (March 1978):91–110.

Although recognizing that differences exist, Pascale argues that there are wide areas of similarity in Japanese and American communication and decision making practices.

410. Pempel, T.J. "The Bureaucratization of Policymaking in Postwar Japan." *American Journal of Political Science* 18 (1974):647–664.

Although dealing with the larger policymaking community in Japan, much of Pempel's study is applicable to education policymaking.

411. Rehder, Robert R. "Education and Training: Have the Japanese Beaten Us Again?" *Personnel Journal* 62 (January 1983):42–47.

Japan is often viewed as an education-based industrial society in which the educational credentials of employees largely determine their social and economic status. Urges close American scrutiny of this model for what maybe learned from it.

412. ———. "Japanese Management: An American Challenge." *Human Resource Management* 18 (Winter 1979):21–27.

Stresses Japanese system of motivating employees by setting high goals and providing in-service training and development opportunities.

413. Rohlen, Thomas P. "Conflict in Institutional Environments: Politics in Education." In *Conflict in Japan*, pp. 136–173. Edited by Ellis S. Krauss, Thomas P. Rohlen and Patricia G. Steinhoff. Honolulu: University of Hawaii Press, 1984.

Rohlen answers two basic questions: (1) How can we account for the effectiveness of postwar Japanese education despite its many intense conflicts? (2) What has happened to the deep political conflicts which divided the public bureaucracies unionized during the American Occupation (1945–1952)?

ORGANIZATIONAL AND STRUCTURE OF JAPANESE EDUCATION II

414. Abe Munemitsu. "Wastage in Primary Education in Asia: An Introduction." *Research Bulletin of the National Institute for Educational Research* 11 (March 1972):51–55.

415. Adachi Kenji. "Education in Question—Educational Reform in Japan." *Bulletin of the UNESCO Regional Office in Asia and the Pacific* 27 (November 1986):17–23.

416. Anderson, Ronald S. "Administration, Supervision and Finance." In *Education in Japan: A Century of Modern Development* (item 20), pp. 261–283.

417. Danielson, Albert, and Okachi Katsuji. "Private Rates of Return to Schooling in Japan." *The Journal of Human Resources* 6 (Summer 1971):391–397.

418. "Educational Ferment in Japan" [3 articles in special issue]. *Japan Christian Quarterly* 35 (Fall 1969):223–246.

419. "Educational Reform in Japan." Translated by Kanaya Toshio. *Bulletin of the UNESCO Regional Office for Education in Asia and the Pacific* 27 (November 1986):69–79.

420. "Educational System in Japan" [Special Issue]. *Education in Japan: A Journal for Overseas* (Hiroshima University) 2 (1967).

421. Gondo Yoshio, and Kengo Machida. "Japanese Educational System and Its Current Problems." *East West Education* 7 (Spring 1986):3–14.

422. Jansen, Marius B. "Educational Policies in Japan." *Education—
      A Bulletin of the Faculty and College of Education,
      University of British Columbia* 2 (March 1958).

423. Japan, Ministry of Education, Science and Culture. *Course of
      Study for Lower Secondary Schools—Japan.* Tokyo:
      Ministry of Education, 1983.

424. ———. *Course of Study for Upper Secondary Schools Japan.*
      Tokyo: Ministry of Education, 1983.

425. ———. *Development of Education in Japan, 1974–1976:
      Report Presented at the 36th International Conference on
      Education, Geneva, 30 August–8 September 1977.* Tokyo:
      Ministry of Education, 1977. In English and French.

426. ———. *Education in Japan: A Brief Outline.* Tokyo: Ministry
      of Education, 1984.

427. ———. *Educational Laws and Regulations in Japan.* Tokyo:
      Ministry of Education, 1955.
      Series I, the Constitution and Fundamental Law on
      Education; Series II, School Education Law.

428. ———. *Educational Standards in Japan, 1964.* Tokyo: Ministry
      of Education, 1965. Same title published in 1975 and 1976.
      See also item 395.

429. ———. *Educational Statistics in Japan.* Tokyo: Research and
      Statistics Division, Minister's Secretariat, Ministry of
      Education, 1976.
      Same title published in 1961 and 1970.

430. ———. *Japan's Growth and Education: Educational
      Development in Relation to Socio-Economic Growth.*
      Tokyo: Ministry of Education, 1963.

431. ———. *Ministry of Education Establishment Law.* Tokyo:
      1969.

432. ———. *Ministry of Education Organization Order.* Tokyo: 1969.

433. ———. *Mombusho: The Ministry of Education, Science and Culture.* Tokyo: Ministry of Education, 1974 and 1981.

434. ———. *National Surveys of Educational Expenditures.* Tokyo: Ministry of Education, 1967.

435. ———. *Outline of Education in Japan.* Tokyo: Ministry of Education, 1972.

    Same title published in 1976, 1979 and 1985.

436. ———. *Report on Educational Planning in Japan.* Tokyo: Ministry of Education, 1969.

437. Japan, National Institute for Educational Research. *Basic Facts and Figures about the Educational System of Japan.* Tokyo: NIER, 1982.

    Same title published in 1983.

438. ———. *Educational Research of Japan: Report of a Survey.* Tokyo: NIER, 1979.

439. ———. *Educational Research: A Perspective.* Tokyo: NIER, 1984.

440. ———. *A List of Documents in English on Education in Japan.* Tokyo: Library of Education, NIER, 1974.

441. ———. *NIER: A Brief History, the Current Status and Future Prospects.* Tokyo: NIER, 1979.

442. ———. *The Standard of Education in Japan.* Tokyo: NIER, 1983.

443. ———. "Survey of Opinions Concerning the Reform of Compulsory Education." *Research Bulletin of the National Institute for Educational Research* (December 1980).

444. Japan, Prime Minister's Office. Statistics Bureau. *Statistical Handbook of Japan*. Tokyo: Prime Minister's Office, 1984.

445. Japanese National Commission for UNESCO. *The Making of Compulsory Education in Japan*. Tokyo: The Commission, 1958.

446. Kameda Yoshiko. "The Kato Gakuen School System of Japan." *Bulletin of the UNESCO Regional Office for Education in Asia and Oceania* 19 (June 1978):113–121.

447. Kato Motofumi. "Organization of Education in Japan." *International Review of Education* 14 (1968):85–91.

448. Kerlinger, Fred. "Decision-Making in Japan." *Social Forces* 30 (October 1951):36–41.

449. Kida Hiroshi. "Development and Present Situation of Educational Administration in Japan." *INF Occasional Paper No. 11*. Bangkok Regional Office for Education in Asia and Oceania, 1982.

450. Levy-Garboua, Louis, et al. *Educational Expenditures in France, Japan and the United Kingdom. Les Depenses d'Enseignement en France, au Japon et au Etats Royaume*. Paris: Organization for Economic Cooperation and Development, 1977. In English and French.

451. Lim, Howard. "A Japanese Agenda for Management Development." *Training and Development Journal* 36 (March 1982):62–67.

452. Mano Miyao. "The Development of the Tasks of Reform of the Educational System of Japan." *East–West Education* 5 (Fall 1984):13–20.

453. Marengo, F.D. "Learning From the Japanese: What or How?" *Management International Review* 4 (1979):39–46.

454. Nagaoka Jun. "The Education Board System in Japan: Its Establishment and Development." *Research Bulletin of the National Institute for Educational Research* 2 (1961):41–48.

455. ———. "How School Affairs are Divided with the Staff in Common School Management." *Research Bulletin of the National Institute for Educational Research* 3 (1962):33–43.

456. ———. "How the Superintendent of a Local Board of Education Performs his Duties." *Research Bulletin of the National Institute for Educational Research* 4 (1963):25–41.

457. Nagaoka Jun and Maki Masami. "Internal Organization and Administration of Schools." *Research Bulletin of the National Institute for Educational Research* 12 (October 1973):29–32.

458. Neumier, Carol. "High School Counselor in Japan." *Personnel and Guidance Journal* 46 (February 1968):602–604.

459. Nishida Kikuo. "Educational Development in Japan." *Meeting of the Experts on Educational Planning in Asia. Tokyo. November 25, 1970. Final Report.* Tokyo: Japanese National Commission for UNESCO, 1971.

460. ———. "Educational Planning in Japan." Bulletin of the UNESCO Regional Office for Education in Asia 3 (August 1968):99–111.

461. Okuda Shinjo. "Educational Planning, Status and Organization in Japan." *Bulletin of the UNESCO Regional Office for Education in Asia* (Bangkok) 16 (June 1975):34–43.

462. Olson, Lawrence. *Dimensions of Japan.* New York: American Universities Field Staff, 1963.
   See Chapter 3: "The Kyoto Superintendent of Schools."

463. Oshima Masanori. "Present Situation of the Study of the School Administration." *Present Status of Educational Research in Japan. Supplement to the Proceedings of the International Conference on Educational Research, 1959.* Tokyo: Organizing Committee, International Conference on Educational Research, 1961, pp. 44–55.

464. Pahg Seong Woo. "The Viewpoints and Characteristics in Studying Action Research." *East West Education* 5 (Spring 1984):27–38.

465. Park Yung H. "The Educational Policy System in Contemporary Japan." *Transactions of the International Conference of Orientalists in Japan* 24 (1979):68–84.

466. Phelps, M. Overton. *Japan: A Guide to the Academic Placement of Students from Japan in Educational Institutions of the United States.* Washington, D.C.: American Association of Collegiate Registrars and Admission Officers, 1976.

467. Sergiovanni, Thomas J. "Ten Principles of Quality Leadership." *Educational Leadership* 39 (February 1982):330–336.

468. Shimada Shigeru. "National Analysis: Japan" *International Review of Education* 15 (1969):163–182.

469. Soramoto Wasuke. "Educational Administration of Japan." *Education in Japan: A Journal for Overseas* (Hiroshima University) 2 (1967):103–106.

470. Takakura Sho. "Current Trends in Educational Administration Research in Japan." *East West Education* 7 (Spring 1986):37–46.

471. Tokyo Metropolitan Government. *An Administrative Perspective of Tokyo.* Tokyo: Tokyo Metropolitan Government, 1971. See pp. 119–123.

472. ———. *Administrative Perspective of Tokyo*. Tokyo: Tokyo Metropolitan Government, 1972.
See Chapter 1, "Education."

473. ———. *Public Education in Tokyo*. Tokyo: Board of Education, 1971.

474. Torrence, Paul E. "Education for 'Quality Circles' in Japanese Schools." *Journal of Research and Development in Japanese Education* 15 (Winter 1982):11–15.

475. Tsuji Shinkichi. "On the Administrative Functions of the Local Boards of Education." *Research Bulletin of the National Institute for Educational Research* 7 (1966):37–51.

476. ———. "The Principal in School Management." *Research Bulletin of the National Institute for Educational Research* 11 (March 1972):43–49.

477. ———. "A Survey on Supervisory Administration." *Research Bulletin of the National Institute for Educational Research* 9 (November 1967):55–56.

478. UNESCO Regional Office for Education in Asia. "Educational Building and Facilities in the Asian Region: Japan." *Bulletin of the UNESCO Regional Office for Education in Asia* 17 (June 1976):71–76.

479. ———. "Japan: Survey of Long-Term Absentees." *Bulletin of the UNESCO Regional Office for Education in Asia* 1 (March 1967):57–58.

CHAPTER IX
HIGHER EDUCATION

Prewar Higher Education

The concept of the modern university was introduced to Japan during the first years of the Meiji period (1868–1912). Like many other modern institutions, the Japanese university had native precursors in the Tokugawa Period (1600–1868).

In 1870, the Japanese authorities established the so-called *Daigaku Nanko* (University South School) whose origins can be traced back to 1684. At that time, the Tokugawa Shogunate established the *Temmon-kata* (Astronomy Office) that was devoted to Dutch Studies. As Nagai Michio has pointed out, the *Daigaku Nanko* was really "the end product of a series of mutations in which the *Temmon-kata* became successively the *Bansho Wakai Goyo* (Office for the Interpretation of Barbarian Books), the *Yogakusho* (Institute for Western Studies), the *Bansho Shirabesho* (Institute for the Investigation of Barbarian Books) and the *Yosho Shirabesho* (Institute for the Investigation of Western Books)."[1] In 1874 this institution evolved into the *Tokyo Kaisei Gakko*, and in 1877 an amalgamation of these and other institutions resulted in the formation of Tokyo University.

Probably the event that most strongly influenced the shaping of the prewar Japanese university was the promulgation of the Imperial University Ordinance of 1886. This Ordinance transformed Tokyo University into Tokyo Imperial University. Based on the German model, the Ordinance defined the university's purpose as "the teaching of, and the fundamental research into, arts and sciences necessary for the state." Thus, from early on in the modern period, fulfilling the needs of the state was the highest priority. The appointment of university presidents by means of an imperial order, also reflected the dominance of the state over imperial universities.

Once again, the Japanese oligarchs had borrowed a Western (German) pattern and, as in similar situations, adapted it to better suit particular Japanese conditions. Although faithful to the original in its research orientation and its formation around a "chair" system in which professors served as civil servants, there were also important differences. The new imperial university included a number of practical faculties not found in Germany, such as agriculture, engineering, etc. And, the most significant difference was the Japanese failure to practice the vital principles of *Lehrfreiheit* (freedom to teach) and *Lernfreiheit* (freedom to learn), which gave the German university its inner strength, vitality, and a measure of academic freedom.

The focus on specialization and research at the university level can be explained by the creation of 32 three-year higher schools (*koto gakko*), which provided the only route into the imperial university. These highly competitive schools were superb *teaching* institutions specializing in general education and, thus, the imperial universities were freed to concentrate on specialization and research.

Founded in 1886, Tokyo Imperial University was both the first and, for over a decade, the only national university. The total number of imperial universities never exceeded nine. In order of their creation (and corresponding prestige) they were, in addition to Tokyo: Kyoto (1897), Kyushu (1903), Hokkaido (1903), Tohoku (1909), Osaka (1931), Nagoya (1931), and also Keijo (1924) and Taihoku (1928) in the overseas colonies of Korea and Formosa. By virtue of prestige and power resulting from both its historical antecedents and its establishment as the first imperial university, Tokyo Imperial University was considered the *crème de la crème* of Japanese higher education. This early advantage was reinforced for many years by the legal exemption of Tokyo's Law Faculty graduates from civil service examinations.[2]

Tokyo University (or Todai) graduates have always held a disproportionate percentage of prestigious posts in governmental ministries. As more and more Todai graduates flowed into the most powerful government ministries, they made sure that their successor generations were also Todai educated. Thus, from the Meiji period, there existed a system in which those who might be expected to carry out periodic reforms of higher education were the very people who benefited from, and had a psychological attachment to, the older system through which they achieved success.

Neither has the private sector of Japanese society been immune to Todai's prestige and power. Early on, it recognized that Todai's graduates were among the most talented in the country and, perhaps more importantly, were well connected with an "old boy" network that could be advantageous to the firms that employed them. From the outset, admission to Todai was widely and quite accurately seen as the key to a young man's future success, whether in government or the business world; virtually every ambitious young man in the empire dreamed of "going up to Tokyo."

The best students competed fiercely to enter Tokyo University and, failing this, other prestigious institutions whose entrance examination they could pass. As the numbers of applicants increased, the difficulty of the entrance examinations grew apace. With a limited number of spaces available, and more and more good candidates sitting for them, the intensity of competition grew. Those who failed entry to the university of their choice often did not give up, but continued cramming to pass the following year's round of examinations. This phenomenon still exists in Japan, and those who engage in it are still referred to as *ronin*, after the masterless samurai of feudal days. The only difference is that these young people are not without a master, but rather without a university.

Although the imperial universities held pride of place on everyone's prestige index, there were a number of excellent private schools, several of which were significantly older than the new imperial universities. As the state universities were explicitly created to fulfill the needs of the state, including the training of government bureaucrats, private universities were often founded by politically liberal, anti-government figures such as Fukuzawa Yukichi (Keio, 1858), Niijima Jo (Doshisha, 1875) and Okuma Shigenobu (Waseda, 1882). The founding of Waseda was, for example, inspired by the "People's Rights Movement" which demanded parliamentary government and greater individual freedom following the Meiji Restoration.

Often recognized by the public for the high quality of education offered, Keio, Waseda and other such elite private institutions failed to receive any official recognition in their early years. Not only were they disqualified from financial support from the government, but they were not even allowed the legal classification of university (*daigaku*) until the University Ordinance of 1918 was promulgated. Furthermore, private school graduates aspiring to enter the governmental bureaucracy faced systematic legal discrimination. These official attitudes served to reinforce the anti-governmental tendencies of many private universities focused on supplying well-trained students to a variety of professions outside of the national bureaucracy. Thus, Keio graduates found success in the world of commerce, and Waseda graduates were successful in politics, journalism and the arts.

The University Code of 1918 provided a legal framework for the establishment of universities other than imperial universities. This code signaled a significant expansion of the system of higher education. In addition to the old multiple-faculty imperial universities, this code provided for the establishment of (a) single-faculty government universities, and (b) the recognition of private and public universities.

In 1919, a six-year plan to expand higher education was launched. It doubled the number of students by establishing new government-operated colleges and universities while, at the same time, expanding existing institutions. The expansion of the private sector was, however, even more impressive. In 1918, for example, there were 65 private colleges serving 34,000 students, while 20 years later there were 25 private universities with 44,000 students and 120 private colleges serving 80,000 students. Most significant, however, is the fact that by 1938 students in the private sector made up almost two-thirds of the total university population, and students in private colleges comprised over 70% of the total population of colleges. This general pattern is one that still exists in Japan a half-century later.

There are several other types of institutions that are important in understanding Japan's prewar system of higher education: technical colleges, women's colleges, and normal schools. Referred to as *semmongakko*, the Japanese special or technical schools were a product of a need for graduates with requisite technical skills to fuel the Meiji modernization. Students could enter these schools directly from lower-middle schools and obtain specialized training without regard for general education. It was possible to obtain qualifications in a variety of fields—including commerce, medicine, dentistry, engineering, etc.—but *not* an academic title. Although not as prestigious as universities, the *semmongakko* provided large numbers of middle-level technicians with the skills needed to fill important economic and social needs.

During the Meiji period, *semmongakko* was also the term used to describe institutions providing higher education in the Japanese language. The long-term goal of their Meiji creators was for these institutions to become the core post-secondary institution, eventually replacing elite schools, teaching in Western languages, which were to be gradually phased out. The decision to establish Tokyo Imperial University in 1886, however, had an important impact on the *semmongakko*. For a variety of reasons, the original *semmongakko* plan was never achieved. Despite this, the *semmongakko* played an important role in providing opportunities for a large number of those unable to afford a university, or to pass its entrance examination. These were terminal institutions, which provided a practical and relevant education for middle-level technicians.

The most important element of women's higher education has clearly been the private, and often missionary-founded, colleges for women. During the first two decades of the Meiji period, Western, primarily American, missionaries were responsible for the establishment of 43 women's educational institutions that evolved into post-secondary schools. The first of these, Ferris Seminary, was founded in Yokohama by James C. Hepburn in 1870. This, and *Kobe Jogakuin* established in Kobe in 1875, were the first to offer higher education to women. Another American, David Murray, a Rutgers Professor of Mathematics who served as National Superintendent of Education from 1873–1878, successfully urged the creation of normal schools for women. The first of these institutions was founded in Tokyo, in 1890, and eventually evolved into Ochanomizu Women's University. The first government college for women was established in Fukuoka in 1922. By 1937, there was a total of 42 private women's colleges.

Probably the most famous Japanese woman to establish a post-secondary institution was Tsuda Umeko, an 1892 graduate of Bryn Mawr. Tsuda Women's College (originally *Joshi Eigaku Juku*, or Women's English College) is still one of the most prestigious women's colleges in contemporary Japan.

This is not to suggest that large numbers of women attended prewar institutions of higher education. Indeed, as in the United States, few did, and their academic options were commonly restricted primarily to the "helping professions," i.e., teaching, nursing, or such fields as music and literature. This, of course, was merely an extension of the concept of educating women to be "good wives and wise mothers."

Finally, although a number of women's institutions were called universities, none was recognized as such. Technically they fell into the category of *semmongakko*, or "special schools." This meant that they could not legally award degrees, only certificates of achievement. Although a handful of men's universities allowed women as "auditors," a woman, no matter how talented, was denied access to the prestigious imperial universities. It was not until the American Occupation of Japan (1945–1952) that university education was open to all regardless of gender.

The normal school sector of prewar Japanese higher education was quasi-militaristic with a strict disciplinary regimen. Depending upon the particular school attended, students received financial support from either the national or prefectural government. A highly structured normal school curriculum concentrated on moral and military training and the inculcation of patriotism. The *quid pro quo* expected from normal school graduates was similar to that of graduates of military academies, i.e., a ten-year obligation to teach in government schools.

Postwar Higher Education

Under the American Occupation, the entire system of education underwent fundamental reorganization. The American authorities viewed prewar Japanese higher education as elitist and hierarchical. Thus, the multi-track system of higher education was scrapped, and steps were taken to democratize access. One of the most important actions was to place the education of women on an equal footing with that of men. Interestingly enough, many parents were not happy to have their daughters attending institutions where they thought they would be corrupted. Coeducation was often seen as undermining traditional family values.

The Report of the First U.S. Education Mission to Japan (March 1946), made a number of recommendations to reform higher education. Among these, the following were probably the most important: (1) the freeing of higher education from excessive government control, (2) the expansion of higher education throughout the nation to improve access based on merit, (3) a greater emphasis on general, or liberal education in the first two years of one's university experience, (4) a guarantee of economic and academic freedom, and (5) an extension of library and research facilities.

In response to these recommendations, the number of universities was increased from 49 (in 1942) to more than 245 (in 1955) and, in addition, many new American-style junior colleges were created. Many of the "new" universities were created by the amalgamation of existing universities, colleges, special and technical schools, higher schools, normal schools, etc. Although access to higher education was much improved as a result, the trade-off was that the quality of higher education was often diluted. Many of these new universities were pejoratively described as "*ekiben daigaku*" (lunch-box universities), after the Japanese custom of selling a lunch box made up of local specialities on the train station platform. The rapid educational expansion, however, did not abate. Between 1960 and 1975, the number of post-secondary institutions (all types) rose from 525 to over 1,000. In the same period, the number of students in these institutions tripled from 710,000 to over 2.1 million.

During the period when new universities were being launched, virtually every town or city wished to have a university. While many existing institutions of higher education did not meet the standard required to become four-year universities, local pride had to be assuaged. The creation of junior colleges satisfied all parties involved.

The period from the end of World War II to the end of the American Occupation in 1952 can fairly be described as the postwar transitional stage of Japanese higher education. The prewar system was scrapped, and the foundations of a new democratic system were put into place. As these events were occurring, a postwar baby boom began after large numbers of military and civilian personnel returned from wartime assignments overseas.

The birthrate rose sharply after 1947. For example, the number of births soared from 1,575,000 in 1945 to 2,718,000 in 1947. This resulted in a virtual flood of children entering elementary school in 1953, along with the certain knowledge that large numbers of these same children would press against university gates in 1965. It was clear to postwar policymakers, therefore, that the current increases in higher education enrollments would not subside in the near future.

As the Occupation wound down (it ended in Spring 1952), powerful business interests argued for educational policies that would be closely aligned to manpower needs. As early as 1952, *Nikkeiren* (Japan

Federation of Employees), an influential federation of some of Japan's largest industrial firms, issued a statement on educational policy that bluntly expressed its unhappiness with the democratically oriented schools and called for an educational system better able to support economic reconstruction. *Nikkeiren* had pinpointed a potentially serious obstacle to Japan's economic development: a serious shortage of well-trained scientific and technical manpower. Industry spokesmen generally agreed on the need for the "functional differentiation of the higher educational structure, and . . . increased specialization in courses and graduation of more science and engineering specialists."[3]

In 1957 the recently established Economic Planning Agency, the coordinating body for overall governmental economic planning, had issued a long-range plan establishing guidelines for economic development and the role of education in achieving it. The Ministry of Education contributed a five-year plan designed to accommodate 8,000 new university places annually for science and technology students, and by 1960, it was close to achieving this goal. Prime Minister Ikeda's scheme to double the national income within a decade, however, required the production of an additional 17,000 scientists and engineers. The Ministry of Education planned to meet this need with a seven-year plan that added 16,000 places annually, but it was subsequently replaced with a four-year plan adding 20,000 places yearly. However, because private schools admitted larger numbers of students than had been anticipated, the plan was realized in three years and, by 1963, there were approximately 100,000 science and technology graduates.

In a similar effort, a new category of higher education was established in 1962. The Ministry of Education created 19 five-year technical schools to train middle-level technicians with a thorough knowledge of their field. After completing the nine years of compulsory education, a student could enter a three-year course at the upper secondary level and a two-year technical course. As of May 1983 there were 62 of these technical schools with a total enrollment of over 47,000 students, of whom 97.2% were male.

Thus, highly differentiated system of technical education was created. At the apex of the system, the universities provided both undergraduate and graduate education for scientists and high-level technical personnel. The technical schools described above were designed to train the large numbers of middle-level technicians essential for the operation of a sophisticated, scientific and technical economy.

In the decade between 1960 and 1970, Japan had succeeded in more than doubling the number of university science and engineering faculties. This, however, tells only part of the story. "In 1960, 18.2 percent of the total [university] enrollment was in the fields of science and engineering; by 1975 this figure was up to 23.2 percent. Even more significantly within national universities, where the government efforts were most direct, the figure rose from 24 percent to 33 percent in these fields."[4]

Student radicals were an important part of the 1945–1968 intellectual ferment in Japan, but during the 1960s their numbers proved to be the heart of the great student protests that shook the nation to its very foundation. The initial "cause" was an attempt to prevent revision of the U.S.–Japan Security Treaty of June 1960. The movement continued, using the American involvement in Vietnam as an emotional focus and culminated in the great Tokyo University struggle of 1968. This event was the high water mark of the Japanese student movement, and student occupation of Todai's physical facilities not only forced the university's closure for several months, but was directly responsible for suspending the 1969 entrance examinations.

The government of Prime Minister Eisaku Sato met this challenge by ramming through the Diet a "Bill for Emergency Measures of University Administration" in August of the same year. The real significance of this bill was that it effectively broke the back of the student movement. As a result, with few exceptions, campus unrest subsided, and the student movement broke into increasingly rival factions, each claiming to be ideologically purer than its opponents.

If the 1960s can be described as a decade of turmoil in which the idealism and enthusiasm for reform reflected the general upheaval occurring in universities of the time, the 1970s were characterized by a much higher degree of stability in which university life became "normalized," and the earlier idealism and enthusiasm was considerably eroded. The kind of cautious realism expressed in the Central Council on Education's guidelines for higher education policies for the period 1976–1986 was typical. Among its major recommendations were: (1) diversifying higher education to meet the increased demand and to protect the quality of higher education; (2) reforming the teaching, research and administration of institutions of higher education; (3) providing government assistance to private universities; (4) reforming the system of entrance examinations; and (5) implementing long-range national planning in higher education.[5] The 1970s and early 1980s, thus, served as a "warm up" period to Japan's current educational reform effort.

Basic Data on Higher Education Today

There are four basic types of higher education institutions in Japan: university (*daigaku*), junior college (*tanki daigaku*), college of technology (*koto semmon gakko*), and special training school (*senshu gakko*).

In 1986, there were 95 national, 36 public, and 334 private four-year universities; and there were 38 national, 52 public, and 459 private two-year junior colleges. Each prefecture has at least one national university.

As of May 1985, there were 1,848,698 students enrolled in universities; of those, 449,373 were attending national universities, 54,944 were attending public universities, and 1,344,281 were attending private universities. Thus, almost 73% of all university students attend private institutions.

Some Major Issues Facing Higher Education Today

I. Entrance Examinations

Despite the student revolt, the widespread acceptance of higher education as a prerequisite to maintaining Japan's economic gains sent increasing numbers of high school graduates through the narrow gates of the universities. The gatekeepers, however, insisted that those admitted first demonstrate their merit by successfully passing rigorous entrance examinations. Although not a new phenomenon in Japanese higher education, one would be hard pressed to disagree with Ezra Vogel's observation that "no single event with the possible exception of marriage, determines the course of a young man's life as much as entrance examinations, and nothing, including marriage, requires as many years of planning and hard work."[6]

Although most Japanese seem to think that there is entirely too much emphasis placed on entrance examinations, a deeply ingrained Confucian legacy, powerful vested interests, and too few places for too many applicants may explain why very little has been done to change the situation.

II. Quality of Undergraduate Education

Passing the entrance examination to the university of one's choice is the key to educational success in Japan. Having worked hard for several years to accomplish this, including attending extra cram schools (*juku*) and, often, supplementary schools (*yobiko*), there is a natural tendency for college students to relax, especially during the first two years of general education. Much of the entrance examination preparation was in the area of general education, so the combination of general academic weariness and what is often an impersonal and boring two years of general education, provides students with a rationale for spending their time in more enjoyable pursuits.

An interesting point can be made about this phenomenon. First, in both the Japanese and American systems of education, students take a rest stop. Whereas the Japanese student works hard to enter the university, the American student works hard to graduate from the university. In other words, the American usually "coasts" through high school and makes up for this holiday if he or she attends a good university; the Japanese pattern is just the opposite, with students taking their "vacation" in the university after working hard in high school.

Although the description above is generally accurate, students in a handful of fields, especially agriculture, engineering, medicine and science, are exceptions. For most students, however, admittance to the university is tantamount to graduating. Former Ambassador Edwin Reischauer, a lifetime student of Japanese society, has put it most bluntly: "The squandering of four years at the college level on poor teaching and very little study seems an incredible waste of time from a nation so passionately devoted to efficiency."[7]

III. Weakness of Graduate Education[8]

Since the first great modern wave of educational reform in the Meiji era, the elite universities have been seen as places of advanced study and research as in the European tradition. Following German academic patterns, the senior professor was a virtual demigod. All academic activities revolved around the "chair" he occupied, and his several subordinates assisted him in pursuing the research activities he formulated. The power of the "chair" resided in his control of the research budget assigned to his chair.

The postwar Occupation reforms sought to change this situation, and American-style graduate schools began to appear throughout the nation. It was not, however, until the mid-1950s that the first master's degrees were offered, and one had to wait until the early 1960s for the first doctorates. For a variety of reasons, graduate student enrollment is concentrated in about 5% of those universities offering graduate work. In fact, only about 65,000 students (4%) of total university enrollment, pursue graduate level education in Japan.

The reality of Japanese graduate education is that the vast majority who do attend, are doing so to gain qualifications for an academic career. The hard truth that potential students understand is that there are only a handful of jobs for which advanced training is useful, and these are at the master's level in engineering and the basic sciences. The major Japanese firms which are fueled by research results generally prefer to provide the equivalent of graduate training within the confines of the firm. As *Japanese Education Today* observes, often "the old apprentice system was merely masked by introduction of new courses that lacked overall program coherence."[9]

As a result of the increasing demand for high-level science and technology, which is expected to escalate in the twenty-first century, the prospects are brighter than the current reality. Even cooperation among academic institutions is a recent phenomenon. The most important development in this area was the 1973 creation of the Tsukuba Science City, northwest of Tokyo. This innovative response to a problem includes 2 universities, 46 national research centers, 8 private research centers and an industrial park in which an impressive, and growing, number of technology-dependent firms have relocated.

Perhaps the most important single obstacle to the rapid improvement of Japanese research is inadequate funding. In 1983, the United States, with a population double that of Japan, provided more than ten times the Japanese figure for research in science and engineering.

IV. Internationalizing Higher Education

Internationalization has been a subject of much debate within Japan and goes far beyond the confines of higher education. This essay, however, will be confined to the higher education sector.

In today's Japan, *kokusaika* (internationalization) is one of the most common buzz words that one hears every day. Not to exhibit internationalism, whether going to bask in the Hawaiian sun, or carrying an expensive Gucci handbag, is to be perceived as unsophisticated and backward. A cursory examination also reveals an increasing number of Japanese colleges and universities with "international" in their names.

Three of the most important indicators of an educational system's international perspective are: (1) the number of foreign students which it accommodates; (2) the number of its students who study abroad; and (3) the number of foreign teachers/researchers who are accepted (on an equal basis) in the dominant employment pattern of the nation's higher education system. In the case of Japan, the results are disappointing. For example, Japan hosts approximately 12,000 foreign students (about 0.5% of her total enrollment) which ranks her close to, or at the bottom among advanced nations.

Also, the flow of faculty and students, by geographical area, to and from Japan resembles Japan's trade balance with the world. The outflow of students and faculty/researchers not only greatly exceeds the inflow, but reflects a major imbalance. At least nine of every ten Japanese students/researchers are attracted to the United States and Western Europe; 82% of the inflow to Japan is from Asia, and 80% of these are from Japan's closest neighbors: Taiwan, China and South Korea. The small number of students from other parts of Asia, let alone the larger world community, means that although American students make up only 6.5% of foreign students in Japan, they constitute the fourth largest group of foreign students. Even this is misleading, since well over half of the Americans are in Japan under exchange agreements between Japanese and American universities, agreements which often provide a ghetto type of education in which the visitors are taught in English using the special facilities of the Japanese universities' "international division."

It is not an exaggeration to say that the number of foreign professors teaching in Japanese universities is truly negligible. Only 1.3% of full-time faculty are foreigners. They seldom are allowed to participate and vote in department meetings, and do not have the same kind of job security as their Japanese colleagues. In fact, it is probably true that the vast majority of these foreigners are teaching English or other foreign languages.

Indeed, until 1982 foreigners could not be employed as tenured faculty members in national or public universities. In that year, however, an important step was taken to allow foreigners some of the rights that their Japanese colleagues teaching in foreign institutions have long enjoyed. The so-called "Foreign Professors Law" of 1982 was passed, and several foreigners received appointments to these universities. The majority of these new appointees were North American or European.

In conclusion, it is fair to say that, although the Japanese have made some efforts toward greater internationalization, Japanese universities have a long way to go before they begin to approach the international character of many American and European universities. It may be well to reflect on the words of one prominent Japanese professor who told the writer that, "International education is the acquisition of international skills and attitudes that enables the person to advance Japan's national interests."

V. The Future of Japanese Higher Education

The current effort to reform Japanese education marks the third major reform attempt in modern Japanese history. One of the most important differences between this attempt and earlier ones, however, is that it is not primarily motivated by external threats (as in the Meiji period), or imposed (as during the Occupation), but is generated by primarily domestic forces. Indeed, the Ad Hoc Council on Educational Reform (*Rinkyoshin*) is a unique body within the Japanese tradition of educational reform. Traditionally, bodies of this sort have been appointed by the ministry of education, assigned a clearly demarcated area of study, and have worked in virtual secrecy until their final reports were submitted to the Minister. The *Rinkyoshin* members, however, were appointed by then Prime Minister Nakasone and reported directly to him, thereby bypassing normal channels. This approach fit Nakasone's political style which, in the words of the University of Washington's Kenneth Pyle, was to appoint "an unusual number of ad hoc commissions . . . to highlight his pet proposals and to bring forth largely predetermined policy recommendations. . . . In this way, he was able to shape the policy agenda and to invest his ideas with the legitimacy that came from the support of distinguished panels."[10]

One of the four areas singled out for reform was higher education. Indeed, many observers have long thought that Japanese higher education was the weakest link in an otherwise strong educational system. The *Rinkyoshin* recommended a list of reforms that would significantly change the Japanese university, if implemented. It is an iron rule of reform, however, that fundamental changes are very difficult to implement even in the best of times. There are always entrenched groups reluctant to risk their power and position, and Japan is no different from other countries in this regard.

Thus, most of the proposed reform measures dealing with higher education will probably recede into the twilight of recent history and be forgotten, but those measures which must be adopted in order for higher education to survive in something like its current form will be embraced by institutions of higher education. At least two changes are likely to occur in the mid-term: lifelong education, and an increased internationalization of higher education. These changes will be embraced, not because policymakers suddenly decide to provide greater educational opportunities to non-traditional and foreign students, but because these measures are a practical means of expanding the pool of potential students.

Japanese higher education enjoyed a rapid and unprecedented expansion in enrollment and financial support during the 1960s. This "golden age" dimmed considerably by the early 1970s, and, before long, entered into a period of no expansion, and then negative growth and decline. Today, Japanese education is faced with a demographic shift which threatens the advances it has made.

The number of kindergarten age children is the lowest since the post-World War II "baby boom," and most kindergartens are being forced to cancel almost half of their classes. The number of kindergartens in Japan has shrunk by 25% since 1979, from some 2.5 million to about 2 million last year. As this declining number of youngsters work their way through the system, there will be a smaller number of children going to all levels of school. It is estimated that the pool of potential college-entering students will increase until 1993, after which their number will decrease sharply, and by 2000 there will be fewer than today. Thus, the question of declining enrollments, which has bedeviled American universities in recent years, will face the Japanese before too long.

Professor Kitamura Kazuyuki, of Hiroshima University's prestigious Research Institute of Higher Education, predicts that the 1990s will be an "age of institutional self-selection" in which the very existence of many educational institutions will be questioned and some may face contraction or even closure. This will be a wrenching experience, as not a single Japanese university was closed between the creation of the first national university in 1868 and 1978, a period of 110 years. Indeed, since the great expansion following World War II only a handful of the 485 universities created since 1950 have been closed, while a mere 42 of 647 private junior colleges have met a similar fate.

In addition to a severe decline of applicants in the traditional pool of students, Japanese society in the 1990s will be characterized by a number of important structural changes. Not the least important of these will be changes in Japanese employment practices. There are already signs that Japanese industry is beginning to transform its traditional system of "lifelong employment," so that major firms will have less incentive to recruit all of its employees fresh out of the university. In addition, diversification of the student population appears to be inevitable. Institutions dependent upon income from entrance examinations and tuition, i.e., the private sector, currently enroll about 75% of all university students. They will need to attract large numbers of non-traditional students, and even foreign students, in an era of sharply decreased traditional student pools. This problem will be exacerbated by increasing competition for Japanese students from foreign, including American, universities that are actively recruiting in Japan, or building branch campuses in many parts of Japan.

Those higher education reform recommendations relevant to this coming crisis will be seen as useful vehicles with which to solve the problem and, thus, are likely to be adopted. Thus, Japanese higher education stands on the brink of a potentially disastrous situation, but implementation of *Rinkyoshin* proposals to provide lifelong learning to a huge pool of non-traditional, adult learners, and to internationalize universities by accepting greater numbers of foreign students may become more important parts of the Japanese system of higher education.

NOTES

1. Michio Nagai, *Higher Education in Japan: Its Takeoff and Crash* (Tokyo: University of Tokyo Press, 1971), p. 25.

2. In the Japanese context, a law faculty does not train attorneys, but prepares students for careers in public administration, constitutional law, politics, etc. Study in a law faculty, therefore, fits one to join a government ministry.

3. T.J. Pempel, *Patterns of Japanese Policymaking: Experiences from Higher Education* (Boulder: Westview Press, 1978), p. 163.

4. Ibid., p. 180.

5. Tetsuya Kobayashi, *Schools, Society and Progress in Japan* (New York: Pergamon Press, 1976), p. 94–95.

6. Ezra F. Vogel, *Japan's New Middle Class: The Salaryman and His Family in a Tokyo Suburb* (Berkeley: University of California Press, 1963), p. 40.

7. Edwin O. Reischauer, Introduction to *The Japanese School: Lessons for Industrial America*, by Benjamin Duke, (New York: Praeger, 1986), p. xviii.

8. Much of this section is based on *Japanese Education Today: A Report From the U.S. Study of Education in Japan*, prepared by a special task force of the OERI Japan Study Team (Washington, D.C.: U.S. Government Printing Office, 1987).

9. Ibid., p. 52.

10. Kenneth B. Pyle, "In Pursuit of a Grand Design: Nakasone Betwixt the Past and Future." *The Journal of Japanese Studies* 13 (Summer 1987):253.

HIGHER EDUCATION: I

480.   Altbach, Philip G., ed. *University Reform: An International Perspective*. Washington, D.C.: American Association for Higher Education, 1980.

Includes material on the Japanese experience.

481.   Amano Ikuo. "Stability and Change in Japanese Higher Education." In *Higher Education for the 1980's: Challenges and Responses* (item 509), pp. 60–71.

Written in 1980, this essay argues that Japanese higher education has escaped the crises facing other systems and enjoyed a period of stability. This can be explained by the increased diversification of higher educational institutions, strong government control, university conservatism, and an industrial employment system which relies heavily on a student's school record.

482. Arimoto Akira. "The Academic Structure in Japan: Institutional Hierarchy and Academic Mobility," Yale Higher Education Research Group, No. 27, August 1978.

Examines the basic characteristics of the Japanese academic structure with special attention to the evolution of its institutional hierarchy, the closed academic structure and the effects of the academic structure upon research.

483. Azumi Koya. *Higher Education and Business Recruitment in Japan*. New York: Teachers College Press, Columbia University, 1970.

An early, but still useful study of how large Japanese firms go about recruiting students, and how graduates go about finding jobs.

484. Bartholomew, James R. "The Acculturation of Science in Japan: Kitasato Shibasaburo and the Japanese Bacteriological Community, 1885–1920." Ph.D. dissertation, Stanford University, 1972.

An important contribution to our understanding of the politics of science in the Meiji Period. It includes important material on Kitasato's founding of the Infectuous Disease Institute in 1893, and its controversial takeover by the Ministry of Education in 1914.

485. ———. "Japanese Culture and the Problem of Modern Science." In *Science and Values*, pp. 99–155. Edited by Arnold

Thackery and Everett Mendelsohn. New York: Humanities Press, 1974.

Good introduction to the problems inherent when a traditional Confucian culture meets modern Western scientific principles.

* ———. "Japan's Modernization and the Imperial Universities, 1876–1920." *Journal of Asian Studies* 37 (February 1978):251–271. Annotated in item 276 above.

* Beauchamp, Edward R. *An American Teacher in Early Meiji Japan*. Annotated in item 148 above.

486. ———. "Griffis and Japanese Higher Education." *Transactions of the Asiatic Society of Japan* Ser. 3, 15 (1980):73–92.

Discusses Griffis's teaching and experiences at the predecessor institution to Tokyo Imperial University from 1872–1874.

487. ———. "*Shiken Jigoku*: The Problem of Entrance Examinations in Japan." *Asian Profile* 6 (December 1978):543–560.

Survey of the problem of "examination hell" and its negative effects on both higher education and pre-university schooling.

488. Bloom, Justin, and Asano Shinsuke. "Tsukuba Science City: Japan Tries Planned Innovation." *Science* 212 (June 12, 1981):1239–1247.

Brief history of Tsukuba and its problems.

489. Bronfenbrenner, Martin. "Economic Education at the University Level." *Journal of Economic Education* 16 (Fall 1985):269–272.

A rather jaundiced view of the teaching of economics in Japanese universities by a long-time student of Japan and the Japanese.

490. Chee Chang-boh. "Development of Sociology in Japan: A Study of the Adaptation of Western Sociological Orientations into the Japanese Social Structure." Ph.D. dissertation, Duke University, 1959.

Covers sociology's development from Meiji period through mid-1950s.

491. Clark, Burton R. "The Japanese System of Higher Education in Comparative Perspective." New Haven: Yale University, Institute for Social Policy Studies, Yale Higher Education Research Group Working Paper 33, January 1979. Also in *Changes in the Japanese University: A Comparative Perspective* (item 497), pp. 217–240.

Examines internal differentiation in Japanese higher education and the problem of coordination effectively, using a comparative perspective.

492. Cummings, William K. "The Aftermath of the University Crisis." *Japan Interpreter* 10 (Winter 1976):350–360.

A leading student of Japanese higher education analyzes Japanese higher education following the great student rebellion of the 1960s and early 1970s.

493. _____. "The Conservatives Reform Higher Education." *Japan Interpreter* (Winter 1974):421–431; reprinted in *Learning to be Japanese: Selected Readings on Japanese Society and Education* (item 22), pp. 316–328.

One observer's interpretation of the role of the conservative government in trying to bring about guided change in Japanese higher education.

494. ———. "Expansion, Examination Fever, and Equality." In *Changes in the Japanese University: A Comparative Perspective* (item 497), pp. 83–106.

Recognizes the criticisms of Japanese education, especially of the infamous examination system, but argues that critics often fail to take into account its inherently egalitarian nature.

495. ———. "The Japanese Private University." *Minerva* 9 (July 1973):303–324.

Japan's private sector is responsible for a majority of Japan's students, yet it receives virtually no support from the government. Cummings details how the private universities have attempted to cope in the face of this and other problems.

496. ———. "The Problems and Prospects of Japanese Universities," in *Japan in the 1980s*, pp. 57–87. Edited by Lewis Austin. New Haven: Yale University Press, 1976.

Treats the politics of Japanese higher education and predicts an increase in financial support for higher education, increasing cooperation between business and higher education, and an end to student radicalism.

497. Cummings, William K.; Amano Ikuo; and Kitamura Kazuyuki, eds. *Changes in the Japanese University: A Comparative Perspective*. New York: Praeger, 1979.

A series of essays on various aspects of the Japanese university written by leading American and Japanese students of Japanese higher education. Contains material difficult to find elsewhere. Contains items 491, 494, 511, 519, 524, 548, 643, 659, 666, 667.

498. Dore, Ronald P. *The Diploma Disease: Education, Qualification, and Development*. Berkeley: University of California, 1976.

Stresses the negative results of overemphasizing formal educational qualifications. Contains material on Japanese case.

499. Frost, Peter. "Examination Hell: Entrance Examinations in Japan's Modernizing Process." *Berkshire Review* 16 (1981):113–121.

Survey of the role of entrance examinations in the development of Japanese higher education.

500. Fukuda Kanichi. "A Professor's View on University Education: The Need for a Democratic Policy." *Journal of Social Political Ideas in Japan* 5 (December 1967):159–224.

A representative left-wing view of Japanese higher education during the two decades following the American Occupation.

501. Geiger, Roger L. "The Limits of Higher Education: Comparative Analysis of Factors Affecting Enrollment Levels in Belgium, France, Japan and the United States." New Haven: Yale University, Institute for Social and Policy Studies, February 1980.

A comparative analysis of enrollment influences in Japan, France, Belgium and the United States.

502. Gramlich, P. Hooper. "The Pattern of Educational Planning for Higher Education in Postwar Japan." *Educational Planning* 4 (October 1977):35–47.

Useful comparative insights on higher education.

503. Griesy, Paul V. "The Doshisha, 1875–1919: The Indigenization of the Institution." 2 vols. Ph.D. dissertation, Columbia University, 1973.

Best history of an important Christian university available in English.

* Hall, Ivan P. *Mori Arinori*. Cited in item 80 above.

Important biographical study of a key Japanese educational statesman who influenced the early growth of higher education in Japan.

504. ———. "Organizational Paralysis: The Case of Todai." In *Organization and Decision-Making in Postwar Japan*, pp. 304–330. Edited by Ezra Vogel. Berkeley: University of California, 1975.

An excellent description of the problems inherent in a system of higher education dominated by a single university.

505. Halpin, Keum Chu. "Reform in University Governance in Japan: Case of the University of Tsukuba." Ph.D. dissertation, University of Washington, 1978.

One of most extensive analyses of the University of Tsukuba which, a decade ago, was seen as an exciting innovation.

506. Havens, Thomas R.H. "Changing Styles of University Life in Japan." *Japan Interpreter* 8 (Autumn 1973):285–191, reprinted in *Learning to be Japanese: Selected Readings on Japanese Society and Education* (item 22), pp. 329–337.

Havens provides a personal view of changes in academic styles in the postwar years.

507. Hiroshima University. *The Changing Functions of Higher Education: Implications for Innovation.* Hiroshima: Hiroshima University, Research Institute for Higher Education, 1984.

Reports from the 1984 OECD/Japan Seminar on Higher Education. Contains items 520, 630, 631, 633, 635.

508. ———. *Comparative Approaches to Higher Education: Curriculum Teaching, and Innovations in an Age of Financial Difficulties.* Hiroshima: Hiroshima University, Research Institute for Higher Education, 1983.

Report of the Hiroshima/OECD Meetings of Experts, 1983. Contains items 518, 610, 634, 653.

509. ———. *Higher Education for the 1980's: Challenges and Response.* Hiroshima: Hiroshima University, Research Institute for Higher Education, 1980.

The annual RIHE seminar focused on the challenges of social change, values crises, societal needs, the internal dynamics of higher education, and future reforms. Contains item 481, 521, 525, 529.

510. ———. *Innovations in Higher Education: Exchange of Experiences and Ideas in International Perspective.* Hiroshima: Hiroshima University, Research Institute for Higher Education, 1981.

Papers from Hiroshima/OECD Meeting of Experts on Higher Education and the Seminar on Innovations in Higher Education.

Contains items 517, 579, 632.

511. Ichikawa Shogo. "Finance of Higher Education." In *Changes in the Japanese University: A Comparative Perspective* (item 497), pp. 40–63.

One of the few English-language materials on how higher education is financed in Japan.

512. Kerr, Clark, et al. *12 Systems of Higher Education: 6 Decisive Issues*. New York: International Council for Educational Development, 1978.

The design, management and effectiveness of systems of higher education in 12 countries, including Japan, are examined in comparative perspective. Underwritten by the Krupp Foundation of West Germany, this volume is available through Interbook, Inc., 13 East 16th Street, New York, New York 10003.

513. Kida Hiroshi. "Higher Education in Japan." *Higher Education* 4 (August 1975):261–272.

Describes and quantifies Japan's present state of higher education development, noting the predominance of private institutions, variety of courses available, wide social base from which students are drawn, highly competitive entrance examinations, and the many challenges including the linked problems of management and finance.

514. ———. "Japanese Universities and Their World, Their Features, and Tasks." NIER Occasional Paper (1–81). Tokyo: National Institute for Educational Research, May 1981.

Discussion of the characteristics of the Japanese university and future issues, including the university's research role. Advocates internationalization of Japan's universities.

515. Kimball, Bruce A. "Japanese Liberal Education: A Case Study in Its National Context." *Teachers College Record* 83 (Winter 1981):245-261.

As its title suggests, this essay focuses on what constitutes a liberal education in Japan.

516. Kitamura Kazuyuki. "A Comparative Essay on the Future of Higher Education in Japan and the United States." *Research in Higher Education/Daigaku Ronshu* 4 (March 19, 1976):17–33.

One of Japan's leading scholars on higher education speculates about the future of higher education in both countries.

517. ———. "Innovations in Higher Education: Issues Definitions and Japanese Experience." In *Innovations in Higher Education* (item 510), pp. 7–17.

Focuses on Japanese innovative attempts in higher education and analyzes their results.

518. _____. "The Internationalization of Higher Education in Japan." *Comparative Approaches to Higher Education: Curriculum, Teaching and Innovations in an Age of Financial Difficulties* (item 508), pp. 12–24.

Argues that Japan can no longer view the world as a market in which skills can be bought and sold, but must play a role in building an international society.

519. ———. "Mass Higher Education." In *Changes in the Japanese University: A Comparative Perspective* (item 497), pp. 64–82.

Surveys Japan's passage from a society with an elite system of higher education to one with a true mass system.

520. ———. "New Implications for the Educational Function of the Japanese University." *The Changing Functions of Higher Education: Implications and Innovations* (item 507), pp. 3–12.

Argues that the traditional view of university students pursuing their own learning needs to be redefined, and research-oriented faculty need to pay more attention to their teaching.

521. ———. "In Search for a System of Post-secondary Education." In *Higher Education for the 1980's: Challenges and Responses.* (item 509), pp. 28–35.

Argues that Japan is not moving toward a "universal" higher education system on the American model.

522. Kitamura Kazuyuki and Cummings, William K. "The 'Big Bang' Theory and Japanese University Reform." *Comparative Education Review* 16 (June 1972):303–324.

Argues that Japanese educational reforms usually follow a "Big Bang" instigated from external forces, such as various political or social crises.

523. Kitamura Kazuyuki and Tomoda Yasumasa. "Patterns of Decision-Making in Japanese Higher Education." *International Journal of Institutional Management in Higher Education* 1 (May 1972):57–63.

Survey of 1,800 faculty members' opinions on the decision-making process.

524. Kobayashi Tetsuya. "The Internationalization of Japanese Higher Education." In *Changes in the Japanese University: A Comparative Perspective* (item 497), pp. 166–184.

Surveys the traditional Japanese attitudes toward internationalization, and argues that Japan must move in that direction in order to play a constructive role in the future.

525. ———. "Japanese Higher Education for the 1980's: Continuity and Change." In *Higher Education for the 1980's: Challenges and Responses* (item 509), pp. 94–101.

A Janus-like look at Japanese higher education which predicts more continuity than change in the short term.

526. Kumagai Fumie. "The Effects of Cross-Cultural Education of
      Attitudes and Personality of Japanese Students." *Sociology
      of Education* 50 (January 1977):40–47.

      Reports the results of a longitudinal study of cross-cultural
      education's effects on the attitudes and personality of 104 male
      graduate students who studied in the United States. Concludes
      that the American experience increased the student's appreciation
      of American culture, but did not lower their appreciation of
      Japanese culture or alter their personalities.

527. Marshall, Byron. "Academic Factionalism in Japan: The Case of
      the Todai Economics Department, 1919–1939." *Modern
      Asian Studies* 12 (October 1978):529–551.

      Case study of the inner workings of a prestigious department
      within Japan's most elite university. Students of American
      higher education will recognize many of the symptoms.

*   ———. "Professors and Politics: The Meiji Academic Elite."
      Journal of Japanese Studies 3 (Winter 1977):71-97.

      Annotated in item 163 above.

528. ———. "The Tradition of Conflict in the Governance of Japan's
      Imperial Universities." *History of Education Quarterly* 17
      (1977):385-406.

      Japan has had a long tradition of turbulence in its elite
      universities and Marshall provides a short, but helpful history of
      this phenomenon.

529. Nagai, Michio. "Higher Education in an Age of
      Internationalization." In *Higher Education for the 1980's:
      Challenges and Responses* (item 509), pp. 8–15.

      Proposes that more research be done outside of universities,
      that there be greater integration of universities and mass
      communication techniques, and that both universities and
      agencies of mass communication have an obligation to educate
      people toward a peaceful world.

* ————. *Higher Education in Japan: Its Take-off and Crash.* Tokyo: University of Tokyo Press, 1971. Annotated in item 165 above.

530. Nakayama Shigeru. *Academic and Scientific Traditions in China, Japan and the West.* Translated by Jerry Dusenberry. Tokyo: Tokyo University Press, 1984.

Excellent comparative study of the development of academic science.

531. Narita Katsuya, ed. *Systems of Higher Education: Japan.* New York: International Council for Educational Development, 1978.

Survey of history, structure and problems of Japanese higher education.

532. Ninomiya Akira. *Private Universities in Japan.* Tokyo: Private Universities Union of Japan, 1975.

Traces the historical development of Japanese universities, with special attention to the Imperial ordinance of 1918 and its resulting influences.

533. Nishimura Hidetoshi. "Universities Under Pressure to Change." *Japan Quarterly* 34 (April–June 1987):179–184.

Argues that Japanese high school students are faced with the alternative of facing the entrance examination competition or accepting a dead-end job requiring little skill or training. The vocational schools established in the mid-1970s to solve this problem have not done so.

534. Pempel, T.J. *Patterns of Japanese Policy-Making: Experiences from Higher Education.* Boulder: Westview Press, 1978.

One of the best studies of the politics of higher education policy-making in Japan. Most valuable for its emphasis on the complexities of higher education policy making.

535. ————. "Patterns of Policymaking in Higher Education." In *Policymaking in Contemporary Japan*, pp. 269–307. Edited

by T.J. Pempel. Ithaca, New York: Cornell University Press, 1977.

A capsule summary of the themes in the above book.

536. Perkin, Harold. "Britain and Japan: Two Roads to Higher Education." *Higher Education Review* 13 (Summer 1981):7–16.

Views each society's universities as embodying its own particular values and meaning. In Japan, it is a spirit of participative self-fulfillment, and in England, it is acquisitive individualism with concern for one's neighbor.

* Roden, Donald T. *Schooldays in Imperial Japan: A Study in the Culture of a Student Elite.* Berkeley: University of California, 1980. Annotated in item 280 above.

537. Rubinger, Richard, ed. *An American Scientist in Early Meiji Japan: The Autobiographical Notes of Thomas C. Mendenhall.* Honolulu: University of Hawaii Press, Asian Studies at Hawaii, No. 35, 1989.

The Japan diary of the first professor of physics at Tokyo University, 1878–1881.

* Spaulding, Robert M. *Imperial Japan's Higher Civil Service Examinations.* Princeton: Princeton University Press, 1967. Annotated in item 52 above.

History of Japan's use of civil service examinations in prewar Japan.

538. Shimahara Nobuo K. "Socialization for College Entrance Examinations in Japan." *Comparative Education* 14 (October 1978):253–266.

Based on field research in Nagoya, this study discusses the pressures for shaping the socialization of Japanese adolescents and secondary schools to meet the requirements of entrance examinations.

539. Shimbori Michiya. "The Japanese Academic Profession." *Higher Education* 10 (January 1981):75–87.

Historical survey focusing on the link between the growth of nationalism and that of the university; the *gakubatsu* (academic cliques), creation of junior colleges, etc.

540. Tsuratani Taketsugu. "Underdevelopment of Social Science in Japan: Causes, Consequences and Remedies." *Social Science Quarterly* 66 (December 1985):805–819.

An interesting, personal view of the state of social science in contemporary Japan. One may not agree with the proposed remedies, but a clear understanding of the problem is presented.

541. Umakoshi Toru et al. "Prospects and Problems in Asian Higher Education: Introductory Presentation by the Secretariat." *Higher Education Expansion in Asia.* Hiroshima: Research Institute for Higher Education, 1985.

Introduction to problems in Asian higher education. See pp. 1–12.

542. Wheeler, Donald F. "Japan." In *Academic Power: Patterns of Authority in Seven National Systems of Higher Education,* pp. 124–144. Edited by John H. Van de Graaf et al. New York: Praeger, 1978.

Prepared for an interdisciplinary seminar at the Institution for Social and Policy Studies at Yale, Wheeler's chapter is one of several that review patterns of academic power in different nations. None of the chapters attempt to cover all aspects of higher education in the country under discussion, but they concentrate on the major institutional forms that carry higher education over time, and the systematic connections that link the forms into society.

543. ———. "The Structure of Academic Governance in Japan." New Haven: Yale University, Institute for Social and Policy Studies, Yale Higher Education Working Paper, August 1976.

Although the Japanese university has been gradually evolving from traditional patterns to more modern ones, the basic patterns of governance and control have changed little. Thus, the Ministry of Education has been forced to use incentives in an attempt to accomplish its reform aims, and it has established some new institutions which it hopes will have considerable influence on Japanese higher education.

HIGHER EDUCATION II

544. Abe Hakaru. "Education of the Legal Profession in Japan." In *Law in Japan: The Legal Order in a Changing Society*, pp. 153–187. Edited by A.T. Von Mehren. Cambridge, Mass.: Harvard University Press, 1963.

545. Altbach, Philip G. *Comparative Perspectives on the Academic Profession.* New York: Praeger Publishers, 1977.

Contains item 564.

546. ———. "Crisis in the Japanese University." *Economic and Political Weekly* (Bombay) 3 (1968):1807–1809.

547. Amagi Isao. "Access versus Admission." *Perspectives for the Future System of Higher Education*. Hiroshima University, Research Institute for Higher Education, 1977.

See pp. 40–47.

548. Amano Ikuo. "Continuity and Change in the Structure of Japanese Higher Education," In *Changes in the Japanese University: A Comparative Perspective* (item 497), pp. 10–39.

549. Aoki Hideo. "The Effect of American Ideas on Japanese Higher Education." Ph.D. dissertation, Stanford University, 1957.

550. Arima Tatsuo. *The Failure of Freedom: A Portrait of the Modern Japanese Intellectual.* Cambridge: Harvard University Press, 1969.

551. "Asahi Shimbun Public Opinion Surveys: Strife in the Universities," *Japan Quarterly* 16 (April–June 1969):157–169.

552. Ayusawa Shintaro. "Geography and Japanese Knowledge of World Geography." *Monumenta Nipponica* 19 (1964).

553. Beauchamp, Edward R. "Recent Trends in the Japanese Student Movement." *Midwest Quarterly* 8 (Spring 1971).

554. Bellah, Robert N. "Intellectual and Society in Japan." *Daedalus* (Spring 1972):89–116.

555. Birnbaum, Henry. "Japanese Educational Patterns in Science and Engineering." *Science* 181 (September 28, 1973):1222–1227.

556. Blewett, John, ed. *Higher Education in Postwar Japan: The Ministry of Education's 1964 White Paper.* Tokyo: Sophia University Press, 1965.

557. Boller, Paul F. "The American Board and the Doshisha, 1875–1900." Ph.D. dissertation, 1947.

558. Bowers, John Z. *Medical Education in Japan.* New York: Harper and Row, 1965.

559. Burnell, Jerrold B. "Public Funds for Private Education in Japan." *Intellect* 102 (April 1974):436–439.

560. Burnstein, Ira J. *The American Movement to Develop Protestant Colleges for Men, 1868–1912.* Ann Arbor: University of Michigan, School of Education, 1967.

561. ———. "Towards a Christian University in Japan." *Japan Christian Quarterly* 34 (Spring 1968):118–122.

562. Cummings, William K. "The Changing Academic Marketplace and University Reform in Japan." Ph.D. dissertation, Harvard University, 1972.

563. ———. "Understanding Behavior in Japan's Academic Marketplace." *Journal of Asian Studies* 34 (February 1975):313–340.

564. Cummings, William K., and Amano Ikuo. "The Changing Role of the Japanese Professor." *Higher Education* 6 (May 1971):209–23; reprinted in *Changes in the Japanese University: A Comparative Perspective* (item 497), pp. 127–148; also in *Comparative Perspectives on the Academic Profession* (item 545), pp. 43–67.

565. Dore, Ronald P. "The Future of Japan's Meritocracy." *Bulletin of the International House of Japan* 26 (October 1970): 30–50.

566. Dornan, Ivan F. "Sendai Student Center." *Japan Christian Quarterly* 46 (Winter 1980):34–39.

567. Dowsey, Stuart, ed. *Zengakuren: Japan's Revolutionary Students.* Berkeley: Ishi Press, 1970.

568. Driver, Christopher. "Japan: The Indefinitely Inflatable Campus." In *The Exploding University*. Edited by Christopher Driver. London: Hodder and Stoughton, 1971.
    See pp. 66–80.

569. Duke, Benjamin C. "The Radical Japanese Student Movement: From Poverty Through Affluence." *Malaysian Journal of Education* (Kuala Lumpur) 11 (1974):33–45.

570. Eto Jun. "The University: Myths and Possibilities." *Journal of Social and Political Ideas in Japan* 5 (December 1967):179–194.

571. Fendrich, James M., and Krauss, Ellis S. "Student Activism and Adult Left-Wing Politics: A Causal Model for Black, White and Japanese Students of the 1960's Generation." *Research in Social Movements, Conflicts and Change* 1 (1978): 231–255.

572. Frost, Peter K. "University Entrance Examinations in Post-War Japan." *The Fourth Kyushu International Culture Conference: Proceedings, Volume 1.* Fukuoka: Fukuoka UNESCO Association, 1977.

    See pp. 1–22.

573. Fukashiro Junio. "Student Thought and Feeling." *Japan Quarterly* 16 (April–June 1969):148–156.

574. Goodman, Grant. "Philippine–Japanese Professorial Exchange in the 1930's." *Journal of Southeast Asian History* 9 (September 1968):229–240.

575. Hiroshima University. *The Internationalization of Higher Education: A Final Summary Report.* Hiroshima: Hiroshima University, Research Institute for Higher Education, 1981.

576. ———. "Recommendations of the Ad Hoc Committee for the Study of Higher Education in Japan." In *Perspectives for the Future System of Higher Education*, pp. 100–103. Hiroshima: Hiroshima University, Research Institute for Higher Education, 1977.

577. Hoosoya Chihiro. "The University Problems in Japan with Special Reference to the Decision-Making Process." *Annual Review. Japan Institute of International Affairs* 5 (1969–1970):185–192.

578. Ichikawa Shogo. "Significance and Characteristics of Private Institutions." In *Systems of Higher Education: Japan.* Edited by K. Narita. New York: ICED, 1978.

579.   Ikado Fujio. "Curriculum Development at Tsukuba." In *Innovations in Higher Education* (item 510), pp. 74–86.

580.   Japan, Ministry of Education, Central Council on Education. "Coping with Student Disorder, Japan: I. Report by the Japanese Central Council on Education; II. Law No. 70 on Provisional Measures Concerning University Administration." *Minerva* 7 (January 1970):116–135.

581.   ———. *The Master Plan for the Reform of Higher Education (Interim Report).* Tokyo: Ministry of Education, 1971.

582.   Kambayashi Kikuko. "A Comparison between Junior Colleges and Special Training Colleges in Japan." *Higher Education* 10 (July 1981):473–486.

583.   Kaneko Motohisa. "The Role of Government in Japanese Higher Education." In *The Role of Government in Asian Higher Education Systems.* Hiroshima: Hiroshima Research Institute for Higher Education, 1988.

584.   Kasahara Yomishi. "'Graduation Phobia' in the Japanese University." In *Youth, Socialization and Mental Health.* Edited by William P. Lebra. Honolulu: University Press of Hawaii, 1974.

585.   Kato Hidetoshi. "Changing Images Among Youth in Modern Japan." In *Listening to Japan: A Japanese Anthology*, pp. 157–165. Edited by Jackson H. Bailey. New York: Praeger, 1973.

586.   Kato Tsuyoshi. "Generational Differences Values and Attitudes Between Japanese College Students and their Fathers." *Monumenta Nipponica* 26 (1971):415–429.

587.   Kim Hong N. "The Sato Government and the University Crisis, 1968–1969." *Asian Profile* 2 (June 1974).

588. ———. "Some Contemporary Issues with Japanese University System." *Journal of East Asiatic Studies* 7 (October 1966):1–6.

589. ———. "The Struggle for Control of the Japanese University." *Journal of Higher Education* 35 (January 1964):19–26.

590. Kobayashi M.J. "Counselor Education in the Counseling Institute of Sophia University, Tokyo." *International Journal for the Advancement of Counseling* 4 (1981): 45-49.

591. Kobayashi Tetsuya. "Changing Policies in Higher Education: the Japanese Case." *World Yearbook of Education 1971–1972.* London: Evans Brothers, 1971.

592 ———. *General Education for Scientists and Engineers in the United States of America and Japan.* Ann Arbor: University of Michigan, School of Education, 1965.

593. Kokusai Bunka Shinkokai. *Higher Education and the Student Problem in Japan.* Tokyo: Kokusai Bunka Shinkokai, 1972.

  See "Chronological Table of Events Related to Higher Education and Student Affairs, 1945–1972," pp. 247–269.

594. Kosaka Masaaki. "The University Problem: A University for the Elite or the Masses." *Education in Contemporary Japan.* Nishinomiya: International Institute for Japanese Studies, 1971.

595. Krauss, Ellis S. *Japanese Radicals Revisited: Student Protest in Postwar Japan.* Berkeley: University of California Press, 1974.

596. Kuwahara Toshikai. "Present Situation and Problems in Higher Education in Japan." *East-West Education* 7 (Spring 1986):15–28.

597. Lifton, Robert J. "Emergent Youth: The Japanese Example." *History and Human Survival.* New York: Vintage, 1971.

598. Long, T. Dixon. "Policy and Politics in Japanese Science."
      Minerva 7 (Spring 1969).

599. Mallea, John R. "The Public Purse and the Private Pocket: The
      Fiscal Crisis in Japanese Higher Education." *Canadian and
      International Education* 4 (June 1975):89–98.

600. Marshall, Byron K. "Radical Students and Militant Teachers: The
      Japanese Edition." *History of Education Quarterly* 17
      (Spring 1977):81–87.
      Essay review of Ellis S. Krauss, *Japanese Radicals Revisited*
      (item 595), Henry D. Smith, *Japan's First Student Radicals*
      (item 282), Benjamin C. Duke, *Japan's Militant Teachers* (item
      308), and Donald R. Thurston, *Teachers and Politics in Japan*.

601. McCormick, Gavan. "The Student Left in Japan." *New Left
      Review* 65 (January–February 1971):37–53.

602. McMahon, M.M. "Legal Education in Japan." *American Bar
      Association Journal* 60 (November 1974):1376–1386.

603. Mitsui Hisashi. "Doshisha and the Kumamoto Band." *Japan
      Christian Quarterly* 25 (April 1959).

604. Morton, Scott. "Japanese Universities and Students Today."
      Current History 75 (November 1978):174–178, 184–185.

605. Murata Suzuko. "Student Pressures in Japanese Education: The
      Problem of Entrance Examination Hell." *Viewpoints in
      Teaching and Learning* 55 (Fall 1979):41–48.

*   ———. "A Study of the Impact of the American Educational
      System on Higher Education in Japan." Ph.D. dissertation,
      Indiana University, 1969.

606. Nagai, Michio. "The Development of Intellectuals in the Meiji
      and Taisho Periods." *Journal of Social and Political Ideas in
      Japan* 2 (April 1964):28–32.

607. ———. "Higher Education in a Free Society Institutional Autonomy and Government Planning." *Japan Quarterly* 24 (July–September 1977):306–312.

608. ———. "Higher Education in Japan." In *Higher Education in Nine Countries*, pp. 227–267. Edited by Barbara Burn et al. New York: McGraw-Hill, 1971.

609. ———. *An Owl Before Dusk.* Berkeley: Carnegie Commission on Higher Education, 1975.
    See pp. 1–10.

610. ———. "The Role of the University in International Understanding." *In Comparative Approaches to Higher Education: Curriculum, Teaching and Innovations in an Age of Financial Difficulties* (item 508), pp. 3–11.

611. ———. "The University and the Intellectual." *Japan Quarterly* 12 (January–March 1965):46–52.

612. Nakano Hideichiro. "The Japanese University Professor Today." *Kwansei Gakuin University Alumni Studies* 23 (December 1974).

*   Nakayama Shigeru. "The Role Played by Universities in the Scientific and Technological Development of Japan." *Journal of World History* 9 (1965):340–362 (also listed in item 191).

613. Narita Katsuya et al. *Japanese Patterns of Institutional Management in Higher Education.* Hiroshima: Research Institute for Higher Education, 1974.

614. Nishimoto Mitoji. "Higher Education in the Age of Communication." *Educational Studies* (Tokyo) 15 (October 1971):149–167.

615. Ohkawa Masazo. "Government-Type and Market-Type Higher Education: A Comparative Survey of Financing Higher

Education in Soviet Union, Great Britain, the United States
and Japan." *Hitotsubashi Journal of Economics* 19
(December 1978):16–32.

616.   Okada Kunio. "Japanese Sociology: Past and Present." *Social
       Forces* 28 (May 1950): 400–409.

617.   Ono Tsutomu. "Student Protest in Japan: What It Means to
       Society." In *Listening to Japan: A Japanese Anthology*, pp.
       166-184. Edited by Jackson H. Bailey. New York: Praeger,
       1973.

*   Organization for Economic Cooperation and Development.
       Reviews of National Policies for Education: Japan. Paris:
       OECD, 1971. Annotated in item 405 above.
       See pp. 69–107 for higher education.

618.   Orihara Hiroshi. "'Test Hell' and Alienation: A Study of Tokyo
       University Freshmen." *Journal of Social and Political Ideas
       in Japan* 5 (1967):225–250.

619.   Owada Yosuyuki; Gleason, Alan H.; and Avery, Robert W.
       "Taishu Danko: Agency for Change, A Japanese
       University." In *Japanese Culture and Behavior*, pp. 443-449.
       Edited by Takie Lebra and William Lebra. Honolulu:
       University of Hawaii Press, 1974.

620.   Passin, Herbert. "Intellectuals in the Decision-Making Process."
       In *Modern Japanese Organization and Decision-Making*, pp.
       251–283. Edited by Ezra Vogel. Berkeley: University of
       California Press, 1975.

621.   ———. "Japan." In *Higher Education: From Autonomy to
       Systems*, pp. 219-227. Edited by James Perkins and Barbara
       Israel. New York: ICED, 1972.

*   ———. "Modernization and the Japanese Intellectual: Some
       Comparative Observations." In *Changing Japanese Attitudes*

Toward Modernization, pp. 447-487. Annotated in item 170 above.

622. Pempel, T. J. "Evaluating Japan's Mass Higher Education." *Japan Quarterly* 18 (October-December 1971):449-454.

623. ————, ed. *Policymaking in Contemporary Japan*. Ithaca: Cornell University Press, 1977.

624. ————. "The Politics of Enrollment Expansion in Japanese Universities." *Journal of Asian Studies* 33 (November 1973):67-86.

625. ————. "The Politics of Higher Education in Postwar Japan." Ph.D. dissertation, Columbia University, 1975.

626. Richards, James M. "Characteristics of U.S., Japanese and British Commonwealth Universities in Offering Education in Agriculture." *Research in Higher Education* 3 (June 1975):99-109.

627. Riggs, Lynne E. *"Ranjuku Jidai"* (The Idioms of Contemporary Japan). *Japan Interpreter* 11 (Spring 1977):541-549.

Good overview of crash schools for university entrance.

628. Rohlen, Thomas P. "The Juku Phenomenon: An Exploratory Essay." *The Journal of Japanese Studies* 6 (Summer 1980):207-242.

629. Sadlak, Jan. "Efficiency in Higher Education: Concepts and Problems." *Higher Education* 7 (May 1978):213-220.

630. Saito Shinroku. "Innovation in Japan's New Type Universities: The Experience of Three Universities." In *The Changing Functions of Higher Education: Implications for Innovation* (item 507), pp. 94-103.

631. Saito Taijun. "Universities and Non-University Higher Education in Japan." In *The Changing Functions of Higher Education: Implications for Innovation* (item 507), pp. 61–66.

632. Sakamoto Takashi. "The Current State and Problems of Teaching Methods at Universities and Colleges in Japan." In *Innovations in Higher Education* (item 509), pp. 87–109.

633. Seki Masao, Matsunaga Yuji, and Maruyama Fumihiro. "Curriculum and Teaching in Japanese Universities: A Report of RIHE National Surveys." In *The Changing Functions of Higher Education* (item 507), pp. 13–29.

634. Shikibu Hisashi. "Curriculum Reform in Hiroshima University: The Case of the Faculty of Integrated Arts and Sciences." In *Comparative Approaches to Higher Education* (item 508), pp. 33–41.

635. Shimahara Nobuo K. "The Puzzle of Higher Education in Japan: A Response." In *The Changing Functions of Higher Education: Implications for Innovation* (item 507), pp. 167–174.

636. ———. "Traditional Patterns of Adaptation and College Entrance Examinations." *Human Organization* 37 (Fall 1978):291–294.

637. Shimbori Michiya. "The Academic Marketplace in Japan. *Developing Economies* 7 (December 1969):617–636.

638. ———. "A Comparison Between Pre and Post-War Student Movements in Japan." *Sociology of Education* 37 (Fall 1963). Reprinted in *Selected Readings on Modern Japanese Society*, pp. 167–175. Edited by George K. Yamamoto and Tsuyoshi Ishida. Berkeley: McCutchan Publishing Company, 1971.

639. ———. "Crisis in the Japanese University." *Economic and Political Weekly* (Bombay) 3 (1968):1807–1809.

640. ———. "Educational Sociology or Sociology of Education." *International Review of Education* 18 (1972):3–12.

641. ———. "Graduate Schools in Japan: Growing Concerns for Graduate Education." *Education in Japan: A Journal for Overseas* (Hiroshima University) 2 (1967):65–74.

642. ——— "An Introduction to Japanese Higher Education." In *Higher Education and the Student Problem in Japan.* pp. 1–51. Edited by Kokusai Bunka Shinkokai. Tokyo: Kokusai Bunka Shinkokai, 1972.

643. ———. "The Productivity of the Japanese Scholar." In *Changes in the Japanese University: A Comparative Perspective* (item 497), pp. 149-165.

644. ———. "The Socialization of a Student Movement: A Japanese Case Study." *Daedalus* 97 (Winter 1968):204–228. Reprinted in *Learning to Be Japanese: Selected Readings on Japanese Society and Education* (item 22), pp. 289–315.

645. ———. "Sociology of Education." *International Review of Education* 25 (1979):393–423.

646. ———. "Strains in the Growing Structure." In *Perspectives for the Future System of Higher Education.* Hiroshima: Hiroshima University, Regional Institute for Higher Education, 1977.

647. ———. "Two Features of Japan's Higher Education Formal and Informal." *Japan Quarterly* 28 (1981):234–244.

648. ———. "Zengakuren: A Japanese Case Study of a Student Political Movement." *Sociology of Education* 37 (Spring 1964): 229–253.

649. Shimizu Y. "Trends in Educational Sociology in Japan." *International Review of Education* 18 (1972):113–117.

650.   Shukan Asahi editorial staff. "Generation Gap." *Japan Interpreter* 7 (Spring 1971): 150–158.

*   Smith, Henry D., II. *Japan's First Student Radicals*. Cambridge: Harvard University Press, 1972. Annotated in item 282 above.

651.   Steinhoff, Patricia G. "Student Conflict." In *Conflict in Japan*, pp. 174–213. Edited by Ellis S. Krauss, Thomas P. Rohlen, and Patricia G. Steinhoff. Honolulu: University of Hawaii Press, 1984.

652.   Takahashi Masao. "The Intellectual in Japan and America." *Japan Quarterly* 13 (1969):319–329.

653.   Takakura Sho. "Innovation of Higher Education in Japan. The Case of the University of Tsukuba." In *Comparative Approaches to Higher Education: Curriculum, Teaching and Innovations in an Age of Financial Difficulties* (item 508), pp. 100–109.

654.   Takane Masaaki. "Competition and Social Emphasis on Higher Education." *Japan Echo* 2 (1975):15–26.

655.   Tamura Shojiro and Matsushita Yasuo. "A Study of College Entrance Examinations Part V." *Research Bulletin of the National Institute for Educational Research* 12 (October 1973):3–11.

656.   Terasaki Masao. "Development of the Study on the History of Universities in Japan." *Japanese Studies in History and Science* (Tokyo) 15 (1976):15–19.

657.   Teichler, Ulrich. "Some Aspects of Higher Education in Japan." *Kokusai Bunka Shinkokai Bulletin* (July 1972).

658. Tominaga Ken'ichi. "The University in Contemporary Society: A View of the Education-Conscious Society." *Japan Echo* 5 (1978): 62–72.

659. Tomoda Yasumasa and Ehara Takekazu. "The Organization and Administration of Individual Universities." In *Changes in the Japanese University: A Comparative Perspective* (item 497), pp. 185–201.

660. Tsuru Shigeto. "Higher Education in Transition." *Perspectives for the Future System of Higher Education.* Hiroshima: Hiroshima University, Research Institute for Higher Education, 1977, pp. 18–26.

661. Tsurumi Kazuko. "The Japanese Student Movement: Value Politics, Student Politics, and the Tokyo University Struggle." Ph.D. dissertation, Columbia University, 1974.

662. ———. *Social Change and Individual: Japan Before and After Defeat in World War II.* Princeton: Princeton University Press, 1970.

    See Chapter 9, "The Student Movement: Its Milieu"; Chapter 10, "The Student Movement Group Portraits"; and Chapter 11, "The Student Movement: Individual Portraits."

663. ———. "Student Movements in 1960 and 1969: Continuity and Change." In *Postwar Trends in Japan: Studies in Commemoration of Rev. Aloysius Miller, S.J.*, pp. 195–227. Edited by Takayangai Shunichi and Miwa Kimitada. Tokyo: University of Tokyo Press, 1975.

664. Ushiogi Morikazu. "A Comparative Study of the Occupational Structure of University Graduates." *Developing Economies* 9 (September 1971):350–363.

665. ———. "Japanese Higher Education in an Age of Financial Difficulties." In *Comparative Approaches to Higher Education: Curriculum, Teaching and Innovations in an Age of Financial Difficulties* (item 508), pp. 195–206.

666. ———. "The Japanese Student and the Labor Market." In
      *Changes in the Japanese University: A Comparative
      Perspective* (item 497), pp. 107–126.

667. Wheeler, Donald F. "Japan's Post-Modern Student Movement."
      In *Changes in the Japanese University: A Comparative
      Perspective* (item 497), pp. 202–216.

CHAPTER X
TEACHER EDUCATION

Historical Context

The history of teacher education in Japan, in the professional sense of the term, dates to the early years of the Meiji Period (1868–1912). Prior to that time, it was assumed that occupations were hereditary and that parents would instruct their children at home, or make a variety of other arrangements for their education.

The recognition by the Meiji leaders that widespread formal educational opportunities would be necessary for the nation's development highlighted the need for a modern mechanism to train teachers. The Ministry of Education was given the authority to establish a school for this purpose, and in July 1872, began to recruit students for the new normal school. In order to enter the new teacher training program one had to be 20 years of age and pass an entrance examination. Successful candidates received a government subsidy and, in return, were obligated to teach in the new elementary schools upon graduation.

The Tokyo Normal School, Japan's first teacher education institution, opened its doors to 54 students in October 1872. The school's site was the building that once housed the *Shoheiko*, the Confucian academy supported for over 200 years by the recently overthrown Tokugawa government. Patterned after Western-style normal schools, it was headed by Morokuzu Nobuzumi (1849–1880). An American educator, Marion M. Scott (1843–1922), a former San Francisco primary school principal, served as the foreign instructor and wielded great influence. Scott, who had been teaching at another institution in Tokyo, "stressed a methodology of teaching that discarded the old individual tutoring-reciting methods. He was the first to introduce the Pestalozzian principles in Japan."[1] Scott not only introduced Western pedagogical theory in Japan, but also imported American-style textbooks, materials, and even school furniture, so that a typical Japanese elementary classroom was virtually identical with those found in such American cities as Boston, New York, or Philadelphia.

An attached elementary school where students could observe real classrooms, and put into practice the pedagogical principles they had been taught, was established at the new Tokyo Normal School the following year. This first teacher-education program was only of a year's duration, and the first class of ten young men graduated in 1873. They were used as teachers in the temporary teacher-training institutes providing short "crash" courses for even less qualified teachers in other parts of the country.

The Tokyo Normal School was charged with more than merely training teachers: "it also concerned itself with the formation of regulations for the course of study for elementary schools and the editing of textbooks."[2] Many of the early graduates of this institution received further education in the United States, while others became the educational leaders of the new public schools being set up throughout Japan.

At this time, the American influence on Japanese education was very strong. In the United States, the educational theories of the Swiss pedagogue, Johann Pestalozzi (1746–1827), were very popular. A hotbed of Pestalozzian thought was the Oswego (New York) Normal School, and the Japanese authorities "with characteristic determination to seize the newest ideas, dispatched three of their brightest young specialists to analyze these ideas firsthand."[3]

To encourage bright young men to become teachers, the government decided that all a candidate admitted to the normal school had to do in return was to agree to teach for several years upon graduation. By 1875 the first normal school for women was established in Ishikawa, and by 1877 there were 92 normal schools throughout the country.

By the turn of the century, the educational theories of the German educator, Johann Friedrich Herbart (1776–1841), became fashionable and played an important role in shaping the nature of Japanese secondary education. Both Pestalozzian and Herbartian ideas were reflected in teacher education. The latter were especially popular because of the emphasis on moral training and values congruent with traditional Confucian notions of sincerity, justice, integrity, etc.

In addition, as Japanese society became increasingly dominated by authoritarian and nationalistic elements, these social and political factors were reflected in the evolution of teacher education. Teachers were taught according to a uniform curriculum, approved by the Ministry of Education, that focused on moral education, military drill, and nationalism. Teachers in training were required to live in dormitories and accept military-like discipline. Upon graduation, the teachers "reimbursed" the government for their education with ten years of teaching service.

The end of World War II, however, marked a 180 degree reversal of Japanese educational practice. One of the earliest American actions was to commission a group of American educators, the First U.S. Education Mission in March 1946, to advise the Japanese on how to democratize their schools. The Mission's report concluded that even if the militarists had not controlled the educational system in the 1930s, revision of that system was long overdue "in accordance with the modern theory of education." In brief, teacher education was badly outdated. As a result of American-inspired reforms, normal schools were absorbed into universities in the form of education faculties.

Teacher Education Since World War II

One of the first acts of the American Occupation authorities was to purge all teachers who actively supported the ultra-nationalistic policies of the prewar and wartime Japanese government. This was a key element in the reformation of teacher education. Japanese teachers were expected to introduce democratic practices in the nation's schools, as well as demonstrating positive democratic behavior to their young charges. In order for this plan to have any prospect for success, it was imperative that the prewar teachers be given as much assistance as possible. With this in mind, in 1947, the Americans introduced a series of seminars, workshops, and short radio courses to re-educate teachers in democratic concepts and methods. Each teacher was required to attend an approved in-service retraining course of some type in order to receive certification to teach.

In 1948, the American authorities introduced an Institute for Educational Leadership (IFEL) Program, staffed by a wide variety of

Japanese specialists and a number of American experts imported to broaden the perspectives of Japanese teachers. The IFEL program continued beyond the end of the Occupation period, and played an important role in changing teacher attitudes and introducing new approaches.

In contrast to the prewar normal school, where teachers were taught, in a quasi-military atmosphere, exactly what to teach and how to teach it, during the Occupation, teacher education was redesigned so that professional preparation was provided at universities. In 1949, the new National School Establishment Law consolidated 249 institutions of higher education into 68 national universities, each of which contained a faculty of education. At the same time, private universities were encouraged to establish teacher education programs within their institutions. A Law for the Certification of Educational Personnel was also passed in 1949. Its purpose was to improve the quality of teaching at the elementary and secondary level. This new system, often called an "open system" by the Japanese, consisted of general education, specialized knowledge of one's teaching field, and professional education.

Critics of "open education," however, question the adequacy of the *professional* training received by teacher education majors. In 1958, for example, the important Central Council on Education (CCE) concluded that certification standards were no longer adequate, and blamed this situation on the American-imposed Occupation reforms. Discussion of the problem continued but, for a variety of reasons, little was done to significantly alter the system.

Beginning in the 1970s an increasing number of college and university students, in order to expand their post-graduation options, took the minimum professional preparation needed to secure teaching certificates. This resulted in a bulge in the number of student teachers, and it was not uncommon for some classroom teachers to supervise three or more of them simultaneously. Thus, the pool of available teachers soon far outstripped openings and a large class of "paper teachers" was created.

In 1971 the Central Council on Education reiterated its earlier concerns and identified teacher education as seriously in need of reform. One of its key recommendations, significantly higher salaries for teachers, became law in 1974 with the passage of the Human Resource Procurement Bill. A few years later, in 1978, another CCE report emerged urging still further teacher education reform. Other agencies have made numerous reforms of a similar nature over the past three decades, but it wasn't until the formation of the Provisional Council on Educational Reform (*Rinkyoshin*), in 1984, that public support for further reform appeared possible.

Teachers and Teacher Education Today

On 17 June 1978, the Diet passed legislation authorizing the establishment of two new institutions of teacher education: Joetsu University of Teacher Education (Niigata prefecture) and Hyogo University of Teacher Education (Hyogo prefecture). The rationale for this action was, in the words of the legislation, "to cope with the social demand for upgrading the quality and ability of teachers for elementary education," and to "encourage practically useful research on school education."[4] Offering both undergraduate and graduate education, the former trains elementary school teachers while the latter is designed to serve as "a university for practicing teachers to enable them to pursue creative research in school education both in theory and practice, and as a center to enhance school education."[5] Approximately two-thirds of the graduate students admitted are practicing teachers with three years of experience.

Earlier reference was made to the emergence of so-called "paper teachers" during the 1970s. By the early 1980s, the Ministry of Education was determined to eliminate as many of these as possible in order to upgrade the quality of those who were teaching. Thus, in 1984, a proposal to reform the 1949 Certification Law was put forward in the Diet. Among its most important provisions was the establishment of a differentiated system of teaching certificates so that one could secure a higher-ranking certificate by taking graduate level courses, etc. Another reform proposal was to increase the number of professional courses required of teachers. This bill was unsuccessful, but it did serve to engender a great deal of discussion and controversy.

In order to teach in Japan, it is still necessary to possess a license to teach at various levels, i.e., elementary, lower secondary, or upper secondary. There are two basic types of licenses at each level, the regular teaching certificate and a temporary teaching certificate. The former is held by those who meet the established criteria and is valid throughout Japan for life. The temporary certificate, however, is good for only three years, and only in the prefecture in which it is granted.

This certificate is used as a short term solution to a particular problem. In addition, there are special certificates for "nursing teachers," special education teachers, etc. As in the case of other teaching certificates, one must attend an approved institution of higher education and earn the number of credits, the amount and content of which are determined by the Educational Personnel Qualification Law.

In any discussion of teachers and teacher education in Japan, two important points have to be borne in mind. Teaching is a respected profession, not easy to enter (only about half who apply are accepted), and teacher compensation is reasonably attractive. For example, persons entering either teaching or an entry level position in a large trading company will begin their careers at approximately the same salary. Although it is true that the business executive will later earn substantially more than a teacher, the teacher's salary is never likely to fall below that of the average salary for a college-educated person.

Nobuo Shimahara writes that, "the total number of applicants who actually took appointment examinations nearly doubled, from 128,000 in 1974 to 245,000 in 1979, although the number of positions increased only 13.5 percent. The competition has declined slightly since 1979, but the prefectural boards of education still enjoy a fivefold oversupply of teacher applicants. . . ." [6]

Two other factors help screen applicants to the teaching profession. First is the competitive appointment examination that is held annually in all 47 prefectures and the 10 largest cities. Even though one has graduated from an appropriate institution with a teaching certificate, and no matter how good one's performance has been, the appointment examination must be passed. Once entry is gained, however, the fledgling teacher can look forward to lifetime employment and regular promotions based on seniority. The second screening variable is that, like most large private-sector corporations, more than half of the 47 prefectures favor recruiting new university graduates exclusively. As a result, they require that applicants be under age 30.

The appointment examination consists of two parts. The first is comprised of written tests of one's general education and knowledge of specialized fields, plus skill tests in appropriate areas, such as physical education, music, foreign language ability, etc. The second portion consists of intensive interviews. In addition, a physical examination may be required and, if one applies to a locality with a large number of *burakumin, dowa* ("assimilation") education may be part of the test (see Chapter XI, "Education of Minorities").

Since World War II, in-service teacher training has been recognized as a key element in maintaining a well-qualified teaching corps. In-service training can be divided into three basic categories. The first, and perhaps most important, consists of out-of-school training in which teachers participate in research projects, study groups and lectures under the auspices of the Ministry of Education, prefectural or local school boards, teacher centers, universities, the Japan Teachers Union (*Nikkyoso*) or a wide range of educational research organizations. School-based training is most often carried out by visiting specialists and, as its title suggests, is carried out in the school environment. Finally, there is teacher self-study which is usually taken quite seriously. The Ministry of Education encourages this approach and has, since 1959, subsidized the overseas travel of almost 5,000 teachers per year.[7]

Current Reform Discussions

The Ad Hoc Council on Educational Reform, created in 1984, issued three reports. The first was issued on 26 June 1985, and listed the "Improvement of the Quality of Teachers" as one of the eight major issues to be considered by the Council. After recognizing that teachers will, of necessity, play a key role in any improvement in the educational system, the Council pledged that it would seek "overall strategies for improving the quality of teachers."[8]

The *Second Report on Educational Reform* was made public on 23 April 1986.[9] A major section of this report was devoted to the topic of the "Improvement of the Quality of Teachers." Among the most important recommendations put forth by the Council, was the immediate review of the teacher training and certification systems. Among the specific proposals was one urging that the current teacher education structure be revised, to prepare teachers "better able to cope with the recent changes in the mental and physical condition of school children."[10]

A common theme running through a number of other recommendations was the need to exhibit greater flexibility. For example, universities should provide half-year or full-year special teacher-training courses for students and adults who have not specialized in education, but who wish to teach. Another proposal of this type was for the creation of a special teacher certificate for people with special knowledge or skills as well as allowing part-time lecturers possessing special knowledge to teach without a certificate. In addition, the Council argued for a carefully planned articulation of those skills "which are expected to be obtained by prospective teachers through preservice [sic] teacher training . . . and those which are expected to be obtained . . . through in-service training"[11] at various stages of one's teaching career.

The Council also opted for new ways of recruiting potential students in order to ensure a broader pool from which to select new teachers. "The methods for selecting new teachers should be diversified to include interviews, essays, practical skills tests, physical fitness tests, aptitude tests. . . . Applicants' record of club activities and social service activities should also be emphasized."[12]

In addition, the Council resurrected a proposal that has been made several times since the end of World War II, i.e., "All beginning teachers should be required to undergo one year of training immediately after their employment under the guidance of supervising teachers."[13] These supervising teachers, it is pointed out, should be part of an ongoing system of in-service teacher education, including "long-term training at regular intervals throughout their career."[14] Whether this idea can be implemented in the face of political and financial constraints is open to question.

On 1 April 1987, the third and final report was released to the public.[15] This report treats "those important issues which were not adequately dealt with in the (two) preceding reports. Such issues include those relating to: a lifelong learning system; reforms in elementary and secondary education; reforms in the organization and management of institutions of higher education; sports and education; and educational costs and financing."[16] Although there are no specific proposals *directly* relating to teacher education in the final report, many of them have ramifications which the Council appears to have ignored.

For example, much is made of the need for Japan to be become an "internationalized" society, and the key role that education must play if that goal is to be achieved. Yet the Ad Hoc Reform Council appears to have been little concerned with the need for teachers to be "internationalized" if they are going to produce "internationalized" citizens. There are a number of similar examples that could be cited, but this one is sufficient to make the point that even in the highly unlikely event that these reports, indeed, do serve as a model for widespread changes in the system, they provide a piecemeal, rather than a comprehensive plan for reform.

NOTES

1. Ronald S. Anderson, *Education in Japan: A Century of Modern Development* (Washington, D.C.: U.S. Government Printing Office, 1975), p. 25.

2. Japan, Ministry of Education, *Japan's Modern Educational System: A History of the First Hundred Years* (Tokyo: Ministry of Education, 1980), pp. 68–69.

3. Anderson, p. 25.

4. Japan, National Institute for Educational Research, *The New Teachers' Training Programme at Hyogo University of Teacher Education* (Tokyo: NIER, 1982), p. 1.

5. Association of International Education, Japan. *Japanese Colleges and Universities, 1987: A Guide to Institutions of Higher Education in Japan* (Tokyo: Maruzen Co., Ltd. 1987), p. 37.

6. Nobuo Shimahara, "The Teaching Profession," (Unpublished Manuscript, 1987), p. 12.

7. For details, see National Institute for Educational Research. *In-Service Training for Teachers in Japan* (Tokyo: NIER, 1985).

8. Provisional Council on Educational Reform. *First Report on Educational Reform* (Tokyo: Government of Japan, June 26, 1985), p. 40.

9. National [Provisional] Council on Educational Reform. *Second Report on Educational Reform* (Tokyo: Government of Japan, April 23, 1986).

10. Ibid., p. 92.

11. Ibid., p. 93.

12. Ibid., p. 98.

13. Ibid., p. 99.

14. Ibid., p. 103.

15. National [Provisional] Council on Educational Reform. *Third Report on Educational Reform* (Tokyo: Government of Japan, April 1, 1987). Page numbers in following material refer to this report.

16. Ibid., p. 1.

TEACHER EDUCATION I

668. Amatsuchi H. *Development of Teacher Training in Japan.* Tokyo: Central Institute of Education, 1967.

   A brief, but useful historical survey of teacher training in modern Japan.

669. Azuma Hiroshi. *Innovation in In-Service Education and the Training of Teachers: Japan.* Paris: OECD, CERI, 1976.

   Concludes that Japan's system of in-service education for teachers is varied, versatile, and all-pervasive.

670. Bartz, Alice. "The Teacher Center and Staff Development." *Drexel Library Quarterly* 14 (July 1978):106–112.

   Defines the concept of a teacher center and traces its development in Japan, England, and the United States.

671. Buxton, Amity P. "Teacher Centers in Japan." *Educational Leadership* 34 (1976):183–189.

   Describes the purpose, scope and activities of teacher centers in Japan using British and American centers as a frame of reference.

672. Cole, Allan B., et al. *Socialist Parties in Postwar Japan.* New Haven: Yale University Press, 1966.

See chapter 2, "Teachers, Police and Foreign Affairs," pp. 65–69.

673. Collins, Kevin A. "Teacher Education in the Ryukyu Islands." Ph.D. dissertation, Michigan State University, 1973.

Probably the only English-language study of the subject. Collins examines both American and Japanese influences on the development of teacher education in Okinawa and evaluates their impact.

674. Dorfman, Cynthia Hearn, ed. *Japanese Education Today: A Report From the U.S. Study of Education in Japan.* Washington, D.C.: U.S Government Printing Office, January 1987.

Up-to-date discussion of Japanese teacher education in the context of the current situation of Japanese teachers.

675. Fukuda Shohachi. "The Four-Year Teacher-Training Project: Its Operation and Achievements." *Tesol Quarterly* 9 (March 1975):15–22.

Detailed description of an intensive training course for teachers of English in Kumamoto Prefecture.

*   Griffith, Harry E. "Japanese Normal School Education." Ed.D. dissertation, Stanford University, 1950. Also listed in item 357 above.

An old but still valuable study, especially on Japanese normal schools between early Meiji and the end of World War II.

676. Inoue Hisao. "The Historical Background and Reforms of Teacher Training." *Education in Japan: A Journal for Overseas* (Hiroshima University) 8 (1975): 69–83.

Description of five major educational societies: The Japanese Society for the Study of Education, the Society for the Philosophy of Education, the Society for Historical Research of Education, Japan Society for the Study of Educational Sociology, The John Dewey Society.

677. Japan, National Institute for Educational Research. *In-Service Training for Teachers in Japan.* Tokyo: NIER Occasional paper (2/85) June, 1985.

After providing the legal framework for in-service teacher education, this report analyzes the roles of the Ministry of Education, and both local and prefectural boards of education vis-a-vis in-service education. Concludes with a description of existing in-service programs for teachers.

678. Japan Teachers' Union. Council on Educational Reform. "What Japan's Education Should Be." In *How to Reform Japan's Education.* Tokyo: Japan Teachers' Union, 1975. Partially reprinted in *Learning to be Japanese; Selected Readings on Japanese Society and Education* (item 22), pp. 349–371.

View of the Japan Teachers' Union on how best to reform teacher education.

679. Kamidera Hisao. "The New Teachers' Training Programme at Hyogo University of Teacher Education." *NIER Occasional Paper* (3/82). Tokyo: National Institute for Educational Research, June 1982.

Includes discussion of the social background for establishing Hyogo University of Teacher Education, the significance of in-service training, the characteristics of the Hyogo University of Teacher Education and concludes with a discussion of its promising potential.

680. Karasawa Tomitaro. "History of Japanese Teachers." *Pedagogical Historica* 6 (1966):300–415.

Survey of the subject by Japan's best known specialist on the history of teachers.

681. Kumura Toshio. *The Development of Modern Education and Teachers Training in Japan.* Tokyo: Japanese National Commission for UNESCO, 1961.

Reprinted and distributed by the Ministry of Education, in 1961, shortly after its publication. An historical survey from the Meiji Restoration through the prewar period, concluding with the situation following the American Occupation and Japan's "reverse course."

682. Miyoshi Nobuhiro. "Controversial Problems of Teacher Education in Japan From a Comparative Viewpoint." *Education in Japan: A Journal for Overseas* (Hiroshima University) 9 (1979):27–41.

Reflects major debates over teacher education that were raging in the 1970s.

683. Morimoto Takiko. "Contrasting Attitudes of Japanese and American Teachers." *Educational Leadership* 39 (March 1982):414.

Reports the results of a 1980 teacher survey in Los Angeles and Tokyo. Concludes that while Japanese teachers identify with their schools and are committed to service, American teachers are more independent and view teaching as a job.

684. ———. "Teachers' Perceptions of Their Roles in Japan and the United States." Ed.D. dissertation. University of California, Los Angeles, 1981.

Comparative study which throws light on some fundamental differences between attitudes of Japanese and American teachers.

685. Morito Tatsuo. "What Constitutes a Good Teacher?" *Journal of Social and Political Ideas in Japan* 1 (1963):95–98.

One view of the characteristics found in good teachers.

686. Pires, Edward A. *Student Teaching Practices in Primary Teacher Training Institutions in Asia.* Bangkok: UNESCO Regional Office for Education in Asia, 1967.

Contains material on Japanese situation in first half of 1960s.

687. Takakura Sho. "Innovative Trends in Teacher Training and Retraining in Japan." *New Patterns of Teacher Education in Canada and Japan.* Paris: OECD, 1975.

Somewhat dated but much material still valuable. Several of his recommendations have been adopted and others anticipated the reports of the Ad Hoc Council on Educational Reform (1983–1987). See pp. 51–88.

688. "Teachers, Children and School." *Outlook* 18 (1975):9–17.

Describes the individual problems and frustrations encountered by three Japanese teachers working within a rigid school system.

689. UNESCO. *New Techniques for Preparing Educational Personnel; Universalizing Education: Selected Innovative Experiences.* New York: UNIPUBS, 1980. Reprinted from "New Techniques for Preparing Educational Personnel; Universalizing Education: Selected Innovative Experiences." Bangkok: UNESCO Regional Office for Education in Asia and Oceania, 1980.

24 Asian case studies that include material on Japan.

690. ———. "Japan." In *Teacher Education in Asia: A Regional Survey.* Bangkok: UNESCO Regional Office for Education in Asia, 1972.

Useful comparative survey of teacher education in Asia. The material on Japan illustrates major differences between Japanese teacher education and other Asian nations. See pp. 143–153.

691. Yuasa Katsumi. "Teacher Training and Its Problems in Japan. *International Review of Education* 4 (1968):479–488.

Description of late-1960s problems; anticipates recommendations of the Ad Hoc Council on Educational Reform (1983–1987).

TEACHER EDUCATION II

692. Asahi Journal Editorial Staff. "The Altered Image of Teachers." *Journal of Social and Political Ideas in Japan* 1 (1963):106–112.

693. Brinkman, Albert R. "Teacher Status in Japan's Schools." *Harvard Educational Review* 24 (1954):176–187.

694. Duke, Benjamin C. "The Japanese Teacher: A Lifetime of Controversy." *Indian Journal of Social Research* (December 1966).

695. Hamada Shunkichi. "Teacher Education Curriculum." *The Educational Sciences* 7 (December 1967):13–22.

696. Igarashi Jiro and Kosuke Tsuneyoshi. "A Description of Professional Education Societies in Japan." *Education in Japan: A Journal for Overseas* (Hiroshima University) 1 (1966):109–121.

697. Japan, Ministry of Education. "How Can Teacher Certificates Be Obtained? How Is the In-Service Training of Teachers Conducted?" In *Education in Japan*. Tokyo: Ministry of Education, 1971.

    See pp. 80–81 and 88–89.

698. ———. "Teacher Training and In-Service Training." In *Educational Standards in Japan*. Tokyo: Ministry of Education, 1971.

    See pp. 113–119.

699. ———. *Training of Science Teachers in Japan: Present and Future*. Tokyo: Ministry of Education, 1970.

700. Japanese National Commission for UNESCO. *Training of Science Teachers in Japan: Present and Future*. Tokyo: Japanese National Commission for UNESCO, 1970.

701. Kakkar, S.B., and Gordon, Leonhard V. "A Cross-Cultural Study of Teacher's Values." *Education and Psychology Review* 6 (1966):172–177.

702. Karasawa Tomitaro. "A New Image for the Teachers in Japan." *Journal of Social and Political Ideas in Japan* 2 (1964):69–72.

703. Kataoka Tokuo. "On the Morals of Teachers in Relation to School Management." *Research Bulletin of the National Institute for Educational Research* 10 (March 1971):1–8.

704. Kawaguchi Tadasu. "Training of Mathematics Teachers." In *Training of Science Teachers in Japan.* Japan: Japanese National Commission for UNESCO, 1970.

     See pp. 53–71.

705. Kobayashi Tetsuya. "Comparative Perspective on Teacher Training, Illustrated by Japan and England." *Yearbook of Education*, London, 1963.

*   ———. *General Education for Scientists and Engineers in the United States of America and Japan.* Also listed in item 592 above.

706. Kumura Toshio and Iwahashi Bunkichi. "Development of the Teacher Training System in Japan." *Education in Japan; A Journal for Overseas* (Hiroshima University) 2 (1967):75–89.

707. Maezima Yasuo. "A Study on the Curriculum of Teacher Education." *Bulletin of the Faculty of Education of the University of Tokyo* 17 (1977):233–253.

708. Morris, Ben. "Japan." In *Some Aspects of Professional Freedom of Teachers; An International Pilot Inquiry.* Paris: UNESCO, 1977.

     See pp. 33–57.

709. Nagai Michio. "What Should be Done About Teachers?" *Journal of Social and Political Ideas in Japan* 1 (1963):99–102.

710. Nakahara Hideo, and Takahashi Genji. "Japan." [Theme Issue on "Status and Position of Teachers"]. *Yearbook on Education.* London: Evans, 1953.

711. Organization for Economic Co-Operation and Development. *Training, Recruitment and Utilization of Teachers:*

Statistical Data, Primary and Secondary Education. Paris: OECD, 1971.

See pp. 51–61.

712. "Re-Examination of the Present System of Teacher Training and Teacher Wages." *Japan Labor Bulletin* 9 (August 1970):2.

713. Sunazawa Kyoji. "Some Points of View on Teaching." *Education in Japan: A Journal for Overseas* (Hiroshima University) 3 (1968):91–97.

714. Takemori Shigekazu. "Training of Science Teachers at the Elementary School Level." In *Training Science Teachers in Japan.* Tokyo: Japanese National Commission for UNESCO, 1970.

See pp. 72–85.

715. Tsuji Shinkichi. "A Study of Teacher Education." *Research Bulletin of the National Institute for Educational Research* 2 (1961):33–40.

716. Tsuji Shinkichi and Ushiogi Morikazu. "Parents' Interest in Education." *Research Bulletin of the National Institute for Educational Research* 5 (1964):25–34.

717. Waki T. "Some Basic Educational Problems in the Teacher-Training Course in a Japanese University Case for Chemistry." *Abstracts of Papers of the American Chemical Society*, April 1979.

718. Yaguchi Hajime. "Character Building and the Role of Teachers." *Journal of Political and Social Ideas in Japan* 2 (1964):73–75.

CHAPTER XI
EDUCATION OF MINORITIES

Compared to most other nations, the number of minority peoples living within Japanese territory is very small; but close analysis suggests that they are not inconsequential to the body politic. For example, in 1980, there were 663,631 Korean residents in Japan. This relative handful of people represents only 0.5% of Japan's total population, but amounts to 86% of all foreign residents in Japan. In addition, Koreans are concentrated in the largest industrial cities, with 186,000 in Osaka alone. The Japanese view of minorities—indeed, of non-Japanese in general—has too often been characterized by insensitivity. One need only recall Prime Minister Nakasone's undiplomatic comment in 1986, about American Blacks and Hispanics lowering the intellectual level of the United States.

In the view of many observers, the Japanese sense of their own uniqueness leads to their being both fascinated by foreigners and repelled by their foreignness. Thus, it is not possible for non-Japanese, no matter how long they have lived in Japan, or how well they speak Japanese or understand Japanese culture, to become "Japanese." Immigration and naturalization are not common in Japan, and a non-Japanese seeking Japanese citizenship embarks on an extremely difficult, time-consuming, and problematic quest.

Many Japanese whose job takes them (and their families) abroad are at a disadvantage when they return home. They have, in the eyes of many of their countrymen, become vaguely foreign or "international" and therefore, no longer "really Japanese." Over the past decade or so, the Ministry of Education has increased its efforts to deal with the problems of the children of these returning Japanese, by establishing several special schools designed to reintegrate them back into Japanese society. If returning Japanese are viewed with this kind of suspicion, one can understand the dimensions of the problems facing non-Japanese minorities living in Japan.

The most important minority groups living in contemporary Japan are *burakumin*, Koreans, and Ainu. The *burakumin*, descended from the outcasts of Tokugawa Japan (1603–1868), are racially and legally Japanese. Once referred to as *eta*, a highly derogatory term suggesting pollution, their status can be traced to their forebears' occupations as butchers and leather tanners, reflecting the Buddhist prohibition against the killing of animals and Shinto ideas of cleanliness. During the premodern era, *burakumin* were required to live in ghetto-like hamlets, resulting in the term *buraku* (hamlet) + *min* (people). They are heavily concentrated in Western Japan, with more than half residing in the Kinki and Chugoku regions, especially in Osaka, Kyoto, and Kobe.

Legally emancipated in 1871, the *burakumin* made no significant educational gains until their agitation for governmental action succeeded in 1969. At that time, inspired by the efforts of the American Civil Rights Movement, the Buraku Liberation Front (BLF) led a protest movement that was instrumental in the passage of the Law of Special Actions for Dowa (assimilation) Policy which, for the first time, provided a legal framework for actions promoting the welfare of the *burakumin*. Although containing no specific educational provisions, it required that both national and local officials identify *burakumin* educational problems and take the necessary steps to solve them. In the same year the government announced a Long-Term Dowa Policy Program effective to March 1979, and later extended it to March 1982. Upon expiration, this law was replaced, only after much debate, with the compromise Area Improvement Measures Law, valid for five years.

The results of these actions have been mixed. On the one hand, whereas only about 30% of *burakumin* children attended senior high school in 1963 (compared to 64% of non-*burakumin* children), studies by Professor Nobuo Shimahara of Rutgers University (see items 763, 764 below) conclude that the situation has significantly improved. The current national high school enrollment is about 95% and the difference in high school enrollment between the eligible minority and majority populations has narrowed to less than 10 percentage points. Important gains have also been made by *burakumin* at the college level, although significant discrimination remains.

Burakumin families, including the children, often tend to exhibit severe identity problems, making a great effort to "pass" as non-*buraku* Japanese as a way of coping with discrimination. This is especially difficult in a society in which the employment of private investigators by potential employers and even spouses is considered a normal precaution.

Japanese public opinion is mixed on the *burakumin* issue. Some recognize the need for social justice, others see such demands as a sign of deleterious social change, and the majority are apathetic because it does not have direct impact on their day-to-day lives. The *burakumin* and their supporters have tried mightily to educate the broader public to the problem, but their success has been limited so far. For example, the director of the Justice Bureau was quoted, in 1982, as telling a group of local government officials that "The rather unsavory parallel has been drawn . . . that public servants are as much a fact of life as the *tokushu buraku*. But public servants are, after all, just human beings." It is attitudes of this sort, not only among government officials who should know better, that need to be changed if *burakumin* are to overcome their historic disability.

Another group that has traditionally faced discrimination is Japan's approximately 700,000 Koreans, many of whom have been born and raised in Japan. Although the barriers existing within the school system are not as great as when Koreans seek employment in the Japanese labor market, it is widely recognized that a Korean problem exists in the school system. There have even been some efforts, in cities with large Korean populations, to inject into the public schools what Americans would call "ethnic studies" for Korean youngsters.

Although Japanese education is highly centralized, especially by American standards, it would be wrong to assume that there is no differentiation among schools. Not all Japanese school boards are identical. For example, Kobe, a city with historic foreign ties and currently controlled by political progressives, has confronted its discrimination problem. The school board has published various anti-discrimination materials for use in both junior and senior high schools in an attempt to deal with discriminatory attitudes toward both *burakumin* and Koreans. Although not entirely successful because many teachers feel uncomfortable discussing such issues, this is an approach that may lend itself to long-term improvements in the situation.

On the other hand, as in the case of the *burakumin*, anti-Korean prejudice is often deep-seated. Some Japanese parents will go to the extremes of changing their residence, or sending their children to private schools in order to avoid having their children attend the same school as Korean youngsters. The irony is that these young Koreans have usually been born in Japan, speak Japanese as their native tongue, and have taken on Japanese cultural patterns. Many have even gone to the extreme of hiding their Korean roots by using a Japanese name. Some Koreans, however, remain wedded to their Korean heritage. In September 1983 there was a heated public controversy over an alleged attempt of school officials in Nagoya to pressure Korean parents into enrolling their son under a Japanese name. The school officials claim that they "suggested" this to the parents for educational reasons, that is, the child was apt to be teased by his classmates because of his "strange" name. Korean organizations and other opponents of discrimination refused to accept this explanation and suggested that it was reminiscent of the Japanese occupation of Korea, when all Koreans were forced to take Japanese names and students were physically punished if caught using Korean with their friends.

Koreans do, however, have the option of sending their children to one of two sets of Korean schools in Japan, one subsidized by the government of South Korea and the other by North Korea. The major problem with attending a Korean school, however, is that graduates are not allowed to take the entrance examination for national or public colleges and universities. This is a major disadvantage in a society in which the most prestigious institutions of higher education are the national universities. This is a contributing cause to the fact that Koreans in Japan have statistically half the average chance of going to a university. Despite this, however, that there is little evidence that this difference in outcome stems primarily from discrimination in the educational and matriculation process itself. This is, however, scant comfort for Japanese educators because the Korean minority does have legitimate grievances which, if not satisfied, contain the potential for serious social discontent.

Because of their aboriginal status, the Ainu are a relatively small but powerful symbol of Japanese discrimination. Accurate figures on the Ainu population are difficult to find, but it is clear that their culture and language are virtually extinct. The few thousand part-Ainu, and far fewer "pure" Ainu still in existence are concentrated on the northern

island, Hokkaido. The Ainu level of educational attainment
significantly trails the general population, and they are often found
selling Ainu arts, crafts and trinkets to tourists in so-called centers of
Ainu culture. In this respect they resemble American Indians in the
Southwest.

In addition to these minorities, Japan is also home to significant
groups of people who physically appear to be Japanese, but are usually
viewed as "different" by most other Japanese. These include more than a
million Okinawans. Finally, there are smaller numbers of Chinese,
konketsujin (offspring of inter-racial parents), Southeast Asian "enter-
tainers" (often bar girls), and a variety of resident foreigners (including
several thousand Americans and Europeans) comprising the nation's
non-Japanese population. Among the special rules governing resident
aliens that has caused a great deal of international controversy in recent
years, is the requirement that these people periodically report to a
government office to be fingerprinted.

Thus, although Japanese claims of racial homogeneity are
understandable in comparative terms, it is important to recognize that
there exist pockets of minorities who are often discriminated against and
whose educational opportunities are circumscribed by the fact of their
minority status.

MINORITY EDUCATION I

The vast majority of Japanese—officials, educators and ordinary
citizens—tend to believe that Japan's society is so homogeneous that
minority problems do not exist or, if they do, they are so few as to lack
importance. As a result, most Japanese scholars avoid writing about
Japan's minorities. Only those Western scholars with a good linguistic
foundation are able to either conduct field work, or even become
familiar with the basic works that are available in Japanese. As a result,
those seeking reliable English-language materials on Japan's minority
groups will not find them in great abundance. A handful of American
scholars (De Vos, Wagatsuma, Rohlen, Shimahara, etc.) remain abreast
of developments in this field.

Those Westerners possessing both an interest and the necessary
linguistic tools, along with a handful of Japanese who write in English,
have produced a literature that is uneven in scope and quality. Much of
the available literature in English is influenced by questions emerging
from the American minority experience. For graduate students and

experienced researchers alike, the field is wide open with all kinds of possible studies waiting to be researched.

719. Brameld, Theodore. *Japan: Culture, Education, and Change in Two Communities.* New York: Holt, Rinehart and Winston, 1968.

Field study conducted by a well-known American anthropologist of education, assisted by extremely capable Japanese research associates. Focuses on two communities, one a fishing village and the other a community of *burakumin.*

720. *Buraku Liberation News.* Published bi-monthly by the Buraku Liberation Research Institute, 1-6-12, Kuboyoshi, Naniwa-ku, Osaka-shi 556, Japan.

Good source of information on *buraku* problems from the *buraku* perspective.

721. Buraku Liberation Research Institute. *Long-Suffering Brothers and Sisters, Unite! The Buraku Problem, Universal Human Rights and Minority Problems in Various Countries.* Osaka: Buraku Liberation Research Institute, 1981.

Consists of papers presented at the December 1980 International Symposium on Human Rights, the first two of the three sections into which the book is divided focus on the Japanese situation. The first part is devoted to "The Present Condition of the Buraku Problem in Japan," and the second to "The Buraku Problem as Viewed from Foreign Countries."

722. ———. *Reality of Buraku Discrimination in Japan: Support Us for the Enactment of the Fundamental Law for Buraku Liberation.* Osaka: Buraku Liberation Research Institute, 1986.

A polemical, but heartfelt, plea for external support for the rights of *burakumin.* Despite its political nature this volume contains useful materials.

723. ———. *The Road to a Discrimination-Free Future: The World Struggle and the Buraku Liberation Movement*. Osaka: Buraku Liberation Research Institute, 1983.

Series of essays on various aspects of the Buraku Movement. Contains several appendices with translations of important documents.

724. Burkhardt, William R. "Institutional Barriers, Marginality and Adaptation Among the American-Japanese Mixed Bloods of Japan." *Journal of Asian Studies* 42 (May 1983):519–544.

One of the legacies of America's postwar involvement with Japan has been the creation of a new minority, the children of American G.I.'s and Japanese women. This article outlines the scope of the problem and the barriers facing these offspring in Japan.

725. Buruma, Ian. *Behind the Mask: On Sexual Demons, Sacred Mothers, Transvestites, Gangsters, Drifters and Other Japanese Cultural Heroes*. New York: Pantheon Books, 1984.

Although not focusing on minority groups or, indeed, explicitly discussing them, Buruma offers insights into the contours of Japanese society that *burakumin* and Koreans have to contend with every day. A valuable book for the context of minority education in Japan.

726. Cornell, John B. "Individual Mobility and Group Membership: The Case of the Burakumin." In *Aspects of Social Change in Modern Japan*, pp. 337–372. Edited by Ronald P. Dore. Princeton: Princeton University Press, 1967.

Follows conventional wisdom about Japanese society in general by arguing that the personal ambitions of individuals in the *buraku* are largely confined to achieving minimal freedoms within the group. The alternative is the always risky attempt to "pass" as a pure Japanese.

727. Cummings, William K. "The Egalitarian Transformation of Postwar Japanese Education." *Comparative Education Review* 26 (February 1982):16–35.

    Evaluates ten features of Japanese education which the author suggests have resulted in egalitarian educational outcomes and egalitarian changes in adult society.

728. De Vos, George A., and Lee Changsoo. "Conclusions: The Maintenance of a Korean Ethnic Minority in Japan." In *Koreans in Japan: Ethnic Conflict and Accomodation*, pp. 354–383. Edited by Changsoo Lee and George De Vos. Berkeley: University of California Press, 1981.

    Summary chapter which provides an excellent overview of the problems of Koreans in Japan, in the context of the widespread Japanese belief that the Japanese must remain ethnically homogeneous. Suggests that the open nature of contemporary Japanese society is shown by the extent of cooperation the authors received in researching extremely sensitive ethnic issues.

729. ———. "Koreans and Japanese: The Formation of Ethnic Consciousness." In *Koreans in Japan: Ethnic Conflict and Accomodation*, pp. 3–30. Edited by Changsoo Lee and George De Vos. Berkeley: University of California Press, 1981.

    A description of six events that constitute an important part of the heritage of Koreans in Japan, and about which Japanese know little or nothing. They summarize, in the words of the authors, "the way that the consciousness of contemporary Japanese differs from the consciousness of those who live in Japan but are aware of their Korean heritage."

730. De Vos, George A., and Wagatsuma Hiroshi, eds. *Japan's Invisible Race: Caste in Culture and Personality.* Berkeley: University of California Press, 1967.

    Essays by ten social scientists provide an interdisciplinary description and analysis of the thesis that "caste and racism are derivatives of identical psychological processes in human personality." An excellent book with which to begin to study Japanese minorities and their problems. Contains items 732–734, 736, 751, 762, 765, 768, 770, 776, 777, 783.

731.   ———. "Minority Status and Delinquency in Japan." In *Socialization for Achievement: Essays on the Cultural Psychology of the Japanese*, pp. 369–390. Edited by George A. De Vos. Berkeley: University of California, 1973.

Argues that there are direct functional parallels between deviant trends in disparaged minority groups in both Japan and the United States. Compares the education of blacks in the United States with *burakumin* in Japan.

732.   ———. "Group Solidarity and Individual Mobility." In *Japan's Invisible Race: Caste in Culture and Personality* (item 730), pp. 241–257.

Suggests that each "outcaste" must determine to take one of three roads: to retain an overt identity with his minority status; to acquire a "selective disguise" in which he retains his affiliation within the *buraku*; or to attempt to "pass" within the broader society as a pure Japanese.

733.   ———. "Minority Status and Attitudes Toward Authority." In *Japan's Invisible Race: Caste in Culture and Personality* (item 730), pp. 258–272.

Most useful for its discussion of the educational deficiences of *burakumin* children.

734.   ———. "Socialization, Self-Perception, and Burakumin Status." In *Socialization for Achievement: Essays on the Cultural Psychology of the Japanese*, pp. 391–419. Edited by George A. De Vos. Berkeley: University of California, 1973. Also in *Japan's Invisible Race: Culture in Caste and Personality* (item 730), pp. 228–240.

Relying heavily on information passed on by *burakumin* informants, this study suggests that *burakumin* children are socialized to exhibit a greater degree of sexual curiosity and freedom, are expected to be more physically aggressive, and learn to cope with the negative self-image of being a *burakumin*. Discusses the psychological dimensions of these and similar elements.

735. De Vos, George A.; Wagatsuma Hiroshi; and Wetherall, William W. *Japan's Minorities: Burakumin, Koreans and Ainu.* London: Minority Rights Group, Report No. 3, 1974.

A full description and analysis of the state of human rights towards minorities in Japan during the mid-1970s.

736. Donoghue, John D. "An Eta Community in Japan: The Social Persistence of Outcaste Groups." *American Anthropologist* 59 (1957):1000–1017. Reprinted in *Japan's Invisible Race: Caste in Culture and Personality* (item 730), pp. 137–152. Also in *Selected Readings in Modern Japanese Society.* Edited by Geroge Yamamoto and Ishida Takeshi. Berkeley: McCutchan Publishers, 1971.

Based on the author's doctoral dissertation.

737. ———. "An Eta Community in Northern Japan." Ph.D. dissertation, University of Chicago, 1956.

Stresses those interpersonal and intergroup elements that help to explain the continued social segregation of the Burakumin as a group.

738. ———. *Pariah Persistence in Changing Japan: A Case Study.* Washington, D.C.: University Press of America, 1977.

Revision of author's dissertation.

739. Goldstein, Michael. "Minority Status and Radicalism in Japan." *Studies in Race and Nations* 3 (University of Denver, 1972).

Goldstein makes a connection between the treatment of minorities in Japan and their levels of radicalism.

740. Hah Chong-Do and Lapp, Christopher. "Japanese Politics of Equality in Transition: the Case of the Burakumin." *Asian Survey* 18 (1978):487–504.

Focuses on changes in Japanese politics and their impact on attitudes toward *burakumin* rights.

741. Hane, Mikiso. *Peasants, Rebels and Outcastes: The Underside of Modern Japan.* New York: Pantheon Books, 1982.

The only full-scale Japanese history text in English that attempts to analyze the evolution of Japan from the point of view of that nation's underclass. See pp. 138–171.

742. Hawkins, John N. "Educational Demands and Institutional Response: Dowa Education in Japan." *Comparative Education Review* 27 (June 1983):204–226. Reprinted in *Education and Intergroup Relations: An International Perspective.* Edited by John N. Hawkins and Thomas La Belle.

Focuses on the role of *dowa* (assimilation) education, the ideological characteristic of *burakumin* organizations, their educational demands, and various levels of the policy process.

743. ———. "Policy Issues in the Education of Minorities: Japan." *Education and Urban Society* 18 (August 1986):412–422.

Discusses the dynamic interaction of the demands of minority groups and the responses of Japanese policy makers.

744. Hilger, M. Inez. *Together with the Ainu: A Vanishing People.* Norman: University of Oklahoma Press, 1971.

A rare look at the process through which an Ainu child is socialized into the world of adults. See Chapter 14, "Learning in Higashi-Shizunai: How the Ainu Child was Reared for Adult Living," pp. 177–200.

745. Lee Changsoo. "Ethnic Discrimination and Conflict: The Case of the Korean Minority in Japan." In *Case Studies on Human Rights and Fundamental Freedoms: A World Survey.* Edited by Willem A. Veenhoven. The Hague: Martinus J. Nijhoff, 1976.

Description of human rights violations of Koreans in Japan and the need to right these wrongs.

746. ———. "Ethnic Education and National Politics." In *Koreans in Japan: Ethnic Conflict and Accomodation*, pp. 159–181. Edited by Changsoo Lee and George De Vos. Berkeley: University of California, 1981.

Describes the efforts undertaken to encourage ethnic studies as a tool to revitalize, or at least maintain, the ethnic consciousness of Korean children born in Japan. The author contends that there were long-term Japanese efforts to assimilate Koreans into Japanese society.

747. ———. "The Legal Status of Koreans in Japan." In *Koreans in Japan: Ethnic Conflict and Accomodation*, pp. 133–158. Edited by Changsoo Lee and George De Vos. Berkeley: University of California Press, 1981.

Analyzes the legal context in which Koreans in Japan must function. The legal status of Koreans in Japan is a precarious one, and this status is complicated by the problems of Korean ethnic identity in an often hostile society.

748. Le Grand, Kathryn B. "Perspective of Minority Education: An Interview with John Ogbu." *Journal of Reading* 24 (May 1981):680–686.

John Ogbu, a Nigerian born anthropologist at the University of California, Berkeley, describes minority group education in U.S. in comparison with five other countries, including Japan.

749. Mackey, William F., and Verdoodt, Albert. *The Multinational Society: Papers of the Ljubljana Seminars.* Rowley, Mass.: Newbury House Publishers, 1975.

Contains 25 papers dealing with minority problems in a wide range of societies. Some information on Japan.

750. Mitchell, Ronald H. "The Korean Minority in Japan, 1910–1963." Ph.D. dissertation, University of Wisconsin, 1963.

Traces the historical development of Koreans in Japan, and analyzes the problems and tensions which have characterized their relationship. Especially good on the origins of the Korean minority problem and the exploitation of Koreans during WW II.

751. Norbeck, Edward. "Little Known Minority Groups in Japan." In *Japan's Invisible Race: Caste in Culture and Personality* (item 730), pp. 183–199.

Discussion of small, virtually unknown minorities in Japan (other than *eta*, Ainu, Koreans, etc.). All of these groups total no more than 30,000-40,000 people; they often work as migrant marine fishermen, woodworkers, hunters, or ironworkers, or are riverine migrants, quasi-religious itinerants, etc.

752. Ogbu, John U. "The Buraku Outcastes of Japan." In *Minority Education and Caste: The American System in Cross-Cultural Perspective*, pp. 307–321. Edited by John U. Ogbu. New York: Academic Press, 1978.

A good survey of the nature of *burakumin* life by a gifted anthropologist. Especially valuable are the comparative insights one receives from reading this chapter in the context of Ogbu's larger book.

753. Peng, Fred C.C. "Education: An Agent of Social Change in Ainu Community Life." *Human Mosaic* 5 (Spring 1972):27–50. Reprinted in *Learning to Be Japanese: Selected Readings on Japanese Society and Education* (item 22), pp. 265–288.

After focusing on the non-formal educational agencies through which Ainu adults traditionally transmitted their culture to the younger generation, the author discusses the often deleterious effects of modern formal education on Ainu life and culture.

754. Peng, Fred C.C., and Geiser, Peter. *The Ainu: The Past in the Present*. Hiroshima: Bunka Hyoron Publishing Co., 1977.

Provides historical context of Ainu prior to discussing demography, residence patterns, religion, and the community political structure.

755. Price, John A. "A History of the Outcastes: Untouchability in Japan." In *Japan's Invisible Race: Caste in Culture and Personality* (item 730), pp. 6–30.

After providing a brief description of outcaste status and untouchability in Asia, Price delineates the outcastes in Japan and traces their development to the official liberation of outcastes in 1871. Price concludes that this group continued to be discriminated against and, indeed, their total population has expanded.

756. Rohlen, Thomas P. "Education: Policies and Prospects." In *Koreans in Japan: Ethnic Conflict and Accomodation*, pp. 182–222. Edited by Changsoo Lee and George A. De Vos. Berkeley: University of California Press, 1981.

An analysis of the Korean ethnic education movement in Japan in which Rohlen concludes that assimilation will continue, but ethnicity will increasingly become an intellectual and symbolic commodity.

757. ———. "Is Japanese Education Becoming Less Egalitarian? Notes on High School Stratification and Reform." *Journal of Japanese Studies* 3 (Winter 1977):37–70.

Topics addressed include high school and university entrance examinations, family backgrounds of students, school subcultures, etc. Suggests that there is an increasing importance between family background and academic success in Japan.

758. ———. "Violence at Yoka High School: Implications for Japanese Coalition Politics of Confrontation Between Communist Party and Buraku Liberation League." *Asian Survey* 16 (1976):682–699.

A case study of the problems faced by young Koreans in Kobe and the violence often characterizing those problems.

759. Ruyle, Eugene E. "Ghetto Schools in Kyoto, Japan." *Integrated Education* 11 (July 1973):29–34.

Kyoto has one of the larger concentrations of Koreans, and Ruyle briefly describes the educational dimensions of this reality.

760. ———. "The Political Economy of the Japanese Ghetto." Ph.D. dissertation, Columbia University, 1971.

Attempts to provide an explanation for the persistence of *eta* communities in modern Japan. Based primarily on data drawn from the Kyoto region.

761. Sasaki Yuzuru and Wagatsuma Hiroshi. "Negative Self-Identity in a Delinquent Korean Youth." In *Koreans in Japan: Ethnic Conflict and Accomodation*, pp. 334–351. Edited by Changsoo Lee and George A. De Vos. Berkeley: University of California, 1981.

A poignant description of the alienation often suffered by young Koreans and the often tragic consequences of that alienation.

762. ———. "A Traditional Urban Outcaste Community." In *Japan's Invisible Race: Caste in Culture and Personality* (item 730), pp. 129–136.

An interesting analysis of the nineteen districts in Kyoto that are officially designated as "Dowa Chiku," or "districts to be integrated."

763. Shimahara Nobuo. *Burakumin: A Japanese Minority and Education*. The Hague: Martinus Nijoff, 1971.

Includes a brief historical description of the development of the *burakumin*, a case study of *burakumin* in one city, the education of *burakumin*, and national policies and local responses.

764. ———. "Toward the Equality of a Japanese Minority: The Case of Burakumin." *Comparative Education* 20 (1984):339–353.

Analyzes the historical development that resulted in the improved condition of the *burakumin* today.

765. Totten, George O. and Wagatsuma Hiroshi. "Emancipation: Growth and Transformation of a Political Movement." In *Japan's Invisible Race: Caste in Culture and Personality* (item 730), pp. 33–67.

Examines the history of *burakumin* from the 1871 abolishment of outcaste status to World War II. Documents the post-emancipation discrimination suffered by this group and the major events which characterized the *burakumin*'s attempts to secure their civil rights.

766. Umakoshi Toru. "The Education of Korean Children in Japan." In *Education and the Integration of Ethnic Minorities*, 36–47. Edited by Dietmar Rothermund and John Simon. London: Francis Printer, 1986.

The author, one of the leading Japanese specialists on the education of Koreans in Japan, describes the continuing assimilationist trend, and calls for the Japanese to do more to help the Koreans, and the Koreans to redouble efforts to retain their cultural heritage.

767. Upham, Frank K. "Instrumental Violence and the Struggle for Buraku Liberation." In *Law and Social Change in Postwar Japan*. Edited by Frank K. Upham. Cambridge: Harvard University Press, 1987.

An analysis of the Burakumin Liberation League's goals and its use of the tactic known as "denunciation struggle." The specifics of this tactic range from friendly persuasion to intimidation and the use of force.

768. Wagatsuma Hiroshi. "Non-Political Approaches: The Influences of Religion and Education." In *Japan's Invisible Race: Caste in Culture and Personality* (item 730), pp. 88–109.

Describes three periods when education was used to accomplish social change: the period of "sympathy education" (1884–1926); the period of "integration education" (1926–1936); and the period of "assimilation education" (1937–1949). The period from 1949 to the mid-1960s was one of further attempts at assimilation but with an American flavor.

769. ———. "Problem of Self-Identity Among Korean Youth in Japan." In *Koreans in Japan: Ethnic Conflict and Accomodation*, pp. 304–333. Edited by Changsoo Lee and

George A. De Vos. Berkeley: University of California, 1981.

Deals with the difficult process by which a young Korean seeks self-identity in an alien society. The author provides writings of students whose quest ended in tragedy.

770.   ———. "Postwar Political Militance." In *Japan's Invisible Race: Caste in Culture and Personality* (item 730), pp. 68–87.

This study provides an excellent supplement to item 767 as it concentrates on the same questions, but from 1947–1961.

771.   Wagatsuma Hiroshi and De Vos, George A. "The Ecology of Special Buraku." In *Japan's Invisible Race: Caste in Culture and Personality* (item 730), pp. 113–128. Edited by George A. De Vos and Wagatsuma Hiroshi. Berkeley: University of California Press, 1966.

772.   ———. "The Outcaste Tradition in Modern Japan: A Problem in Social Self-Identity." In *Aspects of Social Change in Modern Japan*, pp. 373–407. Edited by Ronald P. Dore. Princeton: Princeton University Press, 1967.

Outlines the social-psychological problems faced by the *burakumin* in Japan. Although somewhat dated on details one can learn much from this study.

773.   Wagner, Edward. *Korean Minority in Japan, 1904-1950*. New York: Institute of Pacific Relations, 1951.

An older but still extremely useful study, especially of Koreans in prewar and wartime Japan.

MINORITY EDUCATION II

774.   "The Burakumin." *Japan Quarterly* 22 (July–September 1975):187–190.

775. Cherry, Kittredge. "Burakumin: A Legacy of Prejudice." *PHP* (October 1984):46–52.

776. Cornell, John B. "Buraku Relations and Attitudes in a Progressive Farming Community." In *Japan's Invisible Race: Caste in Culture and Personality* (item 730), pp 153–182.

777. Donoghue, John D. "The Social Persistence of Outcaste Groups." In *Japan's Invisible Race: Caste in Culture and Personality* (item 730), pp 137–152.

778. Duus, Peter. "Japan and Korea in the 20th Century." *Nucleus* 35 (1982):12–37.

779. Forrer, Stephen E., et al. *Racial Attitudes of Japanese University Students. Research in Higher Education* 6 (1977):125–137.

780. Hayashida, Cullen Tadao. "Identity, Race and the Blood Ideology of Japan." Ph.D. dissertation, University of Washington, 1976.

781. Hirasawa Yasumasa. "The Burakumin: Japan's Minority Population." *Integrated Education* 20 (November–December 1983):3–7.

782. ———. "Japan." *Integrated Education* 20 (November–December 1983):18–22.

783. Ito Hiroshi (pseudonym). "Japan's Outcastes in the United States." In *Japan's Invisible Race: Caste in Culture and Personality* (item 730), pp. 200–221.

784. Kawai Hayao. "Egalitarianism in Japanese Education." *Japan Echo* 2 (1975):27–35.

785. Kida Minoru. "'Buraku' in Japan." *Japan Quarterly* 15 (July–September 1968):323–329.

786. ———. "'Buraku' in Japan (2)." *Japan Quarterly* 15 (October–December 1968):472–480.

787. ———. "'Buraku' in Japan (3)." *Japan Quarterly* 16 (January–March 1969):64–70.

788. ———. "'Buraku' in Japan (4)." *Japan Quarterly* 16 (April–June 1969):180–187.

789. Kim Yong Mok. "The Korean Minority in Japan and Their Dilemma of Cultural Identity." *Journal of Asian Affairs* 1 (Spring 1976):54–58.

790. Koyanagai Nobuto. "Give us Back Our Humanity: Report from Kamagasaki." *The Japan Christian Quarterly* 37 (Fall 1971):216–220.

791. Kunimoto Yoshiro. "Okinawans A Minority." *Japan Quarterly* 22 (October–December 1975):327–336.

792. Lewis, James. "Strangers at Home: Koreans in Japan." *East–West Perspectives* (Winter 1981):23–30.

793. Neary, Ian G. "Towards a Reconsideration of the Formation of Buraku Communities and the Development of Discrimination Against Them." In *European Studies on Japan*, pp. 51–57. Edited by Ian Nish and Charles Dunn. Tenterden, Kent: Paul Norbury Publications, 1979.

794. Price, John A. "The Economic Organization of the Outcasts of Feudal Tokyo." *Anthropological Quarterly* 41 (October 1968).

795. "The Racial Problem in Japan." *Japan Quarterly* 15 (July–September 1968):286–289.

796. Shimahara Nobuo. "A Study of the Enculturative Role of Japanese Education." Ed.D. dissertation, Boston University, 1967.

797. Singleton, John. *Nichu: A Japanese School.* New York: Holt, Rinehart and Winston, 1967.

798. Strong, Nathan O. "Patterns of Social Interaction and Psychological Accomodation Among Japan's Konketsujin Population." Ph.D. dissertation, University of California, Berkeley, 1978.

799. Suginohara Juichi. *The Status Discrimination in Japan: Introduction to the Buraku Problem.* Osaka: Buraku Liberation Research Institute, 1983.

800. Suh Il Ro. "The Attitudes of the Japanese Supreme Court Toward the Koreans in Japan." *Journal of Asian Affairs* 1 (Fall 1976):13–22.

801. Taguchi Sumikozu. "A Note on Current Research on Immigrant Groups in Japan." *International Migration Review* 17 (Winter 1983–1984):699–714.

802. Taira Koji. "Japan's Invisible Race Made Visible." *Economic Development and Cultural Change* 19 (1971):663–668.

803. Wagatsuma Hiroshi. "Burakumin in Present-Day Japan: Problems of Ex-Untouchability and Self-Identity." *Journal of Asian Affairs* 1 (Spring 1976):46–53.

804. ———. "Mixed-Blood Children in Japan: An Exploratory Study." *Journal of Asian Affairs* 2 (Spring 1977):9–17.

805. ———. "Political Problems of a Minority Group in Japan: Recent Conflicts in Buraku Liberation Movements." In *Case Studies in Human Rights and Fundamental Freedoms.* The Hague: Foundation for the Study of Plural Societies, 1976.

806. ———. "The Social Perception of Skin Color in Japan." *Daedalus* 96 (Spring 1967):407–443. Reprinted in *Comparative Perspective on Race Relations*, pp. 124–139.

Edited by Melvin M. Tumin. Boston: Little Brown and Co., 1969.

807.   Yoshida Teigo. "The Stranger as God: The Place of the Outsider in Japanese Folk Religion." *Ethnology* 20 (April 1981):87–99.

808.   Yoshino, I. Roger, and Murakoshi Sueo. *The Invisible Visible Minority: Japan's Burakumin.* Osaka: Buraku Liberation Research Institute, 1977.

CHAPTER XII
THE EDUCATION OF WOMEN

A central theme in the education of women in Japan, traceable back to the dawn of Japanese history, has been the differentiation in content even when access and opportunity for training were equal to that of men. Early records suggest that Japanese society was once a matriarchy where women held positions of prestige and authority. Popular lore and early chronicles describe empresses exerting power and influence in the family, government, religion, and, presumably, education as well.

By the seventh century, Japanese society was strongly influenced by Chinese thought, law, writing, and institutional arrangements of many kinds, including education. The teachings of Confucius, which described subordinate roles for females in society, strongly influenced the elite sectors of Japanese society. As a result, the formal power and prestige of women in politics waned, and education was formally separated and substantively differentiated from that of men. By Heian times (794–1185), while men studied the more prestigious Chinese, the official language of court and government, at a Chinese-style university (*Daigaku-ryo*), women studied privately with tutors and wrote in the newly developed native *kana* syllabary. Some, like the tenth-century court ladies, Murasaki Shikibu in *The Tale of Genji* and Sei Shonagon in *The Pillow Book*, made lasting contributions to Japanese literature in their brilliant depictions of court life in the native idiom. This was, to be sure, a period in which the aesthetic accomplishments of women in calligraphy, music, and especially poetry were greatly appreciated, and in which the educational and cultural achievements of aristocratic women were awarded a high place.

By the twelfth century, Heian court culture was replaced as the dominant educational and intellectual force in Japanese society by the concerns of a new aristocracy of provincial warriors. The aesthetic values of the court were displaced by martial virtues of loyalty, obedience, and self-control. The courageous, strong but obedient and loyal samurai woman replaced the aesthetic Heian noblewoman as the aristocratic ideal. The Japanese words for wife, *kanai* and *okusan* meaning persons in the house, came to symbolize the position of women in a feudal society dominated by military concerns. Education was less valued, in general, for both men and women; few samurai were literate. What learning there was took place within the refuge of Buddhist temples or in the households of a few warrior families who maintained libraries, such as the *Kanazawa Bunko* or the *Ashikaga Gakko*.

In the early seventeenth century, Confucian learning was revived when the Tokugawa shogunate sought to impose a value system on its retainers that would insure the continuity of the family's political and military hegemony. Formal education became an important means of disseminating Neo-Confucian orthodoxy. The *bakufu* and the domain lords established special schools with heavily Confucian curricula for the sons of samurai retainers. Upper-class daughters, for the most part, stayed at home and learned characters from copybooks taught by tutors, and memorized the injunctions of the *Onna Daigaku* or "Greater Learning for Women" by the eighteenth-century Confucianist, Kaibara Ekken (see Passin, *Society and Education in Japan* [item 30], pp. 173–176 for an English translation). This work had great influence on the education of women during the Tokugawa period and its traditional message, some would argue, has remained embedded in educational ideology to the present day. It stressed that the primary virtue for women was obedience: to their fathers before marriage, to their husbands afterward, and to their sons in old age.

Despite the limits imposed by law, custom, and teachings of this kind, women at all levels of Japanese society benefitted from the peace and stability, as well as the economic and cultural development fostered by the two and a half centuries of Tokugawa rule (1600–1868). Education spread to the commoner classes—peasants, artisans, merchants, and miscellaneous others such as doctors, priests, *ronin*, teachers—in village schools called *terakoya* which were established by educated, civic-minded elders. These schools grew spontaneously throughout the Tokugawa period and numbered well over 15,000 by the end of it. Women both attended and taught in these schools. It is estimated, nationwide, that about 15% of the women and 40% of the men received some kind of schooling outside the home before 1868.[1]

In rural areas, the percentages were very likely much lower; but in the cities women attended *terakoya* in large numbers. In Tokyo, in the merchant areas of the city, the percentage of girls attending schools was higher than that for samurai girls and roughly the same as that of samurai boys.[2] For girls at the *terakoya*, in addition to the heavy doses of Confucian morality embedded in the readers and copybooks, there was also practical information about household work, infant care, and so on. For females preparing to enter the entertainment professions, special attention was given by tutors to calligraphy, music, dance, and poetry.

The social changes that swept Japan beginning in the 1860s had enormous effects on the education of women. A basic purpose of the Meiji school policy described in the *Gakusei* (Education Law) of 1872 was to increase primary school attendance in general, and to wipe out the distinctions of geography and sex that had characterized educational arrangements of the past. Despite early resistance to the new schools, the graph of attendance gradually moved upward, and by 1905 elementary attendance was close to universal for both boys and girls.

Beyond the primary levels, however, opportunities for girls remained limited. Because the view persisted that women needed little more education than that required to be a good wife and wise mother, facilities beyond compulsory levels lagged badly until the end of World War II. In 1879 the government banned coeducation above the primary level. Differentiation in the education of boys and girls remained the rule. With the exception of teacher-training courses, secondary-level girls high schools became terminal finishing schools, not preparation for the university as were the middle and higher schools for boys. The one outlet for girls with ambitions for higher education was teaching. In 1882, 11 of the 76 prefectural normal schools were for women.

Because of the restrictions placed on secondary and tertiary education for women in the public system, private institutions played a disproportionate role in the secondary and higher education of women before World War II. In the early Meiji period, Christian missionary schools provided the only opportunities for secondary education for women. In 1870 the Ferris Seminary in Yokohama became the first secondary school for Japanese women. By 1900 there were 40 similar schools all across Japan supported by mission funds. In 1882 the

Japanese government established the first public middle school for women, and slowly such schools began to open in other areas. But the private sector continued to carry the heaviest responsibility. In 1899, 20 out of 28 girls high schools were private.

Post-secondary institutions were also founded under private auspices, and some of them were first-rate. Tsuda Umeko (1865–1929) founded *Joshi Eigaku Juku* (now Tsuda College) in 1900 to provide high level training in English language and literature. In the same year Yoshioka Yayoi (1871–1959) founded Tokyo Women's Medical School (*Tokyo Jogakko*). In 1901 Naruse Jinzo (1858–1919) established Japan Women's University (*Nihon Joshi Daigaku*). These schools turned out generations of students and teachers in the fields of medicine, literature, and education.

The spirit of individualism and independence, encouraged by the progressive education movement in Japan during the 1920s, made it possible, for a time, for some women to free themselves from the standard "women's courses" prevalent in both public and private schools. By the 1920s there were numerous experiments in alternative education, particularly at the lower levels, that gave students and teachers the opportunity to break away from the rigid formalities of mainstream educational tradition. During this period, the Japanese experimented with the classroom ideas of John Dewey, Maria Montessori, the Dalton Plan, and other innovative approaches current in the West.

Like the private academies of the Tokugawa period, the progressive schools of the prewar period provided alternatives to public schools; they added diversity and provided options to mainstream offerings in education. They often tended to be iconoclastic, usually reflecting the individual styles and philosophies of their headmasters. Oikawa Heiji (1875–1939) used Deweyan ideas in the elementary school attached to the Akashi Women's Normal School in Hyogo prefecture. In Tokyo, the *Seikei Gakuen*, founded by Nakamura Shunji, and the Imperial Elementary School, founded by Nishiyama Tetsuji in 1912, used progressive ideas from abroad. Kawano Kiyomaru (1873–1941) experimented with self-study methods based on the ideas of Maria Montessori in the Homei Elementary School which was attached to Naruse Jinzo's Japan Women's University. These schools attempted to break down the rigid sex-role-based education of mainstream schools. Great efforts were made to consider the individual differences of the pupils and to respect their freedom. Classes were kept small, and students were encouraged to participate in activities that crossed traditional sex lines: boys, for example, were encouraged to sew at the Imperial Elementary School.

Elementary schools attached to the higher normal schools experimented with progressive methods, as did the schools attached to the prefectural normal schools, but the real innovations came in the private schools. Sawayanagi Masataro (1865–1927) who had held a series of high government posts, including vice-minister of education, gave great prestige to the Dalton Plan in his Seijo Elementary School opened in 1917. Some Seijo teachers broke away to establish their own schools. Former Seijo teachers founded *Seimei Gakuen* in 1930 and *Wako Gakuen* in 1934. Perhaps the best known of all the progressive teachers of this era, Obara Kuniyoshi (1887–1977), left *Seijo Gakuen* and founded his *Tamagawa Gakuen* in the Tokyo suburbs in 1929. His educational philosophy was a synthesis of Christianity, the progressive methods of *Seijo*, and the intimacy of the premodern *terakoya* and private academies. The educational system founded by Obara continues to the present; it is capped by Tamagawa University.

Of particular importance in creating a spirit of intellectual self-reliance and independence in the education of women was the *Jiyu Gakuen*, founded in 1921 by Hani Motoko (1873–1957). Founded originally as a middle school, it was expanded to include an elementary school in 1928, a boy's department in 1935, and a sister school in Peking, China in 1938. The educational goals of the school—independence and individual development—were tied to the aspirations of Japan's early feminist movement. Housed in a building designed by Frank Lloyd Wright, the school was both architecturally and pedagogically anti-establishment. Unlike public schools, there were no school uniforms and no final examinations. Evaluations were done through discussions with students at the end of the year; teachers also sent notebooks of comments to parents. Instead of the usual morals classes (*shushin*) at public schools, the Ministry of Education texts were ignored and students held discussions instead, sometimes interpreting a novel or the newspaper. A point was made of not hanging the Imperial Rescript on Education in a place of honor in the school, which was de rigeur at public institutions.

Another school considered radically progressive, because of its emphasis on self-learning rather than on socializing students to particular sex roles or preparing them for exams, was the Children's Village School established in 1924 by Noguchi Entaro (1868–1941). Like the traditional academies of the Tokugawa period, the school was originally housed in the headmaster's home in the Ikebukuro section of Tokyo. Children came and went according to plans worked out individually with teachers. Pupils were encouraged to experiment, work at their own rates, and use self-study methods. Children jointly evaluated each other's work and no grades were given.

From the outset progressive schools in Japan operated in a hostile and precarious environment. Their existence was constantly threatened by the public system and the Ministry of Education. A particular source of difficulty was the school entrance examination system. The progressive schools found it difficult to maintain programs which jeopardized the futures of pupils by neglecting to prepare them for the next step in the educational ladder. By the end of the 1930s many of the leaders of the progressive movement were out of the picture; they had either died or were retired. Schools that survived were mainly those, like *Tamagawa*, that obviated the need for exam preparation by creating self-contained systems extending from kindergarten through university.

Furthermore, private schooling, by its nature, was limited in scope—existing on the periphery of the mainstream, nationally controlled public school system, and restricted in access by tuition costs. Expansion of educational opportunities for most women had to await the reforms of the public educational system by the Allied Occupation (1945–1952). The Occupation reforms in education had a particular impact on women. Eliminated were the prewar and wartime morals courses (*shushin*), which idealized the traditional family system holding women in an inferior position. The new curriculum supported the democratization of family life and the principle of the equality of women. Coeducation was established at all levels. Structurally, a series of reforms, aimed at destroying the elitist tracking of the prewar system and making all levels of education broadly accessible, opened the way to dramatic increases in educational opportunities for women. Whereas in 1955 only 47% of female students went beyond the compulsory nine years of elementary schooling, by 1975 the rate was 93%, higher than the 91% rate for boys. In 1955 only 15% of female high school graduates entered higher education (21% for males), by 1975 the rate had moved up to 35%, again higher than the male rate of 34%.[3]

To be sure, traditions of segregated education die hard, and traditional attitudes of differentiated sex roles remain. In higher education in particular, a clear differentiation in educational choices between males and females remains. Most women choose junior colleges, which tend to focus on the traditional female subjects of literature, language, domestic arts, nursing, and secretarial skills, rather than the more prestigious and academically oriented four-year universities. In 1975, 86% of junior college students were female; by 1980 the percentage of females at four-year institutions was still under 23%.[4]

There is now a rich literature in English on women in Japan. This material has a far broader focus than education alone, and covers such areas as the changing roles of housewives, socialization patterns, child-rearing, the rise of feminism, the problems and prospects for women in a variety of social roles and occupations. Much of this material touches on educational problems—and to the degree that a particular work does so, it is included in the annotated list that follows. Thus, the list is not a complete survey of materials on women in general, but is a selected list of the work the editors feel best describes educational issues affecting women.

Material on Japanese women that focuses directly on education is far more limited, but breaks down into the following types: descriptions of traditional education aimed at training "good wives and wise mothers"; analyses of advances made, and problems and frustrations still to be overcome; accounts of the educational ramifications within particular life styles, such as farm woman, geisha, urban housewife; the frank, often cathartic reminiscences of liberated Japanese women who have studied abroad; and government statistics and documents related to school attendance.

NOTES

1. Roughly similar estimates were made by R.P Dore in *Education in Tokugawa Japan*, (Berkeley and Los Angeles: University of California Press, 1965), pp. 291–295 and 317–322; and by Herbert Passin in *Society and Education in Japan* (New York: Teachers College Press, 1965), pp. 47–49 and 310–313.

2. Richard Rubinger, "Problems in Research in Literacy in 19th-Century Japan," in *Nihon kyoiku-shi ronso*, ed. Motoyama Yukihiko kyoju taikan kinen ronbun shuhen iinkai (Kyoto: Shibunkaku Shuppan, 1988), p. 9.

3. *Kodansha Encyclopedia of Japan*, Vol. 8, Susan J. Pharr, "Women in Contemporary Japan" (Tokyo: Kodansha, 1983), p. 263.

4. *Kodansha Encyclopedia of Japan*, Vol. 8, E. Patricia Tsurumi, "Women's Education" (Tokyo: Kodansha, 1983), p. 267.

THE EDUCATION OF WOMEN I

*   Ackroyd, Joyce. "Women in Feudal Japan." *Transactions of the Asiatic Society of Japan*. 3rd series. Vol. 7 (November 1959):31–68. Cited in item 133 above.

In contrast to early Japanese history which has been described as matriarchal, owing to the prominence of women in political and social positions, the onset of warrior rule in the twelfth and thirteenth centuries saw a substantially diminished role for women in Japanese society. Through an analysis of feudal military codes, this article describes the place of women and analyzes some of the key writings such as Kaibara Ekken's *Onna Daigaku* where the feminine ideal of dependence and submissiveness, seen as suited to feudal society, was made into a staple of the learning process in the Tokugawa years (1600–1868). The author also argues that some of these attitudes continue into the present.

809.   Beauchamp, Edward R. "The Social Role of Japanese Women: Continuity and Change." *International Journal of Women's Studies* 2 (May–June 1979):244–256.

A useful survey of the great diversity of premodern educational attitudes and practices with regard to women followed by an analysis of the role of women in contemporary Japan. Useful details on educational matters from the historical record and literary sources.

810. Bernstein, Gail Lee. *Haruko's World: A Japanese Farm Woman and Her Community.* Stanford: Stanford University Press, 1981.

Portrait of the feelings, problems, aspirations of a contemporary farm woman based on the author's one-year stay with her family. While educational matters are incidental to the larger story, Chapter 8, "Home and School," describes this woman's attitudes toward her children's education.

811. Bingham, Marjorie Wall, and Gross, Susan Hill. *Women in Japan: From Ancient Times* to the Present. St. Louis: Glenhurst Publications, 1987.

This secondary school textbook (written by teachers with scholar consultants) provides an excellent introduction to a wide range of issues relating to women in Japan and challenges the stereotypes of Japanese women as passive, limited to support roles, with a history dictated by the constraints of Confucianism. Organized chronologically from earliest times, each chapter gives summaries of major points, provocative quotations from a wide range of pertinent historical and literary sources, and questions for discussion. Many photographs and charts accompany the text; there is a good up-to-date bibliography of the better English-language writings. Highly recommended as a starting point for Women's Studies issues for students.

812. Chapman, Christine. "Japan's Women Gain in Struggle for Equality in Higher Education." *The Chronicle of Higher Education.* 19 (Feb. 4, 1980):17.

Increased enrollment of females in higher education, 30% of those surveyed indicating plans for careers, the admittance of females for the first time to technical colleges, talk of opening doors in military schools to women—all suggesting that despite the heavy weight of tradition and continued bias in the marketplace, opportunities in higher education are increasing.

813. Clarke, Elizabeth J. "The Origins of Women's Higher Education in Japan." *Japan Christian Quarterly* 46 (Winter 1980):26–33.

Overview of the growth and development of women's higher education, beginning in private schools of Meiji, expanding in the 1920s under private auspices, and achieving public support in the postwar years. Particularly useful discussions of the roles of Christian mission schools in extending opportunities beyond the elementary level in the Meiji period.

814. Condon, Jane. *A Half Step Behind: Japanese Women of the 80's.* New York: Dodd and Mead and Co., 1985.

A popular, non-academic book that provides a literate, if superficial, introduction to major issues confronting Japanese women in the family, work, and education. In Section II, "Education," problems of education, mothers, schools, and teachers are described. Bibliography has many articles from newspapers and magazines from the early 1980s.

815. Dalby, Liza. *Geisha.* Berkeley: University of California Press, 1983.

Study by an anthropologist, of the world of the contemporary geisha in Kyoto, touching on many aspects of the traditional arts. It also throws light on the apprenticeship system by which young girls are trained in the arcane mysteries of the geisha profession and in so doing provides a glimpse of an important aspect of traditional education in Japan that continues, especially in the arts.

816. *Education in Japan: A Journal for Overseas* (Hiroshima University). Vol. VI (1971).

A special issue devoted to the education of women includes. Contains items 146, 849, 851, 858–860, 865.

817. Fujimura-Fanselow, Kumiko. "Women's Participation in Higher Education in Japan." *Comparative Education Review* 29 (November 1985):471–489.

Based on the author's Teachers College dissertation. A careful, scholarly, analysis of the opportunities for women in higher education in Japan and their use of it. Useful for up-to-date data on changing attitudes of women with optimistic view of future.

818. Herold, Renate. "Problems of Women: The Labor Market (With Special Reference to Japan)." In *Proceedings of the Tokyo Symposium on Women*, pp. 36–49. Edited by Merry I. White and Barbara Malony. Tokyo: International Group for the Study of Women, 1978.

   An important publication from a conference in Tokyo that brought together many of the most prominent specialists in the field (both Japanese and Western, including Pharr, White, Imamura, Vogel, Lebra, Dalby, etc.) to deal with a wide range of topics related to women: social and political change, women and work, women in the arts, community activities of housewives, and the contemporary housewife. Herold's is one of the few contributions that discusses education specifically, showing how public education institutionalizes sex-role stereotypes.

819. Imamura, Anne E. *Urban Japanese Housewives: At Home and in the Community*. Honolulu: University of Hawaii Press, 1987.

   Although not specifically a work on education, this study of the lifestyles of urban Japanese housewives and their changing roles throughout the life cycle, provides much data on educational activities along the way: education as a factor in work after marriage; expectations and attitudes towards the education of children; the PTA as an emotional and social outlet, providing a source of friendships, community involvement, and prestige.

820. Ishimoto, Baroness Shizue. *Facing Two Ways: The Story of My Life*. New York: Farrar and Rinehart, 1935.

   Part II, "Student Days," provides a first-person account of kindergarten, elementary, and high school life at the aristocratic Peers School in prewar days, told by one who at the time completely accepted the mythology of emperor worship.

821. Japan, Ministry of Education, Science, and Culture. *Women and Education in Japan*. Tckyo: Social Education Bureau, Ministry of Education, 1980.

25-page pamphlet with data from census and other sources on: employment trends, volunteer work, political involvement, numbers of women at different levels of school system, non-formal education, and women's groups and organizations. Data only, no interpretative material. Earlier data available in publications for 1969 and 1972.

822. Japan, Ministry of Labor, Women's and Minor's Bureau. *The Status of Women in Japan*. Tokyo: Ministry of Labor, 1972.

Data from 1970 on percentage of males and females entering high school and university; breakdown of numbers of women in junior colleges and universities. Other selected data of limited use. A more comprehensive presentation of data would be welcome. Updates available for 1979 and, presumably, more recently than that.

823. Jones, Hazel J. "Good Wives-Wise Mothers and Pan Pan: Notes on the Position of Japanese Women." *Asian Profile* 3 (December 1975).

Survey of women's role in Japanese society from earliest times, with useful data on schooling opportunities in Tokugawa and Meiji periods. Argues that despite increasing opportunities in quantitative terms, educational quality for women has always remained problematic, and continues to be so in higher education.

*   Kobayashi, Victor Nobuo. *John Dewey in Japanese Educational Thought*. Ann Arbor: University of Michigan Comparative Education Series, No. 2, 1964. Cited in item 278 above.

Includes the best material available in English on the progressive movement in Japanese education during the 1920s and 30s, with descriptions of the leaders of the movement and their alternative schools.

824. Koyama Takashi. *The Changing Social Position of Women in Japan*. Unesco, 1961.

   Chapter II, "Institutional Changes and Redefinition of the Position of Women," cites data that rarely makes its way into secondary works in English. Specifically, comparisions of male and female school attendance rates from 1873 at primary and secondary schools in Japan; data on literacy by sex from the 1951 survey commissioned by the Allied Occupation; a 1954 Ministry of Education survey on student, teacher, and parent attitudes on co-education (not surprisingly, junior high school boys were the most adamantly opposed); 1957 data on graduates of junior high, high school, and university by career and sex. Very short and incomplete but discreet bits of data useful.

825. Kuroyanagi Tetsuko. *Totto-chan: The Little Girl at the Window*. Translated by Dorothy Britton. Tokyo: Kodansha International, 1982.

   A charming account of one little girl's daily experiences at a progessive school in the prewar/wartime period, by one of Japan's most popular TV personalities. A glimpse of opportunities available within the Japanese system for non-mainstream children.

826. Lebra, Takie Sugiyama. *Japanese Women: Constraint and Fulfillment*. Honolulu: University of Hawaii Press, 1984.

   Ethnology of contemporary Japanese women focusing on life cycle and role, and based on life histories of 57 women from a small city southwest of Tokyo. Education discussed within a broad framework under such headings as: school enrollment, examination crisis, nurseries, PTA, programs for mothers, child care, girls schools, and *juku*.

827. Matsui Haru. *Restless Wave: An Autobiography*. New York: Modern Age Books, 1940.

   One woman's childhood and education before the War. See pp. 127–135 for a brief description of Hani Motoko's alternative school, *Jiyu Gakuen*, or "Freedom School."

828. Matsuoka Yoko. *Daughter of the Pacific*. New York: Harper, 1952.

     Chapter 3, "Freedom School," also describes the school founded by Hani Motoko in 1921 as an alternative school.

829. Mishima Sumie Seo. *My Narrow Isle: The Story of a Modern Woman in Japan*. New York: John Day, 1941.

     Chapters 3, 6, and 11 discuss one woman's education in prewar days.

830. Mouer, Elizabeth Knipe. "Women in Teaching." In *Women in Changing Japan*, pp. 157–190. Edited by Joyce Lebra, Joy Paulson, and Elizabeth Powers. Boulder, Colorado: Westview, 1976.

     Changes in women's roles within the educational system since the Occupation reforms. Data on female teachers at all levels of the system, showing rising educational levels of women in the postwar years and increasing opportunities opening for women as men left the profession. Part I is a historical sketch of female teachers, with a description of the life and professional environment of an average teacher in 1975; Part II is three case studies based on interviews of women teachers. Concludes that while much improvement has been seen, blatant job discrimination persists in areas like childcare leave, salaries, promotions to administrative positions, due to the lingering of traditional beliefs.

831. Naruse Jinzo. "The Education of Japanese Women." In *Fifty Years of New Japan*, pp. 192–225. Compiled by Count Shigenobu Okuma. London: Smith, Elder and Co., 1909.

     Survey of the history of women's education from a traditional perspective, up to and including the views of Fukuzawa Yukichi in the early Meiji period.

832. Nuita Yoko. "Continuing Education of Women in Japan." *Improving College and University Teaching* 20 (Winter 1972):66–68. Also published as "Trends in the Continuing

Education of Women in Japan." *Convergence* 2, 2 (1969):26–41.

In an issue devoted entirely to women in higher education, an official of Japan's public broadcast network (NHK) discusses the role of the mass media in the education of women.

833. Pharr, Susan J. "Japan: Historical and Contemporary Perspectives." In *Women: Roles and Status in Eight Countries*, pp. 217–255. Edited by Janet Z. Giele and Audrey C. Smock. New York: John Wiley and Sons, 1977.

Especially useful is the survey of major developments in women's history prior to 1868 and the bibliography of relevant English and Japanese sources related to women in Japan.

834. ———. "The Japanese Women: Evolving Views of Life and Role." In *The Paradox of Progress*, pp. 301–327. Edited by Lewis Austin. New Haven: Yale University Press, 1976. Reprinted in *Asian Women in Transition*, pp. 36–61. Edited by Sylvia A. Chipp and Justin J. Green. University Park: The Pennsylvania State University Press, 1980.

Important and well-known analysis of three categories of contemporary Japanese women: "Neo-traditionalists"—who accept the one-role ideology of women's basic inferiority and natural domesticity; the "New Women"—who claim the right to participate in life in more than one role on a basis of equality and desire to hold jobs and be married in the same manner as men; and "Radical Egalitarians"—who reject traditional sex roles, traditional marriage arrangements, and condemn the government, educational system, and traditional social relations. Pharr sees the latter as a fringe group in an isolated subculture and the real tension between the "Neo-traditionalists" and "New Women" with the latter eventually superseding the former in part due to continuing and improving opportunities for higher education. The author sees the "Radical Egalitarians" gaining strength if accommodation cannot be made with growing numbers of "New Women."

835. ———. *Political Women in Japan: The Search for a Place in Political Life*. Berkeley and London: University of California Press, 1981.

Within the broader context of women in politics, interesting correlations presented between higher education and political activism of different categories of women.

836. Robins-Mowry, Dorothy. *The Hidden Sun: Women of Modern Japan*. Boulder: Westview, 1983.

Probably the best, certainly the most comprehensive and balanced treatment of the manifold issues related to women in Japanese society. Historical section includes the positive legacy of the Confucian tradition; the early modern period includes both sides of the debate over women's role in society and education, roles of overseas education for some women, and the importance in early Meiji of Christian mission schools and Western organizations like the YWCA. A second part treats new possibilities for lifestyles, women's roles in the economy as both producers and consumers, political organization and participation, and international efforts and awareness. The last section, "Designs for the Future," highlights the separation between progressive leaders and the mass of Japanese women, and suggests that Japanese women may be more conservative, but more unified in basic attitudes than women elsewhere. Hence, the author's cautious optimism that women's concerns will be met but that it will be a slow process.

837. Sievers, Sharon. *Flowers in Salt: The Beginnings of Feminist Consciousness in Modern Japan*. Stanford: Stanford University Press, 1983.

The major English language source on the rise of feminism in Japan. Covers a lot of ground not treated elsewhere: Tokugawa period attitudes towards women, Meiji debates within and without government on the role of women, women in the Freedom and People's Rights Movement in early Meiji, the ideas of leading female activists, the influence of women's magazines, and the history of resistance movements. The social costs of Japan's rapid industrialization are seen in terms of the death, suffering, and economic hardships faced by women in factories—which were carefully denied by the cushion of Confucian ideology. Women's place in the rise of the modern labor movement and Socialism, with biographical material on leading women activists often overlooked by others, like Kanno Suga. Particularly interesting are the efforts of politically active women in the establishment of alternative schools—a story which is touched on here and badly needs elaboration in English-language research. Women and education seen in larger perspective of educational standardization, focusing on those who resisted the trend and fell victim to it.

838. Smith, Robert J., and Wiswell, Ella Lury. *The Women of Suye Mura*. Chicago: University of Chicago Press, 1982.

Based on field research in 1935 by Ella Wiswell, wife of John Embree, author of pathbreaking anthropological study of a Japanese village, *Suye Mura*, in which women were largely left out. Here we get a first hand account of the details of women's lives in a prewar village which clearly challenges the traditional image of women as submissive and passive. Education discussed in passing in terms of the prevalence of illiteracy, early socialization, and child care.

839. Sugimoto Etsu. *Daughter of a Samurai*. Garden City: Doubleday, Doran and Co., 1932; new ed. London: Hutchinson, 1960.

Autobiography of a woman who escaped the shackles of traditional Japan by escaping to the West. Descriptions of the kind of home tutoring that characterized upper class Japanese women around the turn of the twentieth century, the benefits of travel and study abroad for a woman who became instructor of Japanese at Columbia University.

840. Vogel, Suzanne H. "Professional Housewife: The Career of Urban, Middle Class Japanese Women." *Japan Interpreter* 12 (1978):16–43.

Lives and social roles of middle-class housewives. Education discussed in terms of socialization for motherhood and in fostering learning in children.

841. Wheeler, Helen Rippier. "Women's Studies, Higher Education, and Feminist Educators in Japan Today." *Journal of the National Association of Women Deans, Administrators, and Counselors* 48 (Summer 1985):31–36.

Very brief introduction to background and current state of Women's Studies in Japanese universities as of 1984.

842. White, Merry I., and Molony, Barbara, eds. *Proceedings of the Tokyo Symposium on Women.* Tokyo: The International Group for the Study of Women, 1978.

An important contribution to the literature on contemporary Japanese women with participation of many leaders in the field. See also item 818.

THE EDUCATION OF WOMEN II

843. Burton, Margaret E. *The Education of Women in Japan.* New York and London: Fleming H. Revell Co., 1914.

844. Fujimura-Fanselow, Kumiko. "Women and Higher Education in Japan: Tradition and Change." Ph.D. dissertation, Columbia University, 1981.

845. Fujimura-Fanselow, Kumiko; Fukutomi Mamoru; Kodama Mieko; Nobuyuki Takenaga; and Yamamoto Yukari. "Learning in the Life Course of Japanese Women." *Tokyo Symposium on Women.* Translated by Hirano Tomako. Tokyo: International Group for the Study of Women and United Nations Asian and Pacific Development Center, 1983.

846. Fujiwara Mariko; Carvell, Kermit; and Fujisaki Tatsuya. *Japanese Women in Turmoil* (Changing Lifestyles in Japan II). Tokyo: Hakuhodo Institute of Life and Living, 1984.

847. Hoshino Ai. *The Education of Women*. Western Influences in Modern Japan series, No. 11. Tokyo: Japanese Council, Institute of Pacific Relations, 1929.

848. Higuchi Keiko. "The PTA—A Channel for Political Activism." *Japan Interpreter* 10 (1975):133–140.

849. Ichibangase Yasuko. "Women's Status and the Task of Education." *Education in Japan: A Journal for Overseas* (Hiroshima University), (item 816), pp. 59–68.

850. Imamura, Anne E. "Kanai or Kagai? The Japanese Urban Housewife—Her Image of and Involvement in Her Community." Ph.D. dissertation, Columbia University, 1980.

851. Inoue Hisao. "A Historical Sketch of the Development of the Modern Educational system for Women in Japan." *Education in Japan: A Journal for Overseas* (Hiroshima University), (item 816), pp. 15–35.

852. Japanese Association of University Women. *Japanese University Women: Issues and Views*. 2 vols. Tokyo: Kenkyusha, 1974.

853. *Kodansha Encyclopedia of Japan*. Vol. 8. "Women in Contemporary Japan," by Susan J. Pharr.

854. *Kodansha Encyclopedia of Japan*. Vol. 8. "Women's Education," by E. Patricia Tsurumi.

855. Oshima Koichi. "Kim Maria and Japan: Korean Women Students in Japan and the March First Independence Movement." *Japan Christian Quarterly* 46 (Winter 1980):40–45.

856. Perry, Linda L. "Mothers, Wives, and Daughters in Osaka: Autonomy, Alliance and Professionalism." Ph.D. dissertation, University of Pittsburgh, 1976.

857. Pharr, Susan J. "Sex and Politics: Women in Social and
      Political Movements in Japan." Ph.D. dissertation,
      Columbia University, 1975.

858. Senju Katsumi. "The Development of Female Education in
      Private Schools." *Education in Japan: A Journal for
      Overseas* (Hiroshima University), (item 816), pp. 37–46.

859. Shibukawa Hisako. "An Education for Making Good Wives and
      Wise Mothers." *Education in Japan: A Journal for Overseas*
      (Hiroshima University), (item 816), pp. 47–57.

*   Shiga Tadashi. "Historical View of the Education of Women
      Before the Time of Meiji." Cited as item 146 above.

860. Shoji Masako. "Women Educators Who Contributed to the
      Education of Women." *Education in Japan: A Journal for
      Overseas* (Hiroshima University), (item 816), pp. 69–83.

861. Smith, Robert J. "Making Village Women into 'Good Wives
      and Wise Mothers' in Prewar Japan." *Japanese Family
      History* 8 (Spring 1983):70–83.

862. Suyematsu Kencho. "Woman's Education." In *Japan by the
      Japanese*. Edited by Alfred Stead. London: William
      Heinemann, 1904.

863. Tamaoka S. "The Tendencies of Girl Students of Nagoya
      Prefecture." *Japanese Journal of Applied Psychology* 5
      (1939).

864. Tomoda Yasumasa. "Educational and Occupational Aspirations
      of Female Senior High School Students." *Bulletin of the
      Hiroshima Agricultural College* 4 (December 1972): 247–
      262.

865. Yamasaki Takako. "Women Educators Who Contributed to the
      Education of Women (II)." *Education in Japan: A Journal for
      Overseas* (Hiroshima University), (item 816), pp. 85–89.

CHAPTER XIII
TEXTBOOKS

Any society whose educational thinking has been as strongly influenced by the Confucian tradition as the Japanese is going to place great emphasis on the contents of the textbooks in its schools. Moreover, the content and selection of textbooks for public schools have become contentious political issues. There is a centralized Ministry of Education, which sees its role as one of establishing uniform national standards, and a significant and vocal political opposition represented by the Japan Teachers Union, which sees the government using education to reassert an outdated and dangerous political ideology. Anyone who believes that Japanese society is essentially harmonious and conflict-free need go no further than the literature on textbooks to understand that important questions of freedom of expression, the control of public education, and the meaning of the Japanese past continue to be vigorously debated.

Prior to 1872, when a national school system was created, textbooks in schools were left to the teachers' discretion. They ranged in content from copybooks to readers incorporating folk traditions, advice for daily tasks and simple moral tales, at the lower levels, to the Confucian classics at the more advanced private academies and official schools. Although the Confucian *Four Books* and *Five Classics* remained the center of the curriculum and the starting point for nearly all formal education in the Tokugawa period, by the 1850s there was a trend to incorporate new areas of knowledge. The private academies were the most innovative in this regard, but official schools also began to reform. National Learning (*kokugaku*) is estimated to have been introduced in about one-third of the domain schools, and Western studies—primarily medicine, military affairs, and shipbuilding—was

adopted in varying degrees in about one-quarter of the official schools.[1]
Consequently, the literary classics of Japan as well as translations of
Dutch-language medical and scientific books became text materials at
academies and some official schools. Although there were heated debates
among scholars of different points of view, since the amount and
substance of one's schooling remained a matter of individual choice
throughout Tokugawa Japan, textbook content and selection did not
become a significant political issue.

When the national system was established in 1872, the tradition of
free choice continued, and teachers were permitted to use either books
written by independent scholars or newly prepared government texts.
Thus, in the early 1870s there was a considerable mix of materials used
in the elementary schools—from the readers, vocabulary lists, and
copybooks used at *terakoya* to the newer texts based on Western
translations that were disseminated by the new publication offices
within the Ministry of Education and the Tokyo Normal School. In
1872 the Ministry of Education published a list of recommended titles,
drawn from translations of Western textbooks and the works of Japanese
writers such as Fukuzawa Yukichi. In 1873 the Ministry published its
own text, *Shogaku tokuhon* (Elementary School Readers) with large
sections based on the American *Willson Readers*.

Local compliance with curriculum guidelines was, at first, weak.
Some prefectures did not immediately introduce geography or science
into their schools; others held back on Western-style methods of
arithmetic, preferring their own time-tested text materials and teachers
guides. A study of the contents of ethics and language texts used during
the 1870s and 1880s suggests that there continued to be a blending of
Western, Japanese, and Confucian values for some time.[2]

In 1881 the Ministry of Education began to take steps to tighten
its control over textbook use and published a list of texts considered
appropriate. By 1883 a "permission system" required the prefectures to
submit for approval lists of texts intended for use. Under minister of
education Mori Arinori's Elementary School Law of 1886 this
procedure was fully implemented, setting up the first nationwide system
for the standardization of textbooks. From this time, all manuscripts
written by private authors required prepublication authorization by the
Ministry of Education.

Because compulsory education had reached nearly universal levels
by 1900, with textbook sales becoming a big business, and also

because local authorities were allowed some discretion in selecting texts from approved lists, the possibilities for abuse became manifest. In the textbook scandal of 1902, local officials were found taking bribes from publishing companies. As a result, local initiatives were restricted, leading to greater national control. The next year, 1903, the Ministry eliminated local selection entirely, and required all elementary schools to adopt identical, state-approved textbooks. The Ministry of Education was granted exclusive copyright for the preparation of texts, giving it final responsibility. From then until the end of World War II, Japanese elementary school textbooks were written, published, and distributed by the Ministry of Education.

At the beginning of the Allied Occupation of Japan (1945–1952), school textbooks were closely scrutinized. Many were banned outright, others were heavily censored for containing material deemed ultranationalistic, militaristic, or critical of Allied policy. History texts were particularly vulnerable because of their treatment of the ancestral mythology. In 1946 the first postwar history text, *Kuni no ayumi* (The Course of Japanese History) was published. Written by Professor Ienaga Saburo and three other Japanese scholars, and authorized by both the Ministry of Education and Occupation authorities, it represented a complete break from earlier ultranationalist texts. By 1946 the American Occupation had, in effect, taken over the role of the Ministry of Education as compiler and authorizer of textbooks. So, although the content of the writing had changed significantly, the prewar system of state authorization continued, now under SCAP control.[3]

In May 1948, the Ministry of Education established a Textbook Authorization Committee to supervise the examination of all manuscripts submitted by independent authors. This meant a return to the pre-1903 procedure (before the Ministry was empowered to compile all textbooks for elementary school use). The new Authorization Committee was made up of teachers, university professors, and members of the publishing world. Specialists on the subject of the text would review it first, then pass it on to the Ministry of Education and then SCAP officials. Then, local educational authorities would choose from the authorized list.

When the Occupation ended in 1952, the Japanese government inherited a system established by American authorities whereby the Ministry of Education commonly would stipulate recommended text revisions before authorization. This became a legal sticking point in

1970, in the Ienaga textbook case, when it was claimed that requiring revisions prior to publication, the method used under Occupation auspices, was a violation of the postwar Japanese Constitution.

By the end of the 1950s, textbook authorization had become more strict owing to political conflicts between the Japan Teachers Union (JTU) and the Ministry of Education. In 1958 a national mandatory curriculum was promulgated by the Ministry of Education. With a required curriculum, the government could stipulate course content and authorize those textbooks that conformed to the mandated curriculum. In 1964 textbooks were made free for the compulsory years and publishing companies were required to register for approval.

The Authorization Process

In the current Japanese system of textbook authorization, individual authors are free to prepare textbook manuscripts which they submit to officially approved textbook publishers. If acceptable at that level, the publisher applies to the Ministry of Education for authorization. Because of the expense of textbook production for the publishers, they have developed elaborate internal authorization systems of their own to insure final acceptance by the Ministry of Education. At the Ministry the manuscript is turned over to a Deliberative Council (*shingikai*) which consists of 120 part-time members—teachers, professor, other educators, and Ministry appointees. It then goes to a subcommittee of area specialists. In addition, there is an advisory committee (*chosakai*) made up of two teachers and one professor which also files a report. Another report comes in from a committee of 41 full-time Ministry of Education textbook inspectors. The full council decision then goes to the Ministry of Education with its recommendation. The council's recommendation may demand mandatory revisions or suggested revisions. Approved materials pass from the Ministry of Education to local boards of education where one textbook for each grade level is adopted. High school texts are selected by principals with the guidance of faculty. The entire authorization process takes about two years.

The Ienaga Case

The constitutionality and legality of Japan's textbook authorization system was challenged in 1965 and in 1967 by Professor Ienaga Saburo, a history professor at Tokyo University of Education. He filed suit in Tokyo District Court against the Japanese government—for alleged violations of his constitutionally guaranteed freedom of expression and academic freedom—when his application for official approval of the fifth edition of his high school textbook, *Shin Nihonshi* (New History of Japan) was rejected. In 1970 the court ruled in Ienaga's favor, finding that rejection of the substance of the ideas of a writer of a textbook constituted unconstitutional censorship and unjust control of education in violation of the law. In 1975 the Ministry of Education's appeal was dismissed, but in 1982 the Supreme Court overturned this judgment and referred the case back for further review.

This case has been under review for over twenty years because it goes to the heart of debates over postwar Japanese education: whether the national government should be determining the content of education as well as the standards for it, whether textbook authorization is being used to set a particular political and ideological agenda in schools, and whether freedom of expression can and should be affected by authorization of school textbooks.

International Repercussions

At the very same time that the Supreme Court was handing down its judgment on the Ienaga case in the summer of 1982, the textbook authorization system became the center of a diplomatic quarrel involving China, South Korea, and Japan. Major Japanese newspapers reported that new elementary and high school texts in Japan had been approved with wording that watered down Japanese actions in China and Korea during World War II. It was charged, for example that the word *shinryaku* (invasion) had been deleted and *shinshutsu* (advance) inserted in descriptions of the movement of Japanese armies into China. The Chinese government lodged a protest, and the Japanese government apologized, taking full responsibility. Later, it was revealed that the facts had been misreported and that such changes had, in fact, not been made in any textbooks.

Although the incident was sparked by press error, it nevertheless revealed the continued regional tensions in Asia and the domestic conflict within Japan between academic and press elites, who generally favor a more liberal system of textbook control, and the government, which believes that central vigilance is essential to maintaining high national standards in education.

NOTES

1. Richard Rubinger, "Education: From One Room to One System," in *Japan in Transition: From Bakumatsu to Meiji*, eds. Marius B. Jansen and Gilbert F. Rozman (Princeton: Princeton University Press, 1986), p. 198.

2. E. Patricia Tsurumi, "Meiji Primary School Language and Ethics Textbooks: Old Values for a New Society," *Modern Asian Studies* 8 (1974): 247–261.

3. Benjamin C. Duke, "The Textbook Controversy," *Japan Quarterly* 19 (July–September 1972): 348.

TEXTBOOKS I

866. The Asia Society. *Asia in American Textbooks: An Evaluation.* New York: The Asia Society, 1976.

The most comprehensive survey and analysis of the treatment of Asia in American elementary and secondary school textbooks up to 1975. Covers 306 books in all 50 states, looking at general characteristics of coverage on Asia, accuracy and authenticity, underlying assumptions, human interest materials, style and tone, and sexism; the conclusion includes recommendations for action.

867. Beer, Lawrence W. "Education, Politics and Freedom in Japan: The Ienaga Textbook Case." *Law in Japan* 8 (1975):67–90.

Details on the legal aspects of decisions handed down by the Tokyo District Court in 1970 and 1974 in the Ienaga textbook case. Clear statement of the issues involved. Also summary of the textbook authorization system in Japan.

868. Bonet, Vicente M., ed. *Religion in the Japanese Textbooks*. 3 vols. Tokyo: Enderle Book Co., 1973.

   Analysis of religious content in 91 elementary and secondary school textbooks in the fields of ethics and society, world history, and Japanese history. Argues that most of what Japanese know about religion is learned from textbook materials.

869. Caiger, John G. "The Aims and Content of School Courses in Japanese History, 1872–1945." In *Japan's Modern Century*, pp. 51–82. Edited by Edmund Skrzypczak. Tokyo: Sophia University Press, 1965.

   Thoughtful analysis which traces the evolution of the government-directed, officially sponsored image of national identity from early Meiji to the end of World War II. Caiger suggests that it was only with defeat in 1945 that it became possible for those with a different view of Japan's national identity to have their view included in historical texts.

870. ———. "Ienaga Saburo and the First Postwar Japanese History Textbook." *Modern Asian Studies* 3 (January 1969):1-16.

   Analyzes the writing and publication in 1946 of *Kuni no ayumi* by Ienaga Saburo and three others, the first history text approved in the postwar period by both the Ministry of Education and SCAP. Suggests that the Ministry of Education's attacks on Ienaga's writings in the 1960s indicate a retreat from the values it espoused when it supported Ienaga's earlier work.

871. Cogan, John J., and Weber, Ronald E. "The Japanese History Textbook Controversy and What We Can Learn From It." *Social Education* 47 (April 1983):253–257.

   Discusses the implications for American teachers of the textbook controversies in Japan in the summer of 1982, when the Supreme Court upheld the Ministry of Education in the Ienaga case, and new controversies swirled around textbook treatments of World War II in China and Korea.

872.   Dore, R.P. "The Content of Terakoya Education." In *Education in Tokugawa Japan* (item 74), pp. 271–290.

Analysis, with excerpts, of the complex combination of superstitions, calendrical lore, traditional medical advice, folk traditions, hints on etiquette, training for basic literacy and numeracy skills, and large doses of Confucian morality that made up the contents of premodern text materials.

873.   ———. "Textbook Censorship in Japan: The Ienaga Case." *Pacific Affairs* 43 (Winter 1970–71):548–556.

Summary of events, analysis of issues, summaries of court arguments in the 1970 court decision in favor of Ienaga Saburo's suit against the Ministry of Education for infringing on his freedom of expression when it refused to authorize his 1965 text unless extensive revisions were made.

874.   Duke, Benjamin C. "The Pacific War in Japanese and American High Schools: A Comparison of the Textbook Teachings." *Comparative Education* 5 (February 1969):73–82.

Uses the Ienaga textbook case as a pretext for comparing the coverage of World War II in American and Japanese high school textbooks. Finds very different treatments in terms of the amount of detail, the level of emotionalism, and coverage of specific events.

875.   ———. "The Textbook Controversy." *Japan Quarterly* 19 (July–Sept. 1972):337–352. Reprinted in *Learning to Be Japanese* (item 22), pp. 240–264.

Substantive and detailed account of the history of textbook authorization system and the steps involved in the progress of Professor Ienaga's lawsuit against the Ministry of Education. A useful summary of the main issues involved for both the principal and the Ministry of Education, and the implications for Japanese education.

*   Fridell, Wilbur M. "Government Ethics Textbooks in Late Meiji Japan." *Journal of Asian Studies* 29 (August 1970):823–833. Annotated in item 153 above.

876.   Huntsberry, Rand. "Suffering History: The Textbook Trial of Ienaga Saburo." *Journal of the American Academy of Religion* 44 (June 1976):239–254.

Uses the Ienaga textbook case to look at the larger issue of the search for values and identity in postwar Japan. Particularly interesting are the autobiographical materials presented on Professor Ienaga and Murao Jiro, an official of the Ministry of Education, showing how each developed entirely different ideas and perspectives on modern Japanese society.

877.   Hurst, G. Cameron, III. "Weaving the Emperor's New Clothes: The Japanese Textbook 'Revision' Controversy." *University Field Staff International, Inc.* No. 46 (1982).

Argues that although the 1982 controversy over Japan's alleged rewriting of history to minimize its imperial past was based on press error, the fact that it occurred reveals continued regional tensions between China, Japan, and Korea and domestic conflict within the academic and press elite and the government.

878.   Ienaga Saburo. "The Historical Significance of the Japanese Textbook Lawsuit." *The Bulletin of Concerned Asian Scholars* 2 (Fall 1970):2–12.

A brief summary of his argument by the principal in the Ienaga textbook case.

879.   *Japan Echo* 9 (Winter 1982):13–51.

See the special section entitled, "The Textbook Flap" which includes a useful introduction by the editors, which summarizes the events of the summer of 1982 when the governments of China and South Korea vigorously objected to the Japanese Ministry of Education's changes in wording in textbook accounts of World War II in Asia. Views on various sides of the issue by prominent writers such as Suzuki Hiroo, Miura Shumon, Okazaki Kaheita, Eto Shinkichi, and Kobori Keiichiro.

880. Karasawa Tomitaro. "Changes in Japanese Education as Revealed in Textbooks." *Japan Quarterly* 2 (July–Sept. 1955):365–383.

Survey of the contents of textbooks from the Tokugawa period, revealing the heavy influence of the prevalent political ethos, by an authority in the field. A much simplified version of the extensive work in this area the author has published in Japanese, and thus not as useful as the title would suggest.

881. Pyle, Kenneth B. "Japan Besieged: The Textbooks Controversy." *Journal of Japanese Studies* 9 (Summer 1983):297–300.

Brief report on the 1982 controversy caused by press accounts of Ministry of Education changes in wording in text accounts of World War II and an introduction to the substantive article by Yayama Taro (see item 886).

*   Steenstrup, Carl. "The Imagawa Letter: A Muromachi Warrior's Code of Conduct Which Became a Tokugawa Schoolbook." *Monumenta Nipponica* 28 (Autumn 1973): 295–316. Annotated in item 57 above.

*   Tsurumi, E. Patricia. "Meiji Primary School Language and Ethics Textbooks: Old Values for a New Society." *Modern Asian Studies* 8 (1974):247–261. Annotated in item 185 above.

882. Uyenaka Shuzo. "The Textbook Controversy of 1911: National Needs and Historical Truth." In *History in the Service of the Japanese Nation*, pp. 94–120. Edited by John S. Brownlee. Toronto: University of Toronto–York University, Joint Center on Modern East Asia, 1983.

Historical, political, and scholarly context of the 1911 textbook incident, where a government text was criticized for supporting a "two courts" position in a chapter on the fourteenth century.

883. Varley, H. Paul. "History Revised." In *Imperial Restoration in Medieval Japan*, pp. 156–183. Edited by H. Paul Varley, New York: Columbia University Press, 1971.

     The history of history teaching in the Meiji period with a focus on the 1911 controversy surrounding the treatment in authorized elementary school textbooks of the theory of "two courts" in the fourteenth century. The text version raised the possibility that imperial authority was divisible, a view which the government could not support.

884. Wray, Harold J. "A Study in Contrasts: Japanese School Textbooks of 1903 and 1941–1945." *Monumenta Nipponica* 2 (Spring 1973):69–86.

     Uses differences in textbooks in two periods to show how educational materials can reflect changes in domestic political context and attitudes to the outside world.

885. Yamazumi Masami. "Textbook Revision: The Swing to the Right." *Japan Quarterly* 28 (Oct.–Dec. 1981):472–478.

     Sees in recent developments in the control of textbooks evidence of conservative and centralizing moves by the Ministry of Education. Particular attention is paid to the growing influence of municipal and prefectural authorities in the selection of textbooks and the waning power of schools and teachers.

886. Yayama Taro. "The Newspapers Conduct a Mad Rhapsody Over the Textbook Issue." *Journal of Japanese Studies* 9 (Summer 1983):301–316.

     Examines the behavior of the press in 1982 including the misreporting of Ministry of Education textbook revisions and the international incident which followed. The author lambasts the Japanese press and supports the authorization system.

TEXTBOOKS II

* Anderson, Ronald S. *Education in Japan: A Century of Modern Development*. Washington, D.C.: U.S. Government Printing Office, 1975. Annotated in item 20 above. See pp. 285–289.

887. Beer, Lawrence W. *Freedom of Expression in Japan: A Study in Comparative Law, Politics and Society.* New York: Kodansha International, 1985. See Chapter 7.

888. ———. "Freedom of Information and the Evidentiary Use of Film in Japan." *American Political Science Review* 65 (1971).

889. Belding, Robert E. "I Am a Japanese Textbook." *Education* 80 (February 1960):359–363.

890. Bellah, Robert N. "Ienaga Saburo and the Search for Meaning in Modern Japan." In *Changing Japanese Attitudes Toward Modernization,* pp. 369–423. Edited by Marius B. Jansen. Princeton: Princeton University Press, 1965.

891. Caiger, J.G. "Education, Values, and Japan's National Identity: A Study of the Aims and Contents of Courses in Japanese History, 1872–1963." Ph.D dissertation, Australian National University, 1966.

892. ———. "The First Postwar History Book in Japan: Japanese or American?" *Journal of the Oriental Society of Australia* 3 (December 1965):2–15.

893. ———. "A 'Reverse Course' in the Teaching of History in Postwar Japan?" *Journal of the Oriental Society of Australia* 5 (December 1967):4–16.

894. Duke, Benjamin C. "Ministry Condemned for Censorship." *Times Educational Supplement* No. 2898 (December 4, 1970):12.

895. ———. "The Pacific War in Japanese and American Schools." *Educational Studies* (International Christian University) 13 (March 1968):158–176.

896. Hook, Glenn D. "Peace Issues in Japanese Textbooks." *Peace Research in Japan* (1977–78):61–65.

897. Hosoya Toshio. *Development of the Modern Textbook System in Japan, 1868–1900.* Tokyo: Japanese National Commission for UNESCO, 1961.

898. Ishii Hidenosuke. "Recent Trends in the Production of School Textbooks." *Asian Printer* 1 (July 1958):28–32.

899. Ishikawa Ken. "Studies in the Teikin Orai Text-Books in Relation to the Development of Teaching Methods." *Japan Science Review—Literature, Philosophy, and History* 3 (1952).

900. Itoh Hirosaki, and Beer, Lawrence W. *The Constitutional Case Law of Japan: Selected Supreme Court Decisions, 1961–1970.* Seattle: University of Washington Press, 1978.

901. Japanese National Commission for UNESCO. *An Analysis of the School Textbooks in Social Studies from the Viewpoint of International Understanding.* Tokyo: Ministry of Education, 1959.

902. ———. *Report of a Survey of School Textbooks in Japan.* Tokyo: Ministry of Education, 1956.

903. ———. *School Textbooks in Japan, 1957: A Report of a Survey from the Standpoint of Education for International Understanding and Cooperation.* Tokyo: Ministry of Education, 1958.

904. ———. *The Treatment of the West in Textbooks.* Tokyo: Ministry of Education, 1958.

905. "Japanese School Textbooks—An Historical Survey." *Proceedings of the International Conference on Educational Research.* Tokyo: Organizing Committee, International Conference on Educational Research, 1961.

See pp. 170–174.

906. Japan, National Institute for Educational Research. *School Textbooks in Japan, 1957*. Tokyo: NIER, 1958.

907. Kambayashi Kikuko. "The Expansion of Treatments of Japan in High School Textbooks in American History, 1951–1972." Ann Arbor: University of Michigan Comparative Education Dissertation Series, No. 26, 1975.

908. Kataoka Tetsuya. "Textbooks and the Specter of Japanese Militarism." *Asian Wall Street Journal*, 12 October 1982.

909. Kaya Michiko. "Japan as Seen in Foreign Textbooks: Some Drawbacks." *Tokyo Book Development Centre Newsletter* 9 (September 1977):1040.

910. Kobayashi, Victor N. "Japan and the United States: What Our Textbooks Teach Us About Each Other." *Today's Education* (Social Studies edition) 70 (November–December 1981):45–57.

911. Koedoot, Gerrit. "Review: *Religion in Japanese Textbooks*." *Japan Christian Quarterly* 43 (Summer 1977):177–182.

912. Lee Sookney. "Primary Arithmetic Textbooks in Korea, Japan, China and the United States." Ed.D. dissertation, University of Iowa, 1954.

913. Miyauchi, Dixon Y. "Textbooks and the Search for New National Ethics in Japan." *Sociology of Education* 28 (March 1964):131–137.

914. Ogata Kazuko. "Mothers and the Textbooks Controversy." Translated by B. Tucker. *Japan Christian Quarterly* 37 (Spring 1971):80–82.

915. Shimada Tatsumi. "Japan in Foreign Textbooks." *Japan Quarterly* 7 (April–June 1966):188–192.

916. Song Un Sun. "A Sociological Analysis of the Value System of Pre-War Japan as Revealed in the Japanese Government Elementary Textbooks, 1932–1941." Ph.D. dissertation, University of Maryland, 1958.

917. Sumeragi Shido. "Report on the Adoption of European Culture and the Development of Textbooks Administration in Japan." *Education in Japan—A Journal for Overseas* (Hiroshima University) 3 (1968):1–5.

918. Takaki Tori. "Education for International Understanding in Shushin Textbooks." *ICU Bulletin of Educational Research* 3 (December 1956):19–42.

919. ———. "The Treatment of Japan and Peoples of Japanese Descent in Senior High School American History Textbooks." Ph.D. dissertation, University of Michigan, 1954.

920. Tamashiro Masamitsu. "Analysis of the Treatment of Selected Aspects of United States—Japan Relations from 1905 to 1960 as Found in High School History Textbooks of Both Nations." Ph.D. dissertation, New York University, 1972.

921. Translation Service Center. "Textbook Furor Due to Careless Reporting." Translation Service Center, No. 264. *Sankei Shimbun* (October 18, 1982):2.

922. Wojtan, Linda S. "Japan in Our Textbooks: The Need for Alternative Resources." *Georgia Social Science Journal* 12 (Summer 1981):7–11.

923. Wray, Harold J. "Changes and Continuity in Images of the Kokutai and Attitudes and Roles Toward the Outside World, A Content Analysis of Japanese Textbooks." Ph.D. dissertation, University of Hawaii, 1971.

924. ———. "China in Japanese Textbooks." In *China and Japan: Search for Balance Since World War I*, pp. 113–131. Edited

by Alvin D. Coox and F. Hilary Conroy. Santa Barbara, Calif.: ABC Clio Books, 1978.

925. ———. "Nationalism and Internationalism in Japanese Elementary Textbooks, 1918–1931." *Asian Forum* 5 (1973):46–62.

926. Wunderlich, Herbert John. "The Japanese Textbook Problem and Solution, 1945–1946." Ph.D. dissertation, Stanford University, 1952.

927. Zolbrod, Leon M. "Kusazoshi: Chapbooks of Japan." *Transactions of the Asiatic Society of Japan* 3rd Series, 10 (August 1968):116–147.

CHAPTER XIV
PROBLEMS, ISSUES, AND REFORM IN JAPANESE EDUCATION

Introduction

The purpose of this final chapter is to describe the most important recent developments in Japanese education and to provide citations and annotations for the best recent English-language writing on significant issues in the field. Since 1984 the focus of discussion and debate on education in Japan—both in scholarly circles and the mass media—has been the government's plans for substantive reform of the educational system. This reform program is discussed, in some detail, in the essay that follows.

Recent literature on Japanese education derives from two distinct perspectives and the bibliography section is divided by topic, reflecting the character of the most recent literature. The materials listed in the first section of the bibliography under the heading, "Problems, Issues, and Reform," are characterized by a critical stance and reformist themes and emanate mostly from Japanese government, media, and scholarly sources. Under the second heading, "Learning from Japan: Western Perspectives," are included recent writings, mostly from Western scholars and journalists, that focus much less on problems and more on those aspects of Japanese education perceived as useful models for the reform of Western educational systems and teaching practices.

It is ironic that at a time when Western interest in Japanese education is intense, when Western writers are holding up Japanese education as a model to be emulated for revitalizing the industrial societies of North America and Europe, the Japanese are consumed with doubts and apparently bent on the most significant reform of their educational system since the Occupation period. From the Japanese side the literature describes a broad spectrum of festering problems calling out for reform: the inegalitarian effects of entrance exam pressures and *juku* attendance; the sacrifice by young children of their emotional and physical well-being; the increase in school violence, bullying, and dropouts; the need to "internationalize" the curriculum, and to better integrate students who have returned from abroad; and the need for greater flexibility in the system as a whole. The reform literature details the many problems and in some cases suggests utopian solutions for them. Whether or not substantive reforms are part of the formal proposals expected from the government in December of 1988, the literature is useful for what it reveals about the hopes and aspirations of many segments of the Japanese public regarding their schools.

Western interest in Japanese education, stimulated by Ezra Vogel's 1979 publication, *Japan as Number One* (item 984 below), has focused not so much on discreet segments of Japanese education but on aggregate statistics on the system as a whole. Figures on school attendance rates, literacy, hours in school per week and per year, scores on international tests of achievement in mathematics and science, and the high standards to which mass education is held accountable in Japanese society are impressive indeed. These basic facts have functioned to stimulate Western interest in further exploration of the sources of educational achievement in Japan.

The Western literature on Japanese education now comes not only from Japan specialists whose interests are in the dynamics of Japanese society, but also from journalists, educators, and government officials who share the belief that Japanese economic success has educational roots. Much of the recent writing is also motivated by a desire to find in superior foreign models incentives for educational reform at home.

In the search for usable models in Japanese education, research has moved beyond aggregate statistics. Bypassing universities and secondary schools—where little of value has been observed—Western social scientists have devoted increasing attention to levels before compulsory schooling takes over—the preschools and nursery schools. While the substantial literature on the socialization process in Japan is beyond the scope of this book, literature on early education is included in the second section of the bibliography.

In many cases it has been social scientists, not Japan specialists, who have done recent work on preschools in Japan. Their interests are either policy oriented—that is, they are interested in the possible benefits of Japanese educational practices for reform at home—or disciplinary—that is, they are gathering data from Japan to test hypotheses developed elsewhere. One possible benefit from this work is that knowledge of Japanese education may be extended beyond the confines of Japanology to the larger contexts of psychological, sociological, and anthropological theory.

The Context of the Current Reform Movement

Japan is now engaged in a major educational reform movement. Its scope is such that if most of the major proposals under consideration are adopted and implemented, the resulting level of change would rank with the two previous watersheds in Japanese educational history, the Meiji and Occupation reforms.[1]

At a time when many Americans are calling for reforms that would restructure American education to more closely resemble the Japanese system, there has been increasing recognition among thoughtful Japanese that their system is beset by serious problems. Japan must, according to a panel of distinguished citizens, "face the harsh reality of the problems in our schools and the serious state of dilapidation or 'desolation' of our educational system which they signal." This desolation, the panel's report continues, "includes bullying, school violence, and excessive competition in entrance examinations."[2]

Most analyses of Japanese education have pointed to Japan's commitment to education as an escalator for success. Now cracks in this commitment are beginning to appear. Professor Amano Ikuo of Tokyo University persuasively argues that Japan is experiencing what he describes as a "crisis in structuration." In his analysis, Amano suggests that postwar Japan was successful in creating a society that was both egalitarian and mobile, but since the economic slowdown following the oil crisis of 1973, opportunities for mobility have been significantly reduced. He believes that the American Occupation's attempt to dismantle the prewar hierarchial system of higher education failed, and that a stable hierarchy of high schools, dominated by the relative handful of high schools providing access to the top universities, has emerged. "The opportunities to the top universities," he writes, "are virtually monopolized by the top high schools, and graduates of these top schools tend to secure jobs leading to the elite positions in society." In an earlier stage of rapid expansion of secondary and higher education, Amano contends, there existed a healthy competition, but, as a result of the changes described above, the number of places in elite universities has decreased, and the number of desirable jobs available upon graduation are fewer. "Although a majority of young people continue to play this game, there are increasing numbers who are unwilling to participate."[3]

Amano's assertion that most Japanese youths continue to play the competition game is undoubtedly accurate, but, for the first time, an increasing number of young people are dropping out of that game. In the past, one of the things that distinguished Japanese schools from their American counterparts was their minuscule number of dropouts. In 1983, for example, 111,531 students of public and private senior high schools in Japan dropped out, an increase of 5.2% over the preceding year. These figures constituted only 2.4% of all senior high school students and is quite low, especially when compared to the 23% of American senior high school students who drop out before graduation. What is troubling, however, is that the Japanese figure has shown an increase every year since 1974, when relevant statistics were first collected.

One of the most interesting dimensions of this phenomenon is the so-called "school refusal syndrome," which in the view of the Ministry of Education is caused by "the rapidity of social change, the proliferation of the nuclear family, loss of community feelings, affluence, and urbanization." Another view, however, "blames the school system which is theoretically designed so that all children of the same group stay at the same level and work at the same pace." The practical result, however, is "great strain on the slower children." These children's complaints of physical ailments that keep them home from school are neither truancy nor delinquency, but "a cry of silence" against the terrible pressures placed on them by an unyielding system."[4] This problem is especially prevalent at the junior high school level where a sharp upsurge has been experienced. The Ministry of Education reports that the number of junior high pupils missing 50 or more days of school for emotional reasons in 1974 was 7,310. By 1983 the number had increased to 24,059.

Others see the problems of contemporary Japan as nothing more than "advanced nation disease" (*senshinkoku-byo*), i.e., the inevitable, if alarming results of modern industrial society: "increases in the rates of divorce, juvenile crime, school violence, and other social ills associated with countries like the United States."[5] It is undeniable that school violence, although still a relatively modest problem when compared to that of the United States, is seen by most Japanese as not only unimaginable, but un-Japanese. The actions of this still small minority have shocked adult Japan because, "their behavior violates the most fundamental code of Confucian-influenced traditional educational values namely respecting and obeying teachers."[6] The first half of 1983 saw a 26% increase in school violence incidents in comparison to 1982. A bewildering increase of violence against teachers occurred and, to the surprise of many, more and more females are engaging in violent activities. The National Police Agency [NPA] reported in 1984 that almost one of every five youngsters taken into custody by the police was female.[7]

Both 1983 and 1984, however, saw a slight decline in school violence (according to NPA reports), but the violence which occurred has been characterized by authorities as more "vicious" than in the past. Indeed, the NPA recorded "an increase in such crimes as kidnapping, arson, and, assaults by minors."[8] The category showing the greatest increase, however, is that of *ijime*, or school "bullying" and both the vernacular and English-language press are filled with reports, editorials, and letters to the editor describing, analyzing, and abhorring it. It has become such a serious problem that the Tokyo Metropolitan Police Department was forced to create a special unit for taking into public custody tormentors in school bullying cases.

By 1985, Ministry of Education statistics indicated that school bullying was again on the rise in Japan, particularly at the junior high school level "where the number of serious incidents reported averaged 5.1 per school." Indeed, bullying was the cause of nine suicides among junior high pupils; between the opening of the school year in April 1985 and October of that year, there were 155,066 reported cases of bullying, affecting 21,899 public schools or 55.6% of the nation's public schools. As might be expected, the majority of these incidents occurred in large urban centers with Tokyo leading the way.[9]

Although media attention to such dramatic incidents as school violence and bullying has galvanized public concern over the public schools, government plans for reform have been under way for some time.

The Current Reform Movement

The late 1970s and early 1980s served as a "warm up" period to Japan's current educational reform movement. In the early 1970s, several important reports calling for educational reforms of various types stirred widespread discussion among thoughtful Japanese and contributed to the ferment that resulted in the appointment of the Ad Hoc Reform Council, or *Rinkyoshin*, in 1984. The first of these early documents, published in 1970, was the Ministry of Education's *Educational Standards in Japan* which provided a comparative framework within which to evaluate Japan's educational achievements. This was soon followed by a report of one of the Ministry's advisory organs, the Central Council for Education, which caused a considerable stir and provoked the Japan Teachers' Union to undertake its own study, which was published in 1975.

The Central Council for Education document took a swipe at both conservative apologists of the existing system and the radical Japan Teachers' Union when it warned that "Education is rapidly falling behind the times because vested interests protect the status quo, because idealists oppose reforms without paying attention to their actual contents, and because much time is spent wastefully on the discussion of reforms which have no possibility of being implemented."[10] The report advocated "long-range fundamental policies and measures for developing the educational system, basing these proposals on an examination of the educational system's achievements over the past twenty years and on its understanding of the system of education appropriate for the years to come, in which rapid technological innovations and national and international changes are anticipated."[11] The then minister of education, Sakata Michita, was impressed enough by this analysis to refer to it as a plan "for the third major educational reform in Japan's history."[12]

Among its proposals, all of which carried hefty price tags, were: extending free public education to four- and five-year-olds; providing teachers with large salary increases; allowing teachers more time to teach by shifting paper work to an expanded clerical staff; expanding special education programs; increasing subsidies to private universities; and others along similar lines. One could probably characterize this report as recognizing that educational expansion had run its course, and there was now a need to move in the direction of improving educational quality. As was to be expected, reactions to specific proposals depended upon whether one's ox was being gored or not.

Still another important document feeding the reform debate was the Organization for Economic Cooperation and Development (OECD) analysis of Japan's educational policies. Falling back on its traditional practice of actively seeking outside advice, Japan invited the Paris-based OECD to send an expert team to advise it on future directions. The OECD report, on balance, probably had the clearest view of Japan's educational problems. The OECD praised the role played by education in the nation's industrial development, but strongly criticized the conformist nature of the Japanese system, overcentralized control, and on overemphasis on standardization in the name of egalitarianism. Instead, it recommended that the time seemed to be ripe "for some practical measures aimed at the development of students' personalities through a more flexible and less pressured scheme of education, with more free time, more curricular freedom, more diversity in extra-curricular activities, and more co-operation among pupils. The time may have come," the OECD examiners continued, "to devote more attention to such matters as *cooperation*, in addition to discipline and competition, and *creativity*, in addition to receptivity and imitation."[13]

Finally, after several years of careful study, the Council on Education Reform of the Japan Teachers' Union, published its own view of the correct path to educational reform. Arguing that Japanese education "is circumscribed" by the government's "high economic growth policy nationally, and Security Treaty setup with the United States internationally," the JTU report suggests that this has resulted in "environmental destruction, soaring prices, housing problems, [a] traffic mess, and energy crisis."[14]

While the reform ferment of the early 1970s was at its height, Japan was hit by the first oil crisis in 1973. As a result of this international economic dislocation, Japan's economy sputtered to a virtual halt and, for a brief period, experienced a negative growth rate. After this sharp decrease in the growth rate, which had averaged 9.1% between 1959–1973, to a mere 4.0% between 1974 and 1980, the government was hard put to provide the resources needed by the education sector and, indeed, has had to find ways to reduce its financial support.

For the reverse of many of the reasons that educational enrollments expanded rapidly during the economic boom of the 1960s, the system began to contract after 1973. The birth rate has dropped sharply in recent years, and there appears to be no good reason to anticipate a turnaround in the near future. The school-age population has been decreasing since 1979 at the kindergarten level, and since 1981 at the lower elementary level, and this negative wave is generally making its way through the entire system. Attendance rates among school age children in the noncompulsory sector have stabilized since 1970s, suggesting that demand may have peaked. Further, "Japan's birth rate for 1980 equaled the record low level for 1966" and, according to a government spokesman, "the proportion of women of childbearing age will decline during the next four or five years."[15] Also, the percentage of Japan's under-15 population decreased from 22.3% in 1984 to 21.8% in 1985.[16]

Recent reports, based on hard data collected and analyzed by the government, have concluded that Japan's population of aged people is rapidly growing, and in 1984, the number of people aged 65 or over reached 9.9% as compared with 5% in 1950. By the year 2000, it is projected that Japan will rank first in the world as the nation with the highest percentage of old people. This "graying" phenomenon is analyzed by government-sponsored research which indicates "that by the year 2001, there will be one citizen 65 or over for every three productive citizens (aged 15 to 64). At present the ratio is one to seven."[17]

The educational implications of this trend are not difficult to see. Japan is now paying the price, in economic and social consequences, for the rapid demographic transition after World War II—from being a country with high death and birthrates to one with low mortality and fertility rates. The aging phenomenon confronts the society in general, and educational planners and policymakers in particular, with a number of problems. One possible scenario is raising the retirement age, enabling workers to stay on the job longer, and reducing the openings for youths who are anxious to enter the labor force. Having more older people in jobs may also serve to decrease productivity at a time when higher productivity is needed to meet increased foreign competition. Finally, it appears certain that the nation's medical bills will increase substantially, and the social implications of all of the above are not easy to predict.

Big business in Japan has also contributed to this situation as a result of its predilection for recruiting new employees from a select group of universities. This causes a downward pressure which distorts pre-university education. One cannot, after all is said and done, blame children and their parents for following the only real path to economic success in Japanese society. They search with a relentless persistence for anything that will give them an "edge" in the great competition for educational certification.

The basic problems facing Japanese policymakers are the maintenance of high standards in education that will continue to foster economic development; and the simultaneous reform of education to provide greater flexibility and defuse public discontent while, at the same time, taking care that revisions take a form that is harmonious with Japanese traditions and values. If the two previous major reforms, in early Meiji and following World War II, are any guide, we can expect reforms of a rather sweeping nature to be made in the next few years, to be followed shortly by a period of reflection in which modifications of the original reforms are made to bring them into closer conformity with the realities of Japanese life.

One of the major differences between the 1980s and the two earlier reform experiences, however, is that in both the Meiji and the Occupation periods there were foreign models available that everyone agreed were worthy of emulation. The foreign models, whether English, French, German or American, were models with which their creators were reasonably satisfied. Today, however, there is no foreign model which stands out as an obvious candidate for adaptation. Virtually all of the countries to which Japan has traditionally looked for educational ideas are themselves engaged in reform efforts to salvage inadequate educational systems. Can Japanese reform creatively cope with this new situation?

The Mechanics of the Current Reform Movement

Prime Minister Nakasone Yasuhiro, facing new elections, determined that he would make educational reform one of the major building blocks in his campaign to be returned to office. In June 1983, he appointed an advisory committee, the Conference on Culture and Education, to examine the problems of Japanese education and to recommend possible actions to remedy the situation. "On the eve of the general election of December 1983, the Prime Minister released a seven-point plan for reform that drew widespread media attention. Among other things, he proposed reform of the university entrance examination system and a reassessment of the 6-3-3 school organization."[18] Following his re-election to office, Nakasone continued to emphasize the need for educational reform. In a February 1984 speech to the Diet, Nakasone reaffirmed his belief that "the time has come to institute sweeping reforms across the entire educational spectrum in preparation for the 21st century."[19]

On 27 March 1984, Nakasone proposed that an ad hoc council on educational reform be "established under his direct control."[20] After lengthy debate on 7 August 1984, the Diet voted to establish the Ad Hoc Council on Educational Reform for a three-year period.[21] The creation of this body, thus, effectively bypassed the existing Central Council for Education and marked a significant departure from the government's long-standing practice of formulating educational policies based on recommendations by the Central Council, which serves as an advisory body to the Minister of Education. It also suggested Nakasone's disenchantment with a body that had long been noted for its moderate approach and general satisfaction with the status quo.

The Ad Hoc Council was chaired by Dr. Okamoto Michio, medical doctor, educational conservative, and former president of Kyoto University who is a long-time close personal friend of Nakasone. In addition, Keio University President Ishikawa Tadao and Industrial Bank of Japan consultant Nakayama Sohei were named vice-chairmen. The remainder of the Council's 25 members were appointed shortly thereafter, and the Council held its first meeting (significantly, at the Prime Minister's residence) on 5 September 1984.

Most of the Council's members were well-known men who have had outstanding careers in a variety of fields. They included three business leaders, two labor-union representatives, a journalist-academician, and a former ambassador. Two women served on the Council, an artist and an essayist. Ages of the Council members ranged from 39 to 78, averaging 59.6 years. Seventeen of the 25 members, or 68%, are graduates of national universities with 40% being alumni of prestigious Tokyo University. Many commented on the scarcity of younger people, women, and those with specialized knowledge and experience in pre-university education.

Although much of the Council's work was carried out in plenary meetings, sub-committees were organized around four specific areas: (1) An Educational System for the Twenty-first Century, (2) Revitalization of the Educational Functions of Society, (3) Reform of Elementary and Secondary Education, and (4) Reform of Higher Education.

Recommendations of the Ad Hoc Council[22]

Early in its deliberations the Council identified eight major issues upon which it would focus its primary attention:

1. Basic Requirements for an Education Relevant to the Twenty-first Century.
2. Organization and Systemization of Lifelong Learning and the Correction of Adverse Effects of Undue Emphasis on the Educational Background of Individuals.
3. Enhancement of Higher Education and Individualization of Higher Education Institutions.
4. Enrichment and Diversification of Elementary and Secondary Education.
5. Improvement of the Quality of Teachers.
6. Coping with Internationalization.
7. Coping with the Information Age.
8. Review of Educational Administration and Finance.

In addition, the Council determined that these issues should be debated within the context of the following concepts: individuality, fundamentals, creativity, expansion of choice, humanization of the educational environment, lifelong learning, internationalism, and dealing with the information age.

Before going out of existence upon the completion of its three-year mandate, the Council published four reports detailing its deliberations. These reports (published in 1985, 1986, and 1987) present a picture of Japanese education that is unfamiliar to the outsider accustomed to the glowing reports presented in the Western media. The four reports are far too detailed for anything but a brief summary of some of their major contents. In addition, there is a great deal of repetition and overlapping throughout all of the reports which makes it very difficult to clearly summarize their contents. Despite this problem, however, these reports are essential reading for anybody wishing to tune in to the education debate still going on within Japanese society. On a positive note, English language translations of these four Reports are readily available from any major library, or through the Japanese Embassy or any of its several Consulates.

The First Report on Educational Reform[23] treats the nation's tendency to attach undue importance to an individual's educational background, especially graduation from the most prestigious institutions of higher education. This, as the Report points out, leads to the excessive competition of the examination system.

In a section titled, "An Educational Wasteland," the Second Report describes the "state of desolation" of Japanese education.[24] This volume does, however, propose three sets of reforms for the consideration of policymakers. The first stresses the need "to invigorate education and inspire public confidence" in the system. The second deals with "coping with the changes of the times" and emphasizes both internationalization and the information age. The final set of proposals concerns educational administration and finance.

The Third Report of the Council[25] offers a number of concrete proposals in regard to those issues not adequately dealt with in the preceding reports. The issues treated include those related to the transition to a lifelong learning system; elementary and secondary education reforms (including textbook reforms); the reform of the organization and management of higher education institutions; reforms associated with coping with internationalization and the age of information; and, finally, the reform of educational finance.

The Council's Fourth Report[26] deals with suggestions for the reform of educational administration and the official start of the school year, as well as recommendations on the future direction of education reforms. While reaffirming many of the earlier reform proposals, the final report calls for the "fostering of a liberal and autonomous mind . . . [whereby] children should be taught to think, judge, and take responsibility for themselves." Following this liberal sentiment is a call for building upon Japan's "unique identity," and a renewed emphasis on a "patriotism" that will "teach the proper sentiment and attitude so that people can understand and respect the meaning of the national flag and the national anthem." Critics of the Council question how critical thinking and an emotional patriotism can be taught side-by-side.

Other major proposals touch upon internationalization, lifelong learning, the reorganization of higher education to ensure greater flexibility to meet both individual and social needs (including entrance examination reforms), reform of the controversial textbook authorization system, encouraging, and assisting foreign students to study in Japan, and the utilization of technology to create an information society.

Conclusions

It is not unknown for highly visible reform commissions to issue a series of recommendations amid great fanfare, and to have them, in effect, disappear, never to be heard from again. The percentage of blue-ribbon panel recommendations (in any country) which has actually been implemented is not impressive. What will occur in Japan is yet to be determined, but it is fair to point out that there are many in the Japanese educational community who feel, to a greater or lesser extent, threatened by these proposals. Any significant change in the examination system, for example, will immediately threaten the financial well-being of, among others, thousands of *juku* and *yobiko*, as well as scores of firms providing sample tests, "how to" books on passing examinations, being accepted at "X" University, and the like. Also faced with the loss of a substantial proportion of income are numerous private universities, whose entrance-examination income can mean the difference between survival and financial disaster. There is also, of course, a substantial number of influential people and organizations which will oppose many reforms on philosophical and pedagogical grounds.

Many older Japanese see a number of the proposed reforms as recycled Occupation proposals, and they argue that Japan would never have achieved her current position in the world had those reforms been implemented in the postwar years. Thus, they see the reform path as one leading to disaster. They argue that although some fine tuning may be needed, there is no need to be stampeded into more than that. To use an American phrase, they argue "If it's not broken, don't fix it."

Perhaps, the most significant element working against a wholesale implementation of the proposed reforms is political reality. First, the Ad Hoc Council was a creation of Prime Minister Nakasone and he staked his personal reputation on its work. Nakasone is no longer in power, and his successor, Prime Minister Takeshita Noboru, is a cautious and conservative politician who lacks Nakasone's interest in, and commitment to major educational reform. Perhaps as important, is the fact that Japan has had six ministers of education since the Council began its work in 1984. With each succeeding minister, the personal commitment to implement a predecessor's reforms is lessened. Finally, as a personal creation of Nakasone, the Council was designed to circumvent the Ministry of Education's bureaucracy. Now five years later, it is unlikely that the Mombusho's bureaucrats have any great interest in pursuing the recommended reforms.

Nevertheless, since the Provisional Council disbanded in 1987 the job of working its recommendations into policy has been taken up by the administration of Prime Minister Takeshita. The proposals are expected to be finalized by December of 1988 and go into effect in the early 1990s. A limited expansion in course offerings and greater freedom for students by expanding elective options are foreseen. There are also likely to be classes in computers added to the curriculum. The draft reforms also stress various areas of traditional culture, such as folk music and classical instuments, as well as training in calligraphy and the abacus. What is likely to arouse the greatest controversy, however, is the advocacy of mandatory use at school events of two sensitive symbols of Japan's miltary past: the national anthem (*Kimigayo*) and the Rising Sun flag.

Exactly which elements of the reform proposals will be implemented is not yet clear. What is certain, however, is that the new reforms will not satisfy all the concerns that were expressed in the debate over them.

NOTES

1. From *Japanese Education Today: A Report from the U.S. Study of Education in Japan* (Washington, D.C.: U.S. Government Printing Office, 1987), p. 63.

2. *Second Report on Educational Reform* (Tokyo: National Council on Educational Reform, 1986), p. 13.

3. Amano Ikuo, "Educational Crisis in Japan," in *Educational Policies in Crisis: Japanese and American Perspectives*, ed. William K. Cummings, et al. (New York: Praeger, 1986), pp. 23–43.

4. Margaret Locke, "Plea for Acceptance: School Refusal Syndrome in Japan," Unpublished paper presented at the Association for Asian Studies

Annual Meeting, Philadelphia, March 1985. To be published in *Social Science and Medicine* (forthcoming).

5. G. Cameron Hurst, III, "Japanese Education: Trouble in Paradise?" *Universities Field Staff International Reports*, No. 40 (1984), p. 10.

6. Nishimura Hidetoshi, "Educational Reform: Commissioning a Master Plan," *Japan Quarterly* 37 (January–March 1985):18–22.

7. *Mainichi Daily News*, 30 December 1984, p. 12.

8. Ibid.

9. *Japan Times*, 22 February 1986, p. 2.

10. *Basic Guidelines for the Reform of Education: On the Basic Guidelines for the Development of an Integrated Educational System Suited to Contemporary Society; Report of the Central Committee for Education* (Tokyo: Ministry of Education, 1972), p. 2.

11. Ibid.

12. *Mainichi Daily News*, 12 June 1971, p. 8.

13. Organization for Economic Cooperation and Development, *Reviews of National Policies for Education: Japan* (Paris: OECD, 1971).

14. Japan Teachers' Union [*Nikkyoso*], *How to Reform Japan's Education* (Tokyo: JTU, 1975), p. 30.

15. *Japan Times*, 26 February 1981, p. 2.

16. *Mainichi Daily News*, 5 May 1985, p. 12.

17. *Japan Times*, 15 September 1985, p. 2.

18. *Japanese Education Today*, p. 64.

19. Ibid.

20. William K. Cummings et al., *Educational Policies in Crisis: Japanese and American Perspectives* (New York: Praeger, 1986), p. 10.

21. *Japanese Education Today*, p. 64.

22. This section relies heavily on *Japanese Education Today*, pp. 64–65.

23. *First Report on Education Reform* (Tokyo: Provisional Council on Educational Reform, 1985).

24. *Second Report on Educational Reform* (Tokyo: Provisional Council on Educational Reform, 1986).

25. *Third Report on Educational Reform* (Tokyo: National Council on Educational Reform, 1987).

26. *Fourth Report on Educational Reform* (Tokyo: National Council on Educational Reform, 1987).

PROBLEMS, ISSUES, AND REFORM I

928. Amano Ikuo. "Educational Crisis in Japan." In *Educational Policy in Crisis: Japanese and American Perspectives* (item 935), pp. 23–43.

Argues that, in the past, Japanese educational reform has been essentially about greater efficiency and equality, but the current debate is a true crisis, i.e., school violence, student apathy, an increasing number of school dropouts, etc.

929. ———. "Educational Reform in Historical Perspective." *Japan Echo* 11 (1984):9–16.

An excellent historical survey of educational reform since the Meiji period.

930. Azuma Hiroshi, Nakagawa Y., and Yamawaki N. "How Returnee Children Feel About Japanese Schools." *Proceedings of the Faculty of Education, Tokyo University* 20 (1980):159–172.

931. Beauchamp, Edward R. "Education." In *Democracy in Japan.* Edited by Ellis Krauss and Takeshi Ishida. Pittsburgh: University of Pittsburgh Press, in press.

Analysis of educational reforms which have resulted in a democratic education system in Japan.

932. ———. *Education in Contemporary Japan.* Bloomington: Phi Delta Kappa Educational Foundations, 1982.

Survey of Japanese education and the impact that educational reforms have had on its development.

933. ———. "Reform Traditions in the United States and Japan." In *Educational Policy in Crisis: Japanese and American Perspectives* (item 935), pp. 3–21.

Historical treatment of reform traditions in the United States and Japan.

* ———. "Shiken Jigoku: The Problem of Entrance Examinations in Japan." *Asian Profile* 6 (December 1978):543–560. Cited as item 487 above.

Analysis of Japan's entrance examination system and attempts to reform it.

934. Cummings, William K. "Patterns of Academic Achievement in the United States and Japan." In *Educational Policies in Crisis: Japanese and American Perspectives* (item 935), pp. 117–135.

After comparing academic achievement in the two countries, Cummings suggests that more and more Japanese youngsters are "opting out of the competition," and "engaging in a variety of antisocial acts." Ironically, the Japanese are beginning to seek ways to reduce the pressure on young people while many American educators are seeking ways to foster greater achievement levels.

935. Cummings, William K; Beauchamp, Edward R., et al., eds.
      *Educational Policies in Crisis: Japanese and America
      Perspectives.* New York: Praeger, 1986

      A conference volume in which leading scholars from Japan
      and America explored the ways each country has perceived and
      learned from the other's educational experiences. The nature and
      process of learning from another educational system was the
      explicit them. Contains items 928, 934, 948, 949, 954, 955.

*   Dore, R. P. *The Diploma Disease: Education, Qualification, and
      Development.* London: Allen and Unwin, 1976. Cited in
      item 498 above.

      A fierce indictment of Japan's over-emphasis on certification
      in its educational system, seen in comparative perspective.

936. Hicks, Joe E. "The Situation of Asian Foreign Students in
      Japan: Can Japanese Universities Handle a 10-Fold
      Increase?" In *Higher Educational Expansion in Asia*, pp.
      141–153. Hiroshima: Hiroshima University, Research
      Institute for Higher Education, 1985.

      A topic little written about that is sure to become an
      important issue very soon.

937. Horio Teruhisa. *Educational Thought and Ideology in Modern
      Japan: State Authority and Intellectual Freedom.* Edited and
      translated by Steven Platzer. Tokyo: University of Tokyo
      Press, 1988.

      A sharply critical perspective on modern educational
      development in Japan, by a noted and influential leftist scholar.
      Horio suggests that the state has joined forces with economic
      leaders to seek reforms to make Japanese schools into principal
      suppliers of trained and docile workers for economic expansion.
      In severely criticizing current reform proposals, Horio offers his
      own reform proposals. A useful introduction by the editor
      provides background on a scholarly viewpoint that seldom
      reaches Western readers and is much at odds with mainstream
      views.

938. Hurst, G. Cameron, III. "Japanese Education: Trouble in Paradise?" *Universities Field Staff International Reports.* No. 40 (1982).

Places educational reform proposals within a larger political and social context. Avoids oversimplification in favor of analysis.

939. Ichikawa Shogo. "American Perceptions of Japanese Education." In *Educational Policies in Crisis: Japanese and American Perspectives* (item 935), pp. 243–261.

940. ———. "Japan." In *Educational Policy: An International Survey.* Edited by J.R. Hough. New York: St. Martin's Press, 1984.

A good introduction to the relationship between education reform and the creation of educational policy.

941. James, Estelle, and Benjamin, Gail. *Public Versus Private Education: The Japanese Experiment.* New Haven: Institution for Social and Policy Studies, Yale University, 1984.

942. Japan, Central Council for Education. *Basic Guidelines for the Reform of Education.* Tokyo: Ministry of Education, 1972.

One of the several earlier reform documents that helped pave the way for the Nakasone Council on Educational Reform in 1984.

943. Japan, National Council on Educational Reform. *First Report on Educational Reform.* Tokyo: Provisional Council on Educational Reform, 1985.

944. Japan, National Council on Educational Reform. *Second Report on Educational Reform.* Tokyo: Provisional Council on Educational Reform, 1986.

945. Japan, National Council on Educational Reform. *Third Report on Educational Reform*. Tokyo: Provisional Council on Educational Reform, 1986.

946. Japan, National Council on Educational Reform. *Fourth Report on Educational Reform*. Tokyo: Provisional Council on Educational Reform, 1987.

947. Japan Teachers' Union. *How to Reform Japan's Education*. Tokyo: Japan Teachers' Union, 1975.

     A dated but still useful paper outlining the JTU position on a variety of educational issues.

948. Kitamura Kazuyuki. "The Decline and Reform of Higher Education in Japan: A Comparative Perspective." In *Educational Policies in Crisis: Japanese and American Perspectives* (item 935), pp. 153–170.

     Kitamura clearly favors the reform of Japanese universities, but points out that a middle ground is needed between resisting change and losing its viability, or yielding too rapidly to change and losing its integrity.

*   Kitamura Kazuyuki. "The Internationalization of Higher Education in Japan." *Japan Foundation Newsletter* (May 1983): 1–9; (September 1983): 6–7 and (August 1984): 9–11). Cited as item 518 above.

949. Kobayashi, Victor N. "Japanese and U.S. Curricula Compared." In *Educational Policies in Crisis: Japanese and American Perspectives* (item 935), pp. 61–95.

     An exhaustive detailing of the differences between American and Japanese curricula, which concluded that, except in the arts, there appears to be a converging of the curricular requirements of the two nations.

950. Murakami Yoshio. "Bullying in the Classroom." *Japan Quarterly* 32 (October–December 1985).

     A Japanese view about a serious problem.

951. Nishimura Hidetoshi. "Educational Reform: Commissioning a Master Plan." *Japan Quarterly* 37 (January–March 1985):18–22.

A skeptical view of the reform of Japanese education that followed the announcement of the Council of Educational Reform.

* Organization for Economic Cooperation and Development. *Review of National Policies for Education, Japan.* Paris: OECD, 1971.

Detailed analysis, by distinguished Western scholars, of the problems facing Japanese education in the late-1960s and early 1970s. Influential in laying the groundwork for the 1980s reform effort. Cited as item 405 above.

952. Ranbom, Sheppard. "Schooling in Japan—The Paradox in the Pattern." *Education Week* (20 and 27 February and 6 March 1985).

* Rohlen, Thomas P. "Is Japanese Education Becoming Less Egalitarian?" *Journal of Japanese Studies* 3 (1977):37–70.

One of the earlier Western analyses of Japanese education that was critical of something other than entrance examinations. Cited above as item 757.

953. ———. *Japan's High Schools.* Berkeley: University of California Press, 1983.

The best study of Japanese high schools in English. Among other things it demonstrates that Japanese high schools are not all the same. Contrary to idealized Western perceptions some Japanese high schools are probably worse than some American high schools.

954. Tobin, Joseph J. "American Images of Japanese Secondary and Higher Education." In *Educational Policies in Crisis: Japanese and American Perspectives* (item 935), pp. 262–274.

Critical of American studies of Japanese education that reveal more about Americans and our education system than about Japan. Proposes a new approach which recognizes the limitations of bicultural studies.

955. Tsukada Mamoru. "A Factual Overview of Japanese and American Education." In *Educational Policies in Crisis: Japanese and American Perspectives* (item 935), pp. 96–116.

The best, recent compilation of educational statistics comparing American and Japanese education.

956. White, Merry I. *The Japanese Overseas: Can They Go Home Again?* New York: Free Press, 1988.

957. Zeugner, John. "Japan's Noneducation." *New York Times*, 24 June 1983.

LEARNING FROM JAPAN: WESTERN PERSPECTIVES

958. Befu, Harumi. "The Social and Cultural Background of Child Development in Japan and the United States." In *Child Development and Education in Japan* (item 976), pp. 13–27.

Interesting, lively, and informative introduction to child development in Japan by a leading anthropologist.

959. Cogan, John J. "Should the U.S. Mimic Japanese Education? Let's Look Before We Leap." *Phi Delta Kappan* 65 (March 1984):464–468.

960. Dore, Ronald P. *Taking Japan Seriously: A Confucian Perspective on Leading Economic Issues.* Stanford: Stanford University Press, 1987.

961. Duke, Benjamin C. *The Japanese School: Lessons for Industrialized America.* New York: Praeger, 1986.

A portrait of the major strengths of Japanese education by relating the way lessons are taught in school to the rhythms of work and play in adult life. Lessons for America from Japanese education discussed. Accessible to the general reader.

962. Fiske, Edward B. "Education in Japan: Lessons for America. Japan's Schools: Intent About the Basics." *New York Times*, 10 July 1986. "Japan's Schools: Stress Group and Discourage Individuality." *New York Times*, 11 July 1986. "Japan's Schools: Exam Ordeal Rules Each Student's Destiny." *New York Times*, 12 July 1986. "Japan's Schools: Not Very Much U.S. Can Borrow." *New York Times*, 13 July 1986.

963. Glazer, Nathan. "There are No Drop-Outs in Japan: The Japanese Educational System." In *Japan's New Giant*. Edited by Hugh Patrick and Henry Rosovsky. Washington, D.C.: The Brookings Institute, 1976.

964. Grilli, Susan. *Preschool in the Suzuki Method*. Tokyo: Harcourt Brace Jovanovich Japan, 1987.

965. Hendry, Joy. *Becoming Japanese: The Work of the Pre-School Child*. Honolulu: University of Hawaii Press, 1986.

966. Hess, Robert, et al. "Family Influences on School Readiness and Achievement in Japan and the United States: An Overview of a Longitudinal Study." In *Child Development and Education in Japan* (item 976), pp. 147–166.

967. LeVine, Robert A., and White, Merry I. *Human Conditions: The Cultural Basis of Educational Development*. London: Routledge and Kegan Paul, 1986.

Includes a discussion of determination of individual attainment and educational development in China, Japan, and the Third World.

968. Lewis, Catherine. "Children's Social Development in Japan: Research Direction." In *Child Development and Education in Japan* (item 976), pp. 186–200.

Methods of cross-cultural research in Japan focusing on preschool and primary schools.

969.   ———. "Cooperation and Control in Japanese Nursery Schools." *Comparative Education Review* 28 (1984): 69–84.

Research that suggests that Japanese experience in socialization at preschool undermines the prevalent American notion that authoritarian control in the early years leads to internalization of values by small children. Indicates that Japanese children learn values best when pressure is least.

970.   ———. "Japanese First Grade Classrooms: Implications for U.S. Theory and Research." *Comparative Education Review* 32, 2 (May 1988):159–172.

The author observed fifteen first-grade classrooms in Japan to seek solutions to questions raised from American experience: how is the transition from the indulged world of the preschooler to the more disciplined world of first grader made?

971.   Lynn, Richard. *Educational Achievement in Japan: Lessons for the West.* Basingstoke: Macmillan Press, 1988.

972.   Nagai Michio. "Postwar Japanese Education and the United States." In *Mutual Images: Essays in Japanese-American Relations*, pp. 169–187. Edited by Akira Iriye. Cambridge, Mass.: Harvard University Press, 1975.

973.   Peak, Lois. "Classroom Discipline and Management in Japanese Elementary Schools." Report to the United States Study of Education in Japan, United States Department of Education, 1985.

974.   ———. "Learning to Go to School in Japan: The Transition from Home to School Life." Ph.D. dissertation, Harvard University School of Education, 1987.

975.   Rohlen, Thomas P. "Japanese Education: If They Can Do It, Should We?" *American Scholar* 55 (Winter 1985–86): 29–43.

976. Stevenson, Harold W., Azuma Hiroshi, and Hakuto Kenji, eds. *Child Development and Education in Japan.* New York: W.H. Freeman, 1986.

A series of short reports from a conference sponsored by the Center for Advanced Study in the Behavioral Sciences at Stanford University. Studies were divided into background studies, empirical studies, and conceptual studies. Useful introduction to psychological, educational, sociological, and anthropological approaches to child development and education focused on Japan. References follow each article. Contains items 958, 966, 968, 977, 978.

977. Stevenson, Harold W.; Stigler, James W.; and Lee Shin Ying. "Achievement in Mathematics." In *Child Development and Education in Japan* (item 976), pp. 201–216.

Differences in mathematics achievement in American and Japanese children attributable to the cultural environments of home and school.

978. ———. "Learning to Read Japanese." In *Child Development and Education in Japan* (item 976), pp. 217–235.

The results of a cross-national reading test given to American and Japanese children show that the Japanese fared no better. The early advantage of a syllabary decreased as the number of Chinese characters increased.

979. Shigaki I. "Child Care Practices in Japan and the United States: How Do They Reflect Cultural Values in Young Children?" *Young Children* 38 (1983):13–24.

980. Taniuchi, L. "Cultural Continuity in an Educational Institution: A Case Study of the Suzuki Method of Music Instruction." In *The Cultural Transition: Human Experience and Social Transformation in the Third World and Japan.* Edited by Merry I. White and Susan Pollak. London: Routledge and Kegan Paul, 1986.

981. Tobin, Joseph Jay; Wu, David Y.H.; and Davidson, Dana H. "Class Size and Student/Teacher Ratios in the Japanese

Preschool." *Comparative Education Review* 31, 4 (November 1987):533–549.

In contrast to Lewis (see item 969), this study focuses not on how large classes are controlled but on why there are such large classes in the first place. By eliciting comments from Japanese teachers on video tapes of American and Japanese preschools, the study suggests that the "benign neglect" of teachers in large classes is a technique used in Japanese culture for bonding in groups.

982.   Torrance, E.P. "Learning About Giftedness and Creativity from a Nation of 115 Million Overachievers." *Gifted Child Quarterly* 24 (Winter 1980):10–14.

983.   U.S. Department of Education. *Japanese Education Today*. Washington, D.C.: U.S. Government Printing Office, 1987.

A Report for the United States Study of Education in Japan prepared by a special task force of the Office of Education Research and Improvement Japan Study Team. While not breaking any new ground, this report provides a useful summary of prevalent attitudes about Japanese education and a wealth of up-to-date figures confirming Japan's stunning successes in many aspects of its education policies.

984.   Vogel, Ezra. *Japan as Number One: Lessons for America*. Cambridge, Mass.: Harvard University Press, 1979.

The book that stimulated much of the recent interest in Japan. The chapter on eduction provides a very rosy, but not inaccurate, picture of the positive side of Japanese educational practice.

985.   White, Merry I. *The Japanese Educational Challenge: A Commitment to Children*. New York: The Free Press, 1987.

A portrait of Japanese education suggesting that learning in Japan is a moral endeavor with intense effort as the mark of virtue. Education thus becomes the key to moral character and cultural continuity. The focus on the cultural context of education in Japan makes its relevance to other cultures problematic.

986. ———. "Japanese Education: How Do They Do It?" *The Public Interest* 76 (1984):87–101.

An interpretive essay that attempts to explain the reasons behind Japan's success in education.

987. White, Merry I., and LeVine, Robert A. "What is an *ii ko* (Good Child)?" In *Child Development and Education in Japan* (item 976), pp. 55–62.

988. White, Merry I., and Pollak, Susan, eds. *The Cultural Transition: Human Experience and Social Transformation in the Third World and Japan.* London: Routledge and Kegan Paul, 1986.

989. Zeugner, John. "The Puzzle of Higher Education in Japan: What Can We Learn from Japan?" *Change Magazine* (1984): 24–31.

AUTHOR INDEX

Note: Numbers in this index are item numbers.

SUBJECT INDEX

Note: Numbers in this index are page numbers.

RECENT STUDIES OF THE EAST ASIAN INSTITUTE

Neighborhood Tokyo. Theodore C. Bestor. (Stanford: Stanford University Press, 1988).

Kim Il Sung: The North Korean Leader. Dae-Sook Suh. (New York: Columbia University Press, 1988).

Japan and the World, 1853-1952: A Bibliographic Guide to Recent Scholarship in Japanese Foreign Relations. Sadao Asada, ed. (New York: Columbia University Press, 1988).

The Japanese Way of Politics. Gerald L. Curtis. (New York: Columbia University Press, 1988).

Border Crossings: Studies in International History. Christopher Thorne. (Oxford and New York: Basil Blackwell, 1988).

The Indochina Tangle: China's Vietnam Policy, 1975-1979. Robert S. Ross. (New York: Columbia University Press, 1988).

Contending Approaches to the Political Economy of Taiwan. Edwin A. Winckler and Susan Greehalgh, eds. (Armonk, N.Y.: M.E. Sharpe, 1988).

Remaking Japan: The American Occupation as New Deal. Theodore Cohen, ed. Herbert Passin. (New York: The Free Press, 1987).

China's Political Economy: The Quest for Development Since 1949. Carl Riskin. (London: Oxford University Press, 1987).

Anvil of Victory: The Communist Revolution in Manchuria. Steven I. Levine. (New York: Columbia University Press, 1987).

Urban Japanese Housewives: At Home and in the Community. Anne E. Imamura. (Honolulu: University of Hawaii Press, 1987).

China's Satellite Parties. James D. Seymour. (Armonk, N.Y.: M.E. Sharpe, 1987).

Security Interdependence in the Asia Pacific Region. James W. Morley, ed. (Lexington, Mass.: Lexington Books–D.C. Heath Co., 1986).

Human Rights in Contemporary China. R. Randle Edwards, Louis Henkin, and Andrew J. Nathan. (New York: Columbia University Press, 1986).

The Manner of Giving: Strategic Aid and Japanese Foreign Policy. Dennis T. Yasutomo. (Lexington, Mass.: Lexington Books–D.C. Heath Co. 1986).

The Pacific Basin: New Challenges for the United States. James W. Morley, ed. (New York: Academy of Political Science, 1986).

Shamans, Housewives and Other Restless Spirits. Laurel Kendall. (Honolulu: University of Hawaii Press, 1986).

Japan's Modern Myths: Ideology in the Late Meiji Period. Carol Gluck. (Princeton: Princeton University Press, 1985).

Japanese Culture. H. Paul Varley. 3rd ed., revised. (Honolulu: University of Hawaii Press, 1984).

Japan Erupts: The London Naval Conference and the Manchuria Incident. James W. Morley, ed. (New York: Columbia University Press, 1984).